UNDERSTANDING AND USING

English Grammar

FOURTH EDITION

UNDERSTANDING AND USING

English Grammar

FOURTH EDITION

VOLUME B

Betty S. Azar
Stacy A. Hagen

PEARSON
Longman

Understanding and Using English Grammar, Fourth Edition
Volume B

Copyright © 2009, 2002, 1989, 1981 by Betty Schrampfer Azar

Azar Associates: Shelley Hartle, Editor, and Sue Van Etten, Manager

Pearson Education, 10 Bank Street, White Plains, NY 10606

Staff credits: The people who made up the *Understanding and Using English Grammar Fourth Edition* team, representing editorial, production, design, and manufacturing, are Janice Baillie, Dave Dickey, Ann France, Amy McCormick, Robert Ruvo, and Ruth Voetmann.

Text composition: S4Carlisle Publishing Services
Text font: 10/12.5 Plantin
Illustrations: Don Martinetti, pages 247, 255, 256, 259, 260 (top), 275, 278, 280, 286, 287, 292, 301, 303, 308, 316, 319, 321, 328, 340, 342, 347, 353, 355, 357, 362, 371, 373, 389, 396, 408, 413, 420, 424, 425, 432, 441, 446; Chris Pavely, pages 251, 257, 260 (bottom), 265, 272, 284, 289, 293, 309, 315, 331, 345, 349, 360, 363, 367, 378, 385, 393, 394, 403, 414, 422, 428

ISBN 13: 978-0-13-233332-0
ISBN 10: 0-13-233332-5

Printed in the United States of America
6 7 8 9 10—V011—14 13 12

For Larry
B.S.A.

For Andy and Julianna
S.H.

Contents

Preface to the Fourth Edition

Understanding and Using English Grammar is a developmental skills text for intermediate to advanced English language learners. It uses a grammar-based approach integrated with communicative methodologies to promote the development of all language skills in a variety of ways. Starting from a foundation of understanding form and meaning, students engage in meaningful communication about real actions, real things, and their own real lives in the classroom context. *Understanding and Using English Grammar* functions principally as a classroom teaching text but also serves as a comprehensive reference text for students and teachers.

The eclectic approach and abundant variety of exercise material remain the same as in the earlier editions, but each new edition incorporates new ways and means. In particular:

- **WARM-UP EXERCISES FOR THE GRAMMAR CHARTS**
  Newly created for the fourth edition, these innovative exercises precede the grammar charts and introduce the point(s) to be taught. They have been carefully crafted to help students *discover* the target grammar as they progress through each warm-up exercise.

- **LISTENING PRACTICE**
  Numerous listening exercises help students interact with the spoken language in a variety of settings that range from the relaxed, casual speech of everyday conversation to the academic content of classroom lectures. An audio CD accompanies the student text, and a full audio script can be found in the back of the book.

- **ACADEMIC READINGS**
  Students can read and respond to a wide selection of carefully crafted readings that focus on the target grammar structure.

- **EXPANDED SPEAKING ACTIVITIES**
  Students have even more opportunities in this fourth edition to share their experiences, express their opinions, and relate the target grammar to their personal lives. The text often uses the students' own life experiences as context and regularly introduces topics of interest to stimulate the free expression of ideas in structured as well as open discussions.

- **CORPUS-INFORMED CONTENT**
  Based on the findings of our corpus researcher, Gena Bennett, grammar content has been added, deleted, or modified to reflect the discourse patterns of spoken and written English.

Understanding and Using English Grammar is accompanied by

- A comprehensive **Workbook**, consisting of self-study exercises for independent work.
- An all-new **Teacher's Guide**, with step-by-step teaching suggestions for each chart, notes to the teacher on key grammar structures, vocabulary lists, and expansion activities and *PowerPoint* presentations for key chapters.
- An expanded **Test Bank**, with additional quizzes, chapter tests, and mid-term and final exams.
- **Test-Generator** software that allows teachers to customize their own tests using quizzes and tests from the *Test Bank*.
- **Azar Interactive**, a computer-based program keyed to the text, provides easily understood content, all-new exercises, readings, listening and speaking activities, and comprehensive tests.
- **PowerPoint** presentations for key chapters. Based on real-world readings, these lessons are designed for use in the classroom as "beyond-the-book" activities. They can be found in the new *Teacher's Guide* or downloaded from AzarGrammar.com.
- A **Chartbook**, a reference book consisting only of the grammar charts.
- **AzarGrammar.com**. This Web site provides a variety of supplementary classroom materials and is a place where teachers can support each other by sharing their knowledge and experience.
- **Fun with Grammar**, a teacher resource text by Suzanne Woodward with communicative activities correlated with the Azar-Hagen Grammar Series. It is available as a text or as a download on *AzarGrammar.com*.

The Azar-Hagen Grammar Series consists of

- *Understanding and Using English Grammar* (blue cover), for upper-level students.
- *Fundamentals of English Grammar* (black), for mid-level students.
- *Basic English Grammar* (red), for lower or beginning levels.

Acknowledgments

A revision of this scope could not have been done without the skills of top-notch professionals. We began with a group of outstanding reviewers whose detailed comments guided our writing. We wish to express our gratitude for their thoughtful reviews. They are Tonie Badillo, El Paso Community College; Edina Bagley, Nassau Community College; Michael Berman, Montgomery College; Elizabeth Bottcher, Columbia University; Eric Clinkscales, Teikyo Loretto Heights University; Cathy Costa, Edmonds Community College; Ms. Carlin Good, Columbia University; Deanna Cecil Ferreira, English Language Institute; Linda Gossard, DPT Business School ESL Program; Dr. Sheila Hakner, St. John's University; Martha Hall, New England School of English; Jennifer Hannon, Massachusetts Community College; Alyson Hanson, Gateway Community College; Joan Heiman, Community College of Denver; Steven Lasswell, Santa Barbara City College; Linda Leary, Albany Education; Louis Lucca, LaGuardia Community College; Kate Masterson, Boston Center for Adult Education; Phyllis McCollum, DPT Business School ESL Program; David Moody, El Paso Community College; Jan Peterson, Edmonds Community College; Antonina Rodgers, Northern Virginia Community College; Lenka Rohls, LaGuardia Community College; Rebecca Suarez, The University of Texas at El Paso; Ann Marie Tamayo, Queens Community College; and Kelly Roberts Weibel, Edmonds Community College.

We would like to thank a terrific support team that allows us to do what we do with enjoyment and ease: Shelley Hartle, managing editor par excellence, who worked magic on every page; Amy McCormick, Azar product manager, who oversaw our project and handled our myriad requests with unfailing grace, humor, and skill; Ruth Voetmann, development editor, whose attention to detail helped polish each chart and exercise; Janice Baillie, expert production editor and copy editor; Sue Van Etten, our skilled and multi-talented business and Web site manager; Gena Bennett, corpus researcher, whose findings helped keep us abreast of the nuances and changes in spoken and written discourse; and Robert Ruvo, our invaluable production liaison at Pearson Education.

Finally, we'd like to thank the dedicated leadership team from Pearson Education that guided this project: JoAnn Dresner, Anne Boynton-Trigg, Rhea Banker, and Sherry Preiss.

For the new design of this fourth edition we were lucky to have had the combined talents of Michael Cimilluca from Lindsay Communications, Ann France from Pearson Education, and freelance artist Kris Wiltse.

Our appreciation also goes to illustrators Don Martinetti and Chris Pavely for their humor and inspired artwork.

Finally, we would like to thank our families for their unflagging patience and encouragement throughout this extensive revision. Their insights and support are a continual source of inspiration.

Betty S. Azar
Stacy A. Hagen

UNDERSTANDING AND USING

English Grammar

FOURTH EDITION

Chapter 12
Noun Clauses

❏ **Exercise 1. Warm-up.** (Chart 12-1)
Check (✓) the complete sentences.

1. _✓_ Jin studies business.
2. ____ What does Jin study?
3. ____ What Jin studies?
4. ____ What Jin studies is business.
5. ____ His books.
6. ____ I don't know how much his books cost.
7. ____ How much his books cost?
8. ____ How much do his books cost?

12-1 Introduction	
independent clause (a) ⌐Sue lives in Tokyo.⌐	A clause is a group of words containing a subject and a verb.* An INDEPENDENT CLAUSE (or *main clause*) is a complete sentence. It contains the main subject and verb of a sentence. Examples (a) and (b) are complete sentences. Example (a) is a statement; (b) is a question.
independent clause (b) ⌐Where does Sue live?⌐	
dependent clause (c) ⌐where Sue lives⌐	A DEPENDENT CLAUSE (or *subordinate clause*) is not a complete sentence. Example (c) is a dependent clause.
noun clause (d) I know ⌐*where Sue lives*.⌐	Example (d) is a complete sentence, with a main subject (*I*) and verb (*know*) followed by a dependent clause. ***Where Sue lives*** is called a *noun clause*.
S **V** **O** (e) I **know** ⌐*what he said*.⌐ **S** **V** (f) ⌐*What he said*⌐ **is** true.	A NOUN CLAUSE has the same uses in a sentence as a noun: it is used as an object or a subject. In (e): The noun clause is the object of the verb ***know***. In (f): The noun clause is the subject of the verb ***is***.

*A *phrase* is a group of words that does NOT contain a subject and a verb.

❏ **Exercise 2. Looking at grammar.** (Chart 12-1)

Underline the noun clause in each sentence. Some sentences do not have one.

1. I couldn't hear <u>what the teacher said</u>.

2. What did the teacher say? *(no noun clause)*

3. No one knows <u>where Tom went</u>.

4. <u>Where Tom went</u> is a secret.

5. What does Nancy want?

6. We need to know <u>what Nancy wants</u>.

❏ **Exercise 3. Looking at grammar.** (Chart 12-1)

Add punctuation and capitalization. <u>Underline</u> the noun clauses.

1. Where did Sara go did she go home → *Where did Sara go?* **D***id she go home?*

2. I don't know <u>where Sara went</u> → *I don't know where Sara went.*
   ⋀

3. What does Alex need do you know

4. Do you know <u>what Alex needs</u>

5. <u>What Alex needs</u> is a new job.

6. We talked about what Alex needs

7. What do you need did you talk to your parents about what you need

8. My parents know what I need

❏ **Exercise 4. Looking at grammar.** (Chart 12-1)

Are these sentences true for you? Circle *yes* or *no*. Discuss your answers.

1. What my family thinks of me is very important to me.   yes   no

2. I always pay attention to what other people think of me.   yes   no

3. Where we live is exciting.   yes   no

4. Where we live is expensive.   yes   no

5. I think how most celebrities behave is admirable.   yes   no

6. I usually don't believe what I read in advertisements.   yes   no

❏ **Exercise 5. Warm-up.** (Chart 12-2)
Choose the correct sentences.

1. Where does Brad live?
   a. I'm not sure where he lives.
   b. I'm not sure where does he live.

2. I'm looking for Brad.
   a. Could you tell me where is Brad?
   b. Could you tell me where Brad is?

12-2 Noun Clauses Beginning with a Question Word

Question	Noun Clause	
Where does she live? What did he say? When do they arrive?	(a) I don't know *where she lives*. (b) I couldn't hear *what he said*. (c) Do you know *when they arrive*?	In (a): *where she lives* is the object of the verb *know*. In a noun clause, the subject precedes the verb. Do not use question word order in a noun clause. Notice: *does*, *did*, and *do* are used in questions but not in noun clauses. See Appendix Chart B-2 for more information about question words and question forms.
S V Who lives there? Who is at the door?	S V (d) I don't know *who lives there*. (e) I wonder *who is at the door*.	In (d) and (e): The word order is the same in both the question and the noun clause because *who* is the subject in both.
V S Who are those men? Whose house is that?	S V (f) I don't know *who those men are*. (g) I wonder *whose house that is*.	In (f): *those men* is the subject of the question, so it is placed in front of the verb *be* in the noun clause.*
What did she say? What should they do?	(h) *What she said* surprised me. S V (i) *What they should do* is obvious.	In (h): *What she said* is the subject of the sentence. Notice in (i): A noun clause subject takes a singular verb (e.g., *is*).

*COMPARE: *Who **is** at the door?* = *who* is the subject of the question.
         *Who **are** those men?* = *those men* is the subject of the question, so *be* is plural.

❏ **Exercise 6. Looking at grammar.** (Chart 12-2)
Change each question in parentheses to a noun clause.

1. (*How old is he?*) I don't know _____how old he is_____ .

2. (*What was he talking about?*) _____ was interesting.

3. (*Where do you live?*) Please tell me _____ .

4. (*Where did she go?*) _____ is none of your business.

5. (*When are they coming?*) Do you know _____ ?

6. (*Which one does he want?*) Let's ask him _____ .

7. (*What happened?*) I don't know _____ .

8. (*Who opened the door?*) I don't know _____ .

9. (*Why did they leave the country?*) _____ is a secret.

10. (*What are we doing in class?*) _____ is easy.

11. (*Who are those people?*) I don't know _____ .

12. (*Whose pen is this?*) Do you know _____ ?

❏ **Exercise 7. Looking at grammar.** (Chart 12-2)
Change the questions to noun clauses. Begin with ***Can you tell me***.

Example: What time does the computer lab close?
→ *Can you tell me what time the computer lab closes?*

1. How is this word pronounced?
2. What does this mean?
3. What was my grade?
4. Who am I supposed to talk to?
5. When is our next assignment due?
6. How much time do we have for the test?
7. When do classes end for the year?
8. Where is our class going to meet?

❏ **Exercise 8. Let's talk.** (Chart 12-2)
Speaker A asks a question. Speaker B responds beginning with ***I don't know*** OR ***I wonder***.
Use the names of your classmates. Work in pairs, in groups, or as a class.

Example: Where is (_____)?
SPEAKER A (*book open*):   Where is Marco?
SPEAKER B (*book closed*): I don't know where Marco is. OR I wonder where Marco is.

(Change roles if working in pairs.)

1. Where does (_____) live?
2. What country is (_____) from?
3. How long has (_____) been living here?
4. What is (_____) telephone number?
5. Where is the post office?
6. How far is it to the South Pole?
7. What kind of watch does (_____) have?
8. Why was (_____) absent yesterday?
9. What is (_____) favorite color?

10. How long has (_____) been married?
11. Why are we doing this exercise?
12. Who turned off the lights?
13. Where are you going to eat lunch/dinner?
14. Where did (_____) go after class yesterday?
15. Why is (_____) smiling?
16. How often does (_____) go to the library?
17. Whose book is that?
18. How much did that book cost?

Exercise 9. Looking at grammar. (Chart 12-2)
Make questions from the given sentences. The words in parentheses should be the answer to the question you make. Begin with a question word (*who, what, how, when, where, why*). Then change the question to a noun clause.

1. Tom will be here (*next week*).
   QUESTION: _____ *When will Tom be here?* _____
   NOUN CLAUSE: Please tell me _____ *when Tom will be here.* _____

2. He is coming (*because he wants to visit his friends*).
   QUESTION: _____
   NOUN CLAUSE: Please tell me _____

3. He'll be on flight (*645, not flight 742*).
   QUESTION: _____
   NOUN CLAUSE: Please tell me _____

4. (*Jim Hunter*) is going to meet him at the airport.
   QUESTION: _____ *Who is going to meet him at the airport?* _____
   NOUN CLAUSE: Please tell me _____ *who he is going to meet at the airport.* _____

5. Jim Hunter is (*his roommate*).
   QUESTION: _____ *Who is Jim Hunter?* _____
   NOUN CLAUSE: Please tell me _____ *Who Jim Hunter is?* _____

6. He lives (*on Riverside Road in Columbus, Ohio, USA*).
   QUESTION: _____ *Where is he living?* *Where does he lives?* _____
   NOUN CLAUSE: Please tell me _____ *where he lives?* _____

7. He was (*in Chicago*) last week.
   QUESTION: _____ *Where was he last week* _____
   NOUN CLAUSE: Please tell me _____ *where he was last week* _____

8. He has been working for Sony Corporation (*since 2000*).
   QUESTION: _____ *Since when has he been working for Sony* _____
   NOUN CLAUSE: Do you know _____ *since when he has been working for Sony.* _____

9. He has (*a Sony*) computer at home.
   QUESTION: _____ *What kind of computer does he have at home?* _____
   NOUN CLAUSE: Do you know _____ *What kind of computer he has at home.* _____

❏ **Exercise 10. Looking at grammar.** (Chart 12-2)

Complete each sentence with the words in parentheses. Use any appropriate verb tense. Some of the completions contain noun clauses, and some contain questions.

1. A: Where (*Ruth, go*) _____*did Ruth go*_____? She's not in her room.

   B: I don't know. Ask her friend Tina. She might know where (*Ruth, go*)

   _____*Ruth went*_____.

2. A: Oops! I made a mistake. Where (*my eraser, be*) _____?

   Didn't I lend it to you?

   B: I don't have it. Ask Sally where (*it, be*) _____. I think I saw her using it.

3. A: The door isn't locked! Why (*Franco, lock, not*) _____ it

   before he left?*

   B: Why ask me? How am I supposed to know why (*he, lock, not*) _____

   _____ it? Maybe he just forgot.

4. A: Mr. Lee is a recent immigrant, isn't he? How long (*he, be*) _____ in

   this country?

   B: I have no idea, but I'll be seeing Mr. Lee this afternoon. Would you like me to ask him

   how long (*he, be*) _____ here?

5. A: Help! Quick! Look at that road sign! Which road (*we, be supposed*) _____

   _____ to take?

   B: Don't look at me! You're the driver. I don't know which road (*we, be supposed*)

   _____ to take. I've never been here before.

---

*Word order in negative questions:
   Usual: *Why didn't you call me?* (with *did + not* contracted)
   Very formal: *Why did you not call me?*

Exercise 11. Listening. (Chart 12-2)

Listen to the dialogues. Choose the completions you hear.

CD 2
Track 1

1. a. how far it is.
    b. How far is it?

2. a. how far it is.
    b. How far is it?

3. a. why we watched the whole thing.
    b. Why did we watch the whole thing?

4. a. why you watched it.
    b. why did you watch it?

5. a. how old she is.
    b. How old is she?

6. a. how this word is pronounced.
    b. How is this word pronounced?

7. a. what the problem is.
    b. what is the problem?

❏ **Exercise 12. Let's talk: interview.** (Chart 12-2)

Ask your classmates if they can answer questions based on the given information. Begin with **Do you know** followed by a question word (**who, what, when, where, how many, how long, how far**). If no one in the class knows the answer to a question, research the answer. Share any information you get with the rest of the class.

Example: the shortest month of the year
SPEAKER A: Do you know *what* the shortest month of the year is?
SPEAKER B: Yes. It's February. OR No, I don't know what the shortest month is.

1. the number of minutes in 24 hours
2. the year the first man walked on the moon
3. the winner of the Nobel Peace Prize last year
4. the place Buddha was born
5. the distance from the earth to the sun
6. the time it takes for the moon to rotate around the earth

❏ **Exercise 13. Warm-up.** (Chart 12-3)

Underline the noun clauses. What words are added when a yes/no question is changed to a noun clause?

QUESTION: Has the mail arrived?
NOUN CLAUSE: I wonder if the mail has arrived.
               I wonder whether the mail has arrived.
               I wonder whether or not the mail has arrived.
               I wonder whether the mail has arrived or not.
               I wonder if the mail has arrived or not.

12-3 Noun Clauses Beginning with *Whether* or *If*

Yes/No Question	Noun Clause	
Will she come? Does he need help?	(a) I don't know *whether she will come*. I don't know *if she will come*. (b) I wonder *whether he needs help*. I wonder *if he needs help*.	When a yes/no question is changed to a noun clause, *whether* or *if* is used to introduce the clause. NOTE: *Whether* is more common than *if* in formal English. Both *whether* and *if* are commonly used in speaking.
	(c) I wonder *whether or not* she will come. (d) I wonder *whether* she will come *or not*. (e) I wonder *if* she will come *or not*.	In (c), (d), and (e): Notice the patterns when *or not* is used.
	(f) *Whether she comes or not* is unimportant to me.	In (f): Notice that the noun clause is in the subject position.

❑ **Exercise 14. Looking at grammar.** (Chart 12-3)
Complete the sentences by changing the questions to noun clauses.

SITUATION: You're at the office.

Example: Let me know if . . .
        Did you finish the sales report? → *Let me know if you finished the sales report.*

Let me know if . . .
1. Is the financial report ready?
2. Will it be ready tomorrow?
3. Does the copy machine need paper? *if the needs paper*
4. Is someone waiting for me? *Someon is wating*
5. Do we need anything for the meeting?
6. Are you going to be there? *are*

Please check whether . . .
7. Did they get my message?
8. Is the copy machine working? *is*
9. Is there any paper left? *is*
10. Is this information correct? *is*
11. Did the fax come in? *came if*
12. Are we going to have Monday off? *are*

❑ **Exercise 15. Let's talk.** (Chart 12-3)
Speaker A asks a question. Speaker B responds beginning with *I wonder*. Work in pairs, in small groups, or as a class.

Example:
SPEAKER A (*book open*):   Does Anna need any help?
SPEAKER B (*book closed*): I wonder whether/if Anna needs any help.

(Change roles if working in pairs.)

1. Where is Tom?
2. Should we wait for him?
3. Is he having trouble?
4. When was the first book written?
5. What causes earthquakes?
6. How long does a butterfly live?
7. Whose dictionary is this?
8. Does it belong to William?
9. Why did dinosaurs become extinct?
10. Is there life on other planets?
11. How did life begin?
12. Will people live on the moon someday?

❑ **Exercise 16. Let's talk: interview.** (Chart 12-3)
Interview students in your class. Ask each one a different question. Begin with *Can*/*Could you tell me*. Share a few of your answers with the class.

1. Have you ever won a prize? What?
2. Have you ever played a joke on someone? Describe it.
3. Have you ever stayed up all night? Why?
4. Have you ever felt embarrassed? Why?
5. Have you ever been in an earthquake? Where? When?
6. Do you have a talent like singing or dancing (*or something else*)? What?
7. Are you enjoying this interview? Why or why not?

❑ **Exercise 17. Let's talk: pairwork.** (Charts 12-1 → 12-3)
Work with a partner to create short dialogues. Partner A asks a question. Partner B answers the question beginning with the words in *italics*.

SITUATION: You're late for school. You need help finding your things.

Example: I don't know . . . .
            Where are my glasses?
PARTNER A (*book open*):   Where are my glasses?
PARTNER B (*book closed*): I don't know where your glasses are.

SITUATION 1: You're late for work.

I don't know . . . .
1. Where did I leave my keys?
2. Where did I put my shoes?
3. Where's my other sock?
4. What did I do with my briefcase?

SITUATION 2: You have a new neighbor.

I'll find out . . . .
5. Where's he from?
6. What does he do?
7. Where does he work?
8. Would he like to come to dinner?

Change roles.
SITUATION 3: You're at a tourist center.

Let's ask . . . .
9. Where is the bus station?
10. How much does the city bus cost?
11. Do the city buses carry bikes?
12. Is this bus schedule correct?

We need to figure out . . . .
13. How far is it from here to town?
14. How much does it cost to take a taxi from here to downtown?
15. How can we get our money changed here?

❑ **Exercise 18. Looking at grammar.** (Charts 12-1 → 12-3)
Correct the errors.
                                    your name is
1. Please tell me what ~~is your name~~ .

                                    will
2. No one seems to know when ~~will~~ Maria arrive.

3. I don't know what ~~does~~ that word mean~~s~~.

            If
4. I wonder ~~does~~ the teacher know the answer?

            wether
5. I'll ask her ~~would~~ she like some coffee or not.
            would.

6. Be sure to tell the doctor where ~~does~~ it hurts.

7. Why ~~am I~~ unhappy is something I can't explain.

8. Nobody cares ~~do~~ whether we stay ~~or~~ leaves.

9. I need to know who ~~is~~ your teacher. is

10. I don't understand why ~~is~~ the car not running properly.

11. My young son wants to know where ~~do~~ the stars go in the daytime.

□ **Exercise 19. Let's talk.** (Charts 12-1 → 12-3)
Work in small groups. What would you say in each situation? Use noun clauses.

Example: Someone asks you about the time the mail comes. You're not sure.
Possible answers: *I'm not sure what time the mail comes.*
I don't know when the mail is supposed to be here.
Etc.

1. You see a restaurant. You can't tell if it's open yet. You ask a man standing outside.
2. You were absent yesterday. You want to know the homework. You ask another student.
3. Someone asks you the date. You don't know, but you tell them you'll find out.
4. Someone asks you about the weather tomorrow. Is it supposed to be sunny? You haven't heard.
5. You're at a clothing store. You're buying a coat and want to know about the return policy. How many days do you have to return it? You ask a salesperson.
6. Your friend asks you if you want to go to a movie or get a DVD to watch at home. Both sound good to you. You tell your friend you don't care which you do.
7. You have a late fee on your bill. You want to know why. You call the company and ask.
8. You are planning a hiking trip with a friend. This friend wants to bring his dog and asks you if it is okay. It doesn't matter to you.

□ **Exercise 20. Warm-up.** (Chart 12-4)
Complete the second sentence of each pair with an infinitive. Use **to get** or **to do**. Is the meaning in each pair the same or different?

What should I do? I don't have any money for the bus. How am I going to get home?

1. a. Susan doesn't know what she should do.

   b. Susan doesn't know what _____.

2. a. She needs to figure out how she will get home.

   b. She needs to figure out how _____ home.

12-4 Question Words Followed by Infinitives

(a) I don't know *what I should do*. (b) I don't know ***what to do***. (c) Pam can't decide *whether she should go or stay home*. (d) Pam can't decide ***whether to go or (to) stay home***. (e) Please tell me *how I can get to the bus station*. (f) Please tell me ***how to get to the bus station***. (g) Jim told us *where we could find it*. (h) Jim told us ***where to find it***.	Question words (***when, where, how, who, whom, whose, what, which***, and ***whether***) may be followed by an infinitive. Each pair of sentences in the examples has the same meaning. Notice that the meaning expressed by the infinitive is either ***should*** or ***can/could***.

❏ **Exercise 21. Looking at grammar.** (Chart 12-4)
Make sentences with the same meaning by using infinitives.

1. Sally told me when I should come. → *Sally told me when to come.*

2. The plumber told me how I could fix the leak in the sink.

3. Please tell me where I should meet you.

4. Robert had a long excuse for being late for their date, but Sandy didn't know whether she should believe him or not.

5. Jim found two shirts he liked, but he had trouble deciding which one he should buy.

6. I've done everything I can think of to help Andy get his life straightened out. I don't know what else I can do.

❏ **Exercise 22. In your own words.** (Chart 12-4)
Complete the sentences with your own words. Use infinitives in your completions.

1. A: I can't decide _____*what to wear*_____ to the reception.

   B: How about your green suit?

2. A: Where are you going to live when you go to the university?

   B: I'm not sure. I can't decide whether _____ or

   _____.

3. A: Do you know how _____?

   B: No, but I'd like to learn.

4. A: I don't know what _____ for her birthday. Got any ideas?

   B: How about a book?

5. My cousin has a dilemma. He can't decide whether _____ or

   _____. What do you think he should do?

6. Before you leave on your trip, read this tour book. It tells you where

   _____ and how _____.

❑ **Exercise 23. Warm-up.** (Chart 12-5)
Check (✓) the grammatically correct sentences.

1. __✓__ We know *that the planets revolve around the sun.*

2. _____ Centuries ago, people weren't aware *that the planets revolved around the sun.*

3. _____ *That the planets revolve around the sun* is now a well-known fact.

4. _____ Is clear *that the planets revolve around the sun.*

12-5 Noun Clauses Beginning with *That*

Verb + *That*-Clause

(a) I **think** *that Bob will come.* (b) I **think** *Bob will come.*	In (a): *that Bob will come* is a noun clause. It is used as the object of the verb ***think***. The word ***that*** is usually omitted in speaking, as in (b). It is usually included in formal writing. See the list below for verbs commonly followed by a *that*-clause.

agree that	*feel* that	*know* that	*remember* that
believe that	*find out* that	*learn* that	*say* that
decide that	*forget* that	*notice* that	*tell* someone that
discover that	*hear* that	*promise* that	*think* that
explain that	*hope* that	*read* that	*understand* that

Person + *Be* + Adjective + *That*-Clause

(c) **Jan is happy** (*that*) *Bob called.*	*That*-clauses commonly follow certain adjectives, such as *happy* in (c), when the subject refers to a person (or persons). See the list below.

I'm *afraid* that*	Al is *certain* that	We're *happy* that	Jan is *sorry* that
I'm *amazed* that	Al is *confident* that	We're *pleased* that	Jan is *sure* that
I'm *angry* that	Al is *disappointed* that	We're *proud* that	Jan is *surprised* that
I'm *aware* that	Al is *glad* that	We're *relieved* that	Jan is *worried* that

It + *Be* + Adjective + *That*-Clause

(d) **It is clear** (*that*) *Ann likes her new job.*	*That*-clauses commonly follow adjectives in sentences that begin with ***it*** + ***be***, as in (d). See the list below.

It's *amazing* that	It's *interesting* that	It's *obvious* that	It's *true* that
It's *clear* that	It's *likely* that	It's *possible* that	It's *undeniable* that
It's *good* that	It's *lucky* that	It's *strange* that	It's *well/known* that
It's *important* that	It's *nice* that	It's *surprising* that	It's *wonderful* that

That-Clause Used as a Subject

(e) *That Ann likes her new job* is clear.	It is possible but uncommon for *that*-clauses to be used as the subject of a sentence, as in (e). The word ***that*** is not omitted when the *that*-clause is used as a subject.
(f) *The fact* (*that*) *Ann likes her new job* is clear. (g) *It is a fact* (*that*) *Ann likes her new job.*	More often, a *that*-clause in the subject position begins with ***the fact that***, as in (f), or is introduced by ***it is a fact***, as in (g).

*To be afraid has two possible meanings:
   (1) It can express fear: *I'm afraid of dogs. I'm afraid that his dog will bite me.*
   (2) It often expresses a meaning similar to "to be sorry": *I'm afraid that I can't accept your invitation. I'm afraid you have the wrong number.*

❏ **Exercise 24. In your own words.** (Chart 12-5)
Complete the sentences with your own words.

1. I recently heard on the news that . . . .
2. When I was young, I found out that . . . .
3. I sometimes forget that . . . .
4. All parents hope that . . . .
5. Most people in my country believe that . . . .
6. Do you feel that . . . ?
7. I recently read that . . . .
8. Scientists have discovered that . . . .
9. Students understand that . . . .
10. Have you noticed that . . . ?

❏ **Exercise 25. Let's talk: interview.** (Chart 12-5)
Interview your classmates. Ask each one a different question. Their answers should follow this
pattern: ***I'm*** + *adjective* + ***that***-*clause*.

Example: What is something in your life that you're glad about?
→ *I'm glad that my family is supportive of me.*

1. What is something that disappointed you in the past? *I am disappinted that*
2. What is something that annoys you? *I'm annoyed that my neighbor's dog is always barks at night.*
3. What is something about your friends that pleases you? *I'm pleased that my friends always is supporting*
4. What is something about nature that amazes you? *I'm amazed that ocean is giant.*
5. What is something about another culture's traditions that surprises you? *I'm surprised that*
6. What is something that you are afraid will happen in the future? *I'm afraid that I couldn't get good TOEFL Score.*
7. What is something about your future that you are sure of?
I'm sure that I will

❏ **Exercise 26. Looking at grammar.** (Chart 12-5)
Make noun clauses using ***it*** and any appropriate word(s) from the list. Make an equivalent
sentence by using a *that*-clause as the subject.

apparent	a pity	surprising	unfair
clear	a shame	too bad	unfortunate
a fact	strange	true	a well-known fact
obvious			

1. The world is round.
   → *It is a fact that the world is round.*
   → *That the world is round is a fact.*
2. Tim hasn't been able to make any friends. *That Tim — is too bad* *It's too bad that*
3. The earth revolves around the sun. *It's*
4. Exercise can reduce heart disease. *a well known fact*
5. Drug abuse can ruin one's health. *true*
6. Some women do not earn equal pay for equal work. *unfair*
7. Irene, who is an excellent student, failed her entrance examination. *surprising*
8. English is the principal language of business throughout much of the world.
   obvious

❏ **Exercise 27. Game.** (Chart 12-5)

Work in teams. Agree or disagree with the given statements. If you think the statement is true, begin with **It's a fact that**. If you think the statement is false, begin with **It isn't true that**. If you're not sure, guess. Choose one person to write your team's statements. The team with the most correct statements wins.*

1. ____It's a fact that____ most spiders have eight eyes.

2. ____It isn't true that____ some spiders have twelve legs.

3. _____ more males than females are colorblind.

4. _____ people's main source of vitamin D is fruit.

5. _____ the Great Wall of China took more than 1,000 years to build.

6. _____ twenty-five percent of the human body is water.

7. _____ a substance called chlorophyll makes plant leaves green.

8. _____ the World Wide Web went online in 2000.

9. _____ elephants have the longest pregnancy of any land animal.

10. _____ the first wheels were made out of stone.

11. _____ a diamond is the hardest substance found in nature.

❏ **Exercise 28. Looking at grammar.** (Chart 12-5)

A *that*-clause is frequently used with **the fact**. Combine the sentences. Introduce each noun clause with **The fact that**.

1. Ann was late. *That* didn't surprise me.
   → *The fact that Ann was late didn't surprise me.*
2. Rosa didn't come. *That* made me angry.
3. Many people in the world live in intolerable poverty. *That* must concern all of us.
4. I was supposed to bring my passport to the exam for identification. I was not aware of *that*.
5. The people of the town were given no warning of the approaching tornado. Due to *that*, there were many casualties.

❏ **Exercise 29. Looking at grammar.** (Chart 12-5)

Restate the sentences. Begin with **The fact that**.

1. It's understandable that you feel frustrated.
   → *The fact that you feel frustrated is understandable.*
2. It's undeniable that traffic is getting worse every year.
3. It's unfortunate that the city has no funds for the project.
4. It's obvious that the two leaders don't respect each other.
5. It's a miracle that there were no injuries from the car accident.

---

*Only the teacher should look at the answers, which can be found in the Answer Key for Chapter 12.

Exercise 30. Let's talk. (Chart 12-5)
Work in small groups. Do you agree or disagree with the statements? Circle *yes* or *no*.

1. It's undeniable that smoking causes cancer.   yes   no

2. It's a well-known fact that young boys are more aggressive than young girls.   yes   no

3. It's unfortunate that people eat meat.   yes   no

4. It's true that women are more nurturing than men.   yes   no

5. That someday all countries in the world will live in peace is unlikely.   yes   no

6. That governments need to pay more attention to global warming is a fact.   yes   no

7. It's clear that life is easier now than it was 100 years ago.   yes   no

8. That technology has given us more free time is clearly true.   yes   no

❏ **Exercise 31. Reading comprehension.** (Chart 12-5)
Part I. Read the article.

canned

fresh

Canned vs. Fresh: Which Is Better?

Do you avoid eating canned fruits and vegetables because you think they may be less nutritious than fresh fruits and vegetables? Do you think they might be less healthy? For many people, the idea of eating canned fruits or vegetables is really not very appealing, and they would rather buy fresh produce. But what are the differences between canned and fresh produce? Let's take a look at the two.

Many people are surprised to hear that canned food can have as many nutrients as fresh. This is true because the fruits and vegetables are put into the cans shortly after being picked. Because the food is canned so quickly, the nutritional content is locked in. Food in a can will stay stable for two years.

Fresh produce, on the other hand, may need to be transported. This can take up to two weeks. Fresh produce will continue to lose important nutrients until it is eaten. The sooner you can eat fresh produce, the more nutritious it will be.

There are also advantages to some fruits when they are first cooked and then canned. Tomatoes, for instance, have a substance called lycopene. This is a cancer-fighting ingredient that is found in cooked tomatoes. Fresh tomatoes do not have a significant amount of lycopene. It is better to eat tomato sauce from a can rather than fresh tomato sauce if you want to have lycopene in your diet.

Of course, there are disadvantages to canned foods. They tend to have a higher salt and sugar content. People who need to watch their salt or sugar intake should try to find cans low in salt or sugar. Also, because the canning process requires heat, some loss of vitamin C may occur, but most essential nutrients remain stable.

Finally, there is the issue of taste. For many, there is no comparison between the taste of fresh fruits and vegetables versus canned. No matter what the benefits of canning, some people refuse to eat anything that isn't fresh. How about you? Which do you prefer?

Part II. Read the statements. Circle "T" for true and "F" for false.

1. According to the article, it's surprising to many people that canned produce can be as nutritious as fresh produce.   T   F

2. It's a fact that food in a can will last for two years.   T   F

3. It's a well-known fact that canned tomatoes contain a cancer-fighting ingredient.   T   F

4. That fresh produce and canned produce taste the same is undeniable.   T   F

5. It's obvious that the writer believes canned food is better than fresh.   T   F

❑ **Exercise 32. Warm-up.** (Chart 12-6)
Read the words in the picture. Then look at the quoted speech below it. Circle the quotation marks. Is the punctuation inside or outside the quotation marks? In item 3, what do you notice about the punctuation?

Watch out! Are you okay? You look like you're going to fall off that ladder.

1. "Watch out!" Mrs. Brooks said.

2. "Are you okay?" she asked.

3. "You look like you're going to fall off that ladder," she said.

12-6 Quoted Speech

Quoted speech refers to reproducing words exactly as they were originally spoken.* Quotation marks ("...") are used.**

Quoting One Sentence

(a) She said, "My brother is a student."	In (a): Use a comma after **she said**. Capitalize the first word of the quoted sentence. Put the final quotation marks outside the period at the end of the sentence.
(b) "My brother is a student," she said.	In (b): Use a comma, not a period, at the end of the quoted sentence when it precedes **she said**.
(c) "My brother," she said, "is a student."	In (c): If the quoted sentence is divided by **she said**, use a comma after the first part of the quote. Do not capitalize the first word after **she said**.

Quoting More Than One Sentence

(d) "My brother is a student. He is attending a university," she said.	In (d): Quotation marks are placed at the beginning and end of the complete quote. Notice: There are no quotation marks after **student**.
(e) "My brother is a student," she said. "He is attending a university."	In (e): Since **she said** comes between two quoted sentences, the second sentence begins with quotation marks and a capital letter.

Quoting a Question or an Exclamation

(f) She asked, "When will you be here?"	In (f): The question mark is inside the closing quotation marks.
(g) "When will you be here?" she asked.	In (g): Since a question mark is used, no comma is used before **she asked**.
(h) She said, "Watch out!"	In (h): The exclamation point is inside the closing quotation marks.
(i) "My brother is a student," *said Anna*. "My brother," *said Anna*, "is a student."	In (i): The noun subject (**Anna**) follows **said**. A noun subject often follows the verb when the subject and verb come in the middle or at the end of a quoted sentence. NOTE: A pronoun subject almost always precedes the verb. *"My brother is a student,"* **she said**. VERY RARE: *"My brother is a student,"* **said she**.
(j) "Let's leave," *whispered* Dave. (k) "Please help me," *begged* the unfortunate man. (l) "Well," Jack *began*, "it's a long story."	*Say* and *ask* are the most commonly used quote verbs. Some others: *add, agree, announce, answer, beg, begin, comment, complain, confess, continue, explain, inquire, promise, remark, reply, respond, shout, suggest, whisper.*

*Quoted speech is also called "direct speech." Reported speech (discussed in Chart 12-7) is also called "indirect speech."

**In British English, quotation marks are called "inverted commas" and can consist of either double marks (") or a single mark ('): She said, 'My brother is a student'.

❑ **Exercise 33. Looking at grammar.** (Chart 12-6)
Add punctuation and capitalization.

1. Henry said   there is a phone call for you

2. There is a phone call for you   he said

3. There is   said Henry a phone call for you

4. There is a phone call for you   it's your sister   said Henry

5. There is a phone call for you   he said   it's your sister

6. I asked him   where is the phone

7. Where is the phone   she asked

8. Stop the clock   shouted the referee   we have an injured player

9. Who won the game   asked the spectator

10. I'm going to rest for the next three hours   she said   I don't want to be disturbed

    That's fine   I replied   you get some rest   I'll make sure no one disturbs you

❑ **Exercise 34. Looking at grammar.** (Chart 12-6)
Add punctuation and capitalization. Notice that a new paragraph begins each time the speaker changes.

When the police officer came over to my car, he said   let me see your driver's license, please

What's wrong, Officer   I asked   was I speeding

No, you weren't speeding   he replied you went through a red light at the corner of Fifth Avenue and Main Street   you almost caused an accident

Did I really do that   I said   I didn't see a red light

❏ **Exercise 35. Let's write.** (Chart 12-6)
Write fables using quoted speech.

Summer

Winter

1. In fables, animals have the power of speech. Discuss what is happening in the illustrations of the grasshopper and the ants. Then write a fable based on the illustrations. Use quoted speech in your fable. Read your fable to a partner or small group.

2. Write a fable that is well known in your country. Use quoted speech.

❏ **Exercise 36. Warm-up.** (Chart 12-7)
Read the conversation between Mr. and Mrs. Cook. Then read the description. What do you notice about the verbs in blue?

DESCRIPTION:
Mr. Cook *said* he knew why Mrs. Cook couldn't find her glasses. He *told* her that they were on her head.

12-7 Reported Speech: Verb Forms in Noun Clauses

Quoted Speech	Reported Speech	
(a) "I *watch* TV every day."	→ She said she *watched* TV every day.	*Reported speech* refers to using a noun clause to report what someone has said. No quotation marks are used.
(b) "I *am watching* TV."	→ She said she *was watching* TV.	
(c) "I *have watched* TV."	→ She said she *had watched* TV.	
(d) "I *watched* TV."	→ She said she *had watched* TV.	If the reporting verb (the main verb of the sentence, e.g., *said*) is simple past, the verb in the noun clause will usually also be in a past form, as in these examples.
(e) "I *had watched* TV."	→ She said she *had watched* TV.	
(f) "I *will watch* TV."	→ She said she *would watch* TV.	
(g) "I *am going to watch* TV."	→ She said she *was going to watch* TV.	
(h) "I *can watch* TV."	→ She said she *could watch* TV.	
(i) "I *may watch* TV."	→ She said she *might watch* TV.	
(j) "I *must watch* TV."	→ She said she *had to watch* TV.	
(k) "I *have to watch* TV."	→ She said she *had to watch* TV.	
(l) "I *should watch* TV."	→ She said she *should watch* TV.	In (l): ***should***, ***ought to***, and ***might*** do not change.
"I *ought to watch* TV."	→ She said she *ought to watch* TV.	
"I *might watch* TV."	→ She said she *might watch* TV.	
(m) Immediate reporting: — What did the teacher just say? I didn't hear him. — He said he *wants* us to read Chapter 6. (n) Later reporting: — I didn't go to class yesterday. Did Mr. Jones give any assignments? — Yes. He said he *wanted* us to read Chapter 6.		Changing verbs to past forms in reported speech is common in both speaking and writing. However, sometimes in spoken English, no change is made in the noun clause verb, especially if the speaker is reporting something immediately or soon after it was said.
(o) "The world *is* round."	→ She said the world *is* round.	Also, sometimes the present tense is retained even in formal English when the reported sentence deals with a general truth, as in (o).
(p) "I *watch* TV every day."	→ She *says* she *watches* TV every day.	When the reporting verb is simple present, present perfect or future, the noun clause verb is not changed.
(q) "I *watch* TV every day."	→ She *has said* that she *watches* TV every day.	
(r) "I *watch* TV every day."	→ She *will say* that she *watches* TV every day.	
(s) "*Watch* TV."	→ She *told* me *to watch* TV.★	In reported speech, an imperative sentence is changed to an infinitive. ***Tell*** is used instead of ***say*** as the reporting verb. See Chart 14-6, p. 313, for other verbs followed by an infinitive that are used to report speech.

★NOTE: ***Tell*** is immediately followed by a (pro)noun object, but ***say*** is not: *He told **me** he would be late. He said he would be late.*
Also possible: *He said **to me** he would be late.*

Exercise 37. Looking at grammar. (Chart 12-7)
Complete the sentences by reporting the speaker's words. Use noun clauses. Use past verb forms in noun clauses if appropriate.

1. Pedro said, "I will help you." Pedro said . . . .
   → *Pedro said (that) he would help me.*
2. "Do you need a pen?" Elena asked. Elena asked me . . . . *If I need a pen.*
3. Jennifer asked, "What do you want?" Jennifer asked me . . . . *that what I wanted*
4. Talal asked, "Are you hungry?" Talal wanted to know . . . . *that If I was hungry*
5. "I want a sandwich," Elena said. Elena said . . . . *that she wants a sandwich*
6. "I'm going to move to Ohio," said Bruce. Bruce informed me . . . . *the he is moving to*
7. "Did you enjoy your trip?" asked Kim. Kim asked me . . . . *if I enjoyed my trip*
8. Oscar asked, "What are you talking about?" Oscar asked me . . . . *that what was I was talking about*
9. Maria asked, "Have you seen my grammar book?" Maria wanted to know . . . . *that If I had seen her book*
10. Amy said, "I don't want to go." Amy said . . . . *that she*
11. "Can you help me with my report?" asked David. David asked me . . . .
12. "I may be late," said Mitch. Mitch told me . . . .
13. Felix said, "You should work harder." Felix told me . . . . *I should work H*
14. Nadia said, "I have to go downtown." Nadia said . . . .
15. "Why is the sky blue?" my young daughter often asks. My young daughter often asks me . . . . *whe the sky is blue.*
16. My mother asked, "Where is everyone?" My mother wondered . . . .
17. "I will come to the meeting," said Pavel. Pavel told me . . . .
18. Ms. Adams just asked Ms. Chang, "Will you be in class tomorrow?" Ms. Adams wanted to know . . . .
19. "I think I'll go to the library to study." Joe said . . . .
20. "Does Omar know what he's doing?" I wondered . . . .
21. "Is what I've heard true?" I wondered . . . . *If what I had heard was true.*
22. "The sun rises in the east," said Mr. Clark. Mr. Clark, an elementary school teacher, explained to his students that . . . .
23. "Someday we'll be in contact with beings from outer space." The scientist predicted that . . . .

Exercise 38. Let's talk. (Chart 12-7)
Students A and B have their books open. They read the dialogue aloud. Student C's book is closed. Your teacher asks Student C about the dialogue.

Example:
STUDENT A (*book open*):   What time is it?
STUDENT B (*book open*):   Two-thirty.
TEACHER: What did Manuel (*Student A*) want to know?
STUDENT C (*book closed*): He wanted to know what time it was (OR is).
TEACHER: What did Helen (*Student B*) say?
STUDENT C (*book closed*): She told him that it was (OR is) two-thirty.

1. STUDENT A: Can you speak Arabic?
   STUDENT B: A little.
   TEACHER: What did (*Student A*) ask?
                     What did (*Student B*) say?

2. STUDENT A: Where is your grammar book?
   STUDENT B: In my backpack.
   TEACHER: What did (*Student A*) want to know?
   What did (*Student B*) tell (*Student A*)?

3. STUDENT A: What courses are you taking?
   STUDENT B: I'm taking three science courses this term.
   TEACHER: What did (*Student A*) want to know?
   What did (*Student B*) say?

4. STUDENT A: Did you finish your assignment?
   STUDENT B: Oh, no, my assignment! I totally forgot about it.
   TEACHER: What did (*Student A*) ask?
   What did (*Student B*) tell (*Student A*)?

5. STUDENT A: Have you had lunch already?
   STUDENT B: Yes, I just finished.
   TEACHER: What did . . . ?

6. STUDENT A: Where will you be tomorrow around three o'clock?
   STUDENT B: I have a doctor's appointment at 2:45.

7. STUDENT A: How do you like living here?
   STUDENT B: It's okay.

8. STUDENT A: Is what you said really true?
   STUDENT B: Yes, it's the truth. I'm not making it up.

9. STUDENT A: How many people have you met since you came here?
   STUDENT B: Lots. People here have been very friendly.

10. STUDENT A: Is what you want to talk to me about really important?
    STUDENT B: Yes, it's very important. We need to sit down and have a serious conversation.

❏ **Exercise 39. Let's talk.** (Charts 12-1 → 12-7)
Speaker A asks a question — whatever comes to mind — using each item and a question word (**when, how, where, what, why,** *etc.*). Speaker B answers the question in a complete sentence. Speaker C reports what Speaker A and Speaker B said. Work in small groups or as a class.

Example: tonight
SPEAKER A (*Rosa*): What are you going to do tonight?
SPEAKER B (*Ali*): I'm going to study.
SPEAKER C (*Yung*): Rosa asked Ali what he was going to do tonight. Ali replied that he was going to study.

1. this evening	5. book	9. television
2. music	6. this city	10. dinner
3. courses	7. population	11. next year
4. tomorrow	8. last year	12. vacation

□ **Exercise 40. Looking at grammar.** (Chart 12-7)
Complete the sentences with a past form of the verbs in parentheses.

1. A: The test is scheduled for Monday.
   B: Really? I heard it (*schedule*) ___was scheduled___ for Tuesday.

2. A: It's raining outside.
   B: Really? I thought it (*snow*) ___was snowing___.

3. A: Tony needs to borrow your bike for Saturday.
   B: Are you sure? I heard he (*need*) ___was needed___ to borrow it for Sunday.

4. A: Marita hasn't applied for a job yet.
   B: That's not what I heard. I heard she (*apply*) ___had applyed___ for work
   at her uncle's company.

5. A: Mikhail can't come tonight.
   B: Are you sure? I heard he (*come*) ___would come. / could come / is coming___ tonight.

6. A: Ms. Alvarez is going to retire.
   B: Really? I thought she (*continue*) ___was continued / continuing.___ in her sales
   position for another year. ___

□ **Exercise 41. Listening.** (Chart 12-7)

CD 2
Track 2

Listen to the sentences. Complete them using past verb forms to report speech.

1. The speaker said that she ___wasn't going___ to the personnel meeting
   because she ___had to___ finish a report.

2. The speaker said that he _____ Marta any money because his
   wallet _____ in his coat pocket back at home.

3. The speaker said that someone in the room _____ very strong
   perfume and it _____ her a headache.

4. The speaker said that he _____ Emma at the coffee shop at 9:00.
   He said he _____ not to be late.

5. The speaker said she _____ looking for a new job and asked
   her friend what he _____ she _____.

6. The speaker said that they _____ late for the concert
   because his wife _____ attend a business function after work.

264 CHAPTER 12

❏ **Exercise 42. Looking at grammar.** (Chart 12-7)
Change quoted speech to reported speech. Study the example carefully and use the same pattern: *said that . . . and that*.

1. "My father is a businessman. My mother is an engineer."

    He said that _____ *his father was a businessman and that his mother was an engineer.* _____

2. "I'm excited about my new job. I've found a nice apartment."

    I got an email from my sister yesterday. She said _____

    _____

3. "I expect you to be in class every day. Unexcused absences may affect your grades."

    Our sociology professor said _____

    _____

4. "Highway 66 will be closed for two months. Commuters should seek alternate routes."

    The newspaper said _____

    _____

5. "Every obstacle is a steppingstone to success. You should view problems in your life as

    opportunities to prove yourself."

    My father often told me _____

    _____

❏ **Exercise 43. Let's write.** (Charts 12-1 → 12-7)
Read each dialogue and write a report about it. Your report should include an accurate idea of the speaker's words, but it doesn't have to use the exact words.

Example: Jack said, "I can't go to the game."
Tom said, "Oh? Why not?"
"I don't have enough money for a ticket," replied Jack.

Possible written reports:
→ Jack told Tom that he couldn't go to the game because he didn't have enough money for a ticket.
→ When Tom asked Jack why he couldn't go to the game, Jack said he didn't have enough money for a ticket.
→ Jack said he couldn't go to the game. When Tom asked him why not, Jack replied that he didn't have enough money for a ticket.

Write reports for these dialogues.
1. "What are you doing?" Alex asked.
   "I'm drawing a picture," I said.

2. Asako said, "Do you want to go to a movie Sunday night?"

Cho said, "I'd like to, but I have to study."

3. "How old are you, Mrs. Robinson?" the little boy asked.

   Mrs. Robinson said, "It's not polite to ask people their age."

   "How much money do you make?" the little boy asked.

   "That's impolite too," Mrs. Robinson said.

4. "Is there anything you especially want to watch on TV tonight?" my sister asked.

   "Yes," I replied. "There's a show at eight that I've been waiting to see for a long time."

   "What is it?" she asked.

   "It's a documentary on green sea turtles," I said.

   "Why do you want to see that?"

   "I'm doing a research paper on sea turtles. I think I might be able to get some good information from the documentary. Why don't you watch it with me?"

   "No, thanks," she said. "I'm not especially interested in green sea turtles."

☐ **Exercise 44. Check your knowledge.** (Charts 12-1 → 12-7)
Correct the errors.

1. Tell the taxi driver where do you want to go.

2. My roommate came into the room and asked me why aren't you in class? I said I am *[was]*
   waiting for a telephone call from my family.

3. It was my first day at the university, and I am *[was]* on my way to my first class. I wondered who
   else will *[would]* be in the class. What the teacher would be like?

4. He asked me that what did I intend to do after I graduate? *[graduation]*

5. What does a patient tell a doctor it is confidential.

6. What my friend and I did it was our secret. We didn't even tell our parents what did we do. *[did]*

7. The doctor asked that I felt okay. *[If]* I told him that I don't *[didn't]* feel well.

8. I asked him what kind of movies does he like, he said me, "I like romantic movies." *[told]*

9. "Is true you almost drowned?" my friend asked me. "Yes," I said. "I'm really glad to be alive. It
   was really frightening."

10. It is a fact that I almost drowned makes me very careful about water safety whenever I go
    swimming.

11. I didn't know where am *[was]* I supposed to get off the bus, so I asked the driver where is the
    science museum. She tell *[was]* me the name of the street. She said she will *[would]* tell me when should
    I get off the bus.

12. My mother did not live with us. When other children asked me where was my mother,
was
I told them she ~~is~~ going to come to visit me very soon.

" would
13. When I asked the taxi driver to drive faster, he said I ~~will~~ drive faster if you pay me more. *"*

At that time I didn't care how much would it cost, so I told him to go as fast as he can.

14. My parents told me is essential to know English if I want to study at an American
it
university.

☐ **Exercise 45. Let's talk.** (Charts 12-1 → 12-7)
Give a one-minute impromptu speech on any topic that interests you (insects, soccer, dogs, etc.). Your classmates will take notes as you speak. Later, in a short paragraph or orally, they will report what you said.

☐ **Exercise 46. Let's talk and write.** (Charts 12-1 → 12-7)
You and your classmates are newspaper reporters at a press conference. You will all interview your teacher or a person whom your teacher invites to class. Your assignment is to write a newspaper article about the person whom you interviewed.

Take notes during the interview. Write down some of the important sentences so that you can use them for quotations in your article. Ask for clarification if you do not understand something the interviewee has said. It is important to report information accurately.

In your article, try to organize your information into related topics. For example, if you interview your teacher, you might use this outline:

I. General introductory information
II. Professional life
   A. Present teaching duties
   B. Academic duties and activities outside of teaching
   C. Past teaching experience
   D. Educational background
III. Personal life
   A. Basic biographical information (e.g., place of birth, family background, places of residence)
   B. Free-time activities and interests
   C. Travel experiences

This outline only suggests a possible method of organization. You must organize your own article, depending upon the information you have gained from your interview.

When you write your report, most of your information will be presented in reported speech; use quoted speech only for the most important or memorable sentences.

NOTE: When you use quoted speech, be sure you are presenting the interviewee's *exact words*. If you are simply paraphrasing what the interviewee said, do not use quotation marks.

❑ **Exercise 47. Let's talk and write.** (Charts 12-1 → 12-7)
Work in small groups. Discuss one (or more) of the given statements. Write a report of the main points made by each speaker in your group. (Do not attempt to report every word that was spoken.)

In your report, use words such as **think, believe, say, remark**, and **state** to introduce noun clauses. When you use **think** or **believe**, you will probably use present tenses (e.g., *Omar* **thinks** *that money* **is** *the most important thing in life.*). When you use **say, remark**, or **state**, you will probably use past tenses (e.g., *Olga* **said** *that many other things* **were** *more important than money.*).

Do you agree with these statements? Why or why not?
1. Money is the most important thing in life.
2. A woman can do any job a man can do.
3. When a person decides to get married, his or her love for the other person is the only important consideration.
4. A world government is both desirable and necessary. Countries should simply become the states of one nation, the Earth. In this way, wars could be eliminated and wealth could be equally distributed.

❑ **Exercise 48. Warm-up.** (Chart 12-8)
Read the sentences. Then substitute the phrases in the list for the words in blue.

SITUATION: Mr. and Mrs. Smith plan to retire soon and travel around the world.

in any way that	anything that	any place that	at any time that

1. They'll go wherever they want.
2. They'll leave whenever they want.
3. They'll do whatever they want.
4. They'll help people however they can.

12-8 Using *-ever* Words

The following **-ever** words give the idea of "any." Each pair of sentences in the examples has the same meaning.

whoever	(a) **Whoever** wants to come is welcome. *Anyone who* wants to come is welcome.
	(b) He makes friends easily with **whoever** he meets.* He makes friends easily with *anyone who* he meets.
whatever	(c) He always says **whatever** comes into his mind. He always says *anything that* comes into his mind.
whenever	(d) You may leave **whenever** you wish. You may leave *at any time that* you wish.
wherever	(e) She can go **wherever** she wants to go. She can go *anyplace that* she wants to go.
however	(f) The students may dress **however** they please. The students may dress *in any way that* they please.

*In (b): **whomever** is also possible; it is the object of the verb **meets**. In American English, **whomever** is rare and very formal. In British English, **whoever** (not **whomever**) is used as the object form: *He makes friends easily with whoever he meets.*

○ **Exercise 49. Looking at grammar.** (Chart 12-8)
Complete the sentences with *-ever* words.

1. Mustafa is free to go anyplace he wishes. He can go _____*wherever*_____ he wants.

2. Mustafa is free to go anytime he wishes. He can go _____ he wants.

3. I don't know what you should do about that problem. Do _____ seems best to you.

4. I want you to be honest. I hope you feel free to say _____ is on your mind.

5. _____ leads a life full of love and happiness is rich.

6. If you want to rearrange the furniture, go ahead. You can rearrange it _____ you want. I don't care one way or the other.

7. Those children are wild! I feel sorry for _____ has to be their babysitter.

8. I have a car. I can take you _____ you want to go.

9. Irene does _____ she wants to do, goes _____ she wants to go, gets up _____ she wants to get up, makes friends with _____ she meets, and dresses _____ she pleases.

Chapter 13
Adjective Clauses

❏ **Exercise 1. Warm-up.** (Chart 13-1)
The sentences are all correct. The words in blue are all pronouns. What nouns do they refer to? How does the noun affect the choice of the pronoun?

1. a. We helped the man. He was lost in the woods.
   b. We helped the man who was lost in the woods.
   c. We helped the man that was lost in the woods.

2. a. The new computer is fast. It is in my office.
   b. The new computer which is in my office is fast.
   c. The new computer that is in my office is fast.

13-1 Adjective Clause Pronouns Used as the Subject

<table>
<tr>
<td colspan="2">

I thanked the woman.
She helped me.
↓

(a) I thanked the woman   **who** *helped me.*
(b) I thanked the woman   **that** *helped me.*
</td>
<td>

In (a): ***I thanked the woman*** = a main clause;
      who helped me = an adjective clause.★

An adjective clause modifies a noun.

In (a): the adjective clause modifies ***woman***.
</td>
</tr>
<tr>
<td colspan="2">

The book is mine.
It is on the table.
↓

(c) The book ***which*** *is on the table* is mine.
(d) The book ***that***   *is on the table* is mine.
</td>
<td>

In (a): ***who*** is the subject of the adjective clause.

In (b): ***that*** is the subject of the adjective clause.

NOTE: (a) and (b) have the same meaning; (c) and (d) have the same meaning.
</td>
</tr>
<tr>
<td colspan="2"></td>
<td>

who = used for people
which = used for things
that = used for both people and things
</td>
</tr>
<tr>
<td colspan="2">

(e) CORRECT: The book ***that is on the table*** is mine.
(f) *INCORRECT:* The book is mine ~~that is on the table.~~
</td>
<td>

An adjective clause closely follows the noun it modifies.
</td>
</tr>
</table>

★A *clause* is a structure that has a subject and a verb. There are two kinds of clauses: **independent** and **dependent**.
  In example (a):
  • The main clause (*I thanked the woman*) is also called an **independent** clause. An independent clause is a complete sentence and can stand alone.
  • The adjective clause (*who helped me*) is a **dependent** clause. A dependent clause is NOT a complete sentence and cannot stand alone. A dependent clause must be connected to an independent clause.

❏ **Exercise 2. Looking at grammar.** (Chart 13-1)
Choose all the possible completions for each sentence. Do not add any commas or capital letters.

1. I met the doctor _____ helped my father after the accident.
   (a.) who   (b.) that   c. which   d. she

2. Where is the magazine _____ has the story about online theft?
   a. who   b. that   c. which   d. it

3. Did I tell you about the car salesman _____ tried to sell me a defective truck?
   a. who   b. that   c. which   d. he

4. The house _____ is across the street from us is going to be rented soon.
   a. who   b. that   c. which   d. it

❏ **Exercise 3. Looking at grammar.** (Chart 13-1)
Combine the two sentences. Use the second sentence as an adjective clause.

1. I saw the man. He closed the door. → *I saw the man* $\begin{Bmatrix} who \\ that \end{Bmatrix}$ *closed the door.*
2. The girl is happy. She won the race.
3. The student is from China. He sits next to me.
4. The students are from China. They sit in the front row.
5. We are studying sentences. They contain adjective clauses.
6. I am using a sentence. It contains an adjective clause.

❏ **Exercise 4. Let's talk.** (Chart 13-1)
Make true statements. Use *who* as the subject of an adjective clause. Work in pairs, in small groups, or as a class.

Example: I like teachers who . . . .
            I like teachers who have a good sense of humor.
            I like teachers who don't give tests. Etc.

1. People who . . . amaze me.
2. I don't like people who . . . .
3. Friends who . . . frustrate me.
4. Famous athletes who . . . are not good role models for children.

❏ **Exercise 5. Listening.** (Chart 13-1)
Part I. When *who* is contracted with an auxiliary verb, the contraction is often hard to hear. Listen to the following sentences. What is the full, uncontracted form of the *italicized* verb?

CD 2
Track 3

1. He has a friend *who'll* help him. (*full form = who will*)
2. He has a friend *who's* helping him.
3. He has a friend *who's* helped him.
4. He has friends *who're* helping him.
5. He has friends *who've* helped him.
6. He has a friend *who'd* helped him.
7. He has a friend *who'd* like to help him.

Part II. Complete the sentences with the verbs you hear, but write the full, uncontracted form of each verb.

Example: You will hear: I know a man who's lived in 20 different countries.

You will write: I know a man who _____*has lived*_____ in 20 different countries.

8. We know a person who _____ great for the job.

9. We know a person who _____ to apply for the job.

10. That's the man who _____ the speech at our graduation.

11. I know a nurse who _____ around the world helping people.

12. Let's talk to the people who _____ the protest march.

13. There are people at the factory who _____ there all their adult lives.

14. The doctor who _____ care of my mother retired.

❑ **Exercise 6. Warm-up.** (Chart 13-2)
Read the passage and complete the sentences.

    When William and Eva started their family, they decided that Eva would continue to work and William would quit his job to stay home with the children.

    William has been a stay-at-home dad for the last seven years, but now both children are in school, and he's going back to work. He's looking for a job that will still allow him to spend time with his children. What kind of job do you think he is looking for?

He is looking for a job that/which . . . OR *He is not looking for a job that/which . . .*

1. leave him free on weekends
2. require him to work on weekends
3. include a lot of long-distance travel
4. have minimal travel requirements
5. have a long commute
6. be close to home
7. demand sixteen-hour work days
8. have flexible hours

13-2 Adjective Clause Pronouns Used as the Object of a Verb

The man was Mr. Jones. I saw **him**. ↓ (a) The man **who(m)** *I saw* was Mr. Jones. (b) The man **that** *I saw* was Mr. Jones. (c) The man Ø *I saw* was Mr. Jones.	Notice in the examples: The adjective clause pronouns are placed at the beginning of the clause.
The movie wasn't very good. We saw **it** last night. ↓ (d) The movie **which** *we saw last night* wasn't very good. (e) The movie **that** *we saw last night* wasn't very good. (f) The movie Ø *we saw last night* wasn't very good.	In (a): **who** is usually used instead of **whom**, especially in speaking. **Whom** is generally used only in very formal English. In (c) and (f): An object pronoun is often omitted (Ø) from an adjective clause. (A subject pronoun, however, may not be omitted.) **who(m)** = used for people **which** = used for things **that** = used for both people and things

(g) *INCORRECT:* The man who(m) I saw ~~him~~ was Mr. Jones.
                    The man that I saw ~~him~~ was Mr. Jones.
                    The man I saw ~~him~~ was Mr. Jones.
	In (g): The pronoun **him** must be removed. It is unnecessary because *who(m)*, *that*, or Ø functions as the object of the verb **saw**.

❑ **Exercise 7. Looking at grammar.** (Chart 13-2)
Choose all the possible completions for each sentence. Do not add any commas or capital letters.

1. Tell me about the people _____ you visited when you were in Oxford.
   (a.) who   (b.) that   c. which   d. she   (e.) whom   (f.) Ø

2. Do you want to see the pictures _____ the photographer took?
   a. who   b. that   c. which   d. they   e. whom   f. Ø

3. The people _____ I call most often on my cell phone are my mother and my sister.
   a. who   b. that   c. which   d. she   e. whom   f. Ø

4. The apartment _____ we wanted to rent is no longer available.
   a. who   b. that   c. which   d. it   e. whom   f. Ø

5. The children _____ the Smiths adopted are from three different countries.
   a. who   b. that   c. which   d. they   e. whom   f. Ø

❑ **Exercise 8. Looking at grammar.** (Chart 13-2)
Combine the two sentences. Use the second sentence as an adjective clause. Give all the possible patterns, orally or in writing.

1. The book was good. I read it.
   → *The book that/which/Ø I read was good.*
2. I liked the woman. I met her at the party last night.
3. I liked the composition. You wrote it.
4. The people were very nice. We visited them yesterday.
5. The man is standing over there. Ann brought him to the party.

□ **Exercise 9. Warm-up.** (Chart 13-3)
Compare the <u>underlined</u> adjective clause in sentence a. with the one in sentence b. What differences do you notice? NOTE: Both sentences are correct.

1. a. I think Lee is a person <u>who you can have fun with</u>.
   b. Do you think Lee is a person <u>with whom you can have fun</u>?

2. a. The art school <u>which Lori applied to</u> is very demanding.
   b. Do you know the name of the art school <u>to which Lori applied</u>?

13-3 Adjective Clause Pronouns Used as the Object of a Preposition

	She is the woman. I told you **about her**.		In very formal English, the preposition comes at the beginning of the adjective clause, as in (a) and (e). Usually, however, in everyday usage, the preposition comes after the subject and verb of the adjective clause, as in the other examples.
(a)	She is the woman	*about whom*	*I told you.*
(b)	She is the woman	*who(m)*	*I told you about.*
(c)	She is the woman	*that*	*I told you about.*
(d)	She is the woman	Ø	*I told you about.*

	The music was good. We listened **to it** last night.		NOTE: If the preposition comes at the beginning of the adjective clause, only **whom** or **which** may be used. A preposition is never immediately followed by **that** or **who**.
(e)	The music	*to which*	*we listened*	*last night*	was good.
(f)	The music	*which*	*we listened to*	*last night*	was good.
(g)	The music	*that*	*we listened to*	*last night*	was good.
(h)	The music	Ø	*we listened to*	*last night*	was good.

INCORRECT: She is the woman ~~about who~~ I told you.

INCORRECT: The music ~~to that~~ we listened last night was good.

□ **Exercise 10. Looking at grammar.** (Chart 13-3)
Choose all the possible completions for each sentence. Which one seems the most formal?

1. The sunglasses _____ were under the sofa.
   a. which I was looking for
   b. that I was looking for
   c. I was looking for
   d. I was looking
   e. I was looking for them

2. The health-care workers _____ were helpful.
   a. who I spoke to
   b. that I spoke to
   c. who I spoke to them
   d. to whom I spoke
   e. to who I spoke
   f. I spoke to

□ **Exercise 11. Looking at grammar.** (Chart 13-3)
Combine the two sentences. Use the second sentence as an adjective clause. Give all the possible patterns, orally or in writing.

1. The man is standing over there. I was telling you about him.
2. I must thank the people. I got a present from them.
3. The meeting was interesting. Omar went to it.

❏ **Exercise 12. Looking at grammar.** (Charts 13-1 → 13-3)
Give all the possible completions for each sentence.

1. The dress ____*that / which / Ø*____ she is wearing is new.

2. Did I tell you about the woman _____ I met last night?

3. The report _____ Joe is writing must be finished by Friday.

4. The doctor _____ examined the sick child was gentle.

5. Did you hear about the earthquake _____ occurred in California?

6. The woman _____ I was dancing with stepped on my toes.

❏ **Exercise 13. Looking at grammar.** (Charts 13-1 → 13-3)
<u>Underline</u> the adjective clause in each sentence. Give all other possible patterns.

1. The woman <u>that I spoke to</u> gave me good advice.
   → *who(m) I spoke to*
   → *I spoke to*
   → *to whom I spoke*

2. I returned the money which I had borrowed from my roommate.

3. Yesterday I ran into an old friend I hadn't seen for years.

4. Marie lectured on a topic she knew very little about.

5. I read about a man who keeps chickens in his apartment.

❏ **Exercise 14. Check your knowledge.** (Charts 13-1 → 13-3)
Correct the errors in the adjective clauses.

1. In our village, there were many people didn't have much money.

2. I enjoyed the book that you told me to read it.

3. I still remember the man who he taught me to play the guitar when I was a boy.

4. I showed my father a picture of the car I am going to buy it as soon as I save enough money.

5. The woman about who I was talking about suddenly walked into the room.
   I hope she didn't hear me.

6. The people appear in the play are amateur actors.

7. I don't like to spend time with people which loses their temper easily.

8. While the boy was at the airport, he took pictures of people which was waiting for their planes.

9. People who works in the hunger program they estimate that 45,000 people worldwide die from starvation and malnutrition-related diseases every single day of the year.

10. In one corner of the marketplace, an old man who was playing a violin.

❑ **Exercise 15. Looking at grammar: pairwork.** (Charts 13-1 → 13-3)
Work with a partner. Speaker A looks at the cue briefly. Then, without looking at the text, Speaker A says the cue to Speaker B. Speaker B begins the answer with *Yes*.

Examples:
SPEAKER A (*book open*): You drank *some* tea. Did it taste good?
SPEAKER B (*book closed*): Yes, *the* tea I drank tasted good.

SPEAKER A (*book open*): A police officer helped you. Did you thank her?
SPEAKER B (*book closed*): Yes, I thanked *the* police officer who helped me.

1. You are sitting in a chair. Is it comfortable?
2. You saw a man. Was he wearing a brown suit?
3. A woman stepped on your toes. Did she apologize?
4. Some students took a test. Did most of them pass?
5. You were reading a book. Did you finish it?
6. A taxi driver took you to the bus station. Did you have a conversation with her?

Change roles.
7. You stayed at a hotel. Was it in the center of town?
8. A waiter served you at a restaurant. Was he polite?
9. A woman came into the room. Did you recognize her?
10. Some students are sitting in this room. Can all of them speak English?
11. You were looking for a dictionary. Did you find it?
12. A clerk cashed your check. Did he ask for identification?

❑ **Exercise 16. Warm-up.** (Chart 13-4)
Check (✓) the sentences that are grammatically correct .

1. ___ I have a friend. His purpose in life is to help others.

2. ___ I have a friend whose purpose in life is to help others.

3. ___ I have a friend who his purpose in life is to help others.

4. ___ I have a friend that his purpose in life is to help others.

13-4 Using *Whose*

I know the man. ***His bicycle*** was stolen. ↓ (a) I know the man ***whose bicycle*** *was stolen*.	***Whose*** is used to show possession. It carries the same meaning as other possessive pronouns used as adjectives: *his, her, its,* and *their*.

	Like *his, her, its,* and *their,* ***whose*** is connected to a noun:
	   his bicycle → *whose bicycle*
	   her composition → *whose composition*

The student writes well. I read ***her composition***. ↓ (b) The student ***whose composition*** *I read* writes well.	Both ***whose*** and the noun it is connected to are placed at the beginning of the adjective clause. ***Whose*** cannot be omitted.
(c) I worked at a ***company whose employees*** wanted to form a union.	***Whose*** usually modifies people, but it may also be used to modify things, as in (c).
(d) That's the boy ***whose parents*** you met. (e) That's the boy ***who's*** in my math class. (f) That's the boy ***who's been living*** at our house since his mother was arrested.*	***Whose*** and ***who's*** have the same pronunciation. ***Who's*** can mean ***who is***, as in (e), or ***who has***, as in (f).

*When ***has*** is a helping verb in the present perfect, it is usually contracted with ***who*** in speaking and sometimes in informal writing, as in (f).
When ***has*** is a main verb, it is NOT contracted with ***who***: *I know a man* ***who has*** *a cook*.

❑ **Exercise 17. Looking at grammar.** (Chart 13-4)
Complete the sentences with ***who*** or ***whose***.

1. I know a doctor _____*whose*_____ last name is Doctor.

2. I know a doctor _____*who*_____ lives on a sailboat.

3. The woman _____ wallet was stolen called the police.

4. The woman _____ found my wallet called me immediately.

5. The professor _____ teaches art history is excellent.

6. The professor _____ course I am taking is excellent.

7. I apologized to the man _____ coffee I spilled.

8. I made friends with a man _____ is in my class.

Adjective Clauses **277**

❏ **Exercise 18. Looking at grammar.** (Chart 13-4)
Combine the two sentences. Use the second sentence as an adjective clause.

1. I met the woman. Her husband is the president of the corporation.
   → *I met the woman whose husband is the president of the corporation.*
2. Mrs. North teaches a class for students. Their native language is not English.
3. The people were nice. We visited their house.
4. I live in a dormitory. Its residents come from many countries.
5. I have to call the man. I accidentally picked up his umbrella after the meeting.
6. The man poured a glass of water on his face. His beard caught on fire when he lit a cigarette.

❏ **Exercise 19. Listening.** (Chart 13-4)
Circle the words you hear: ***who's*** or ***whose***.

CD 2
Track 4

Example: You will hear: The man who's standing over there is Mr. Smith.
            You will choose: (who's)   whose

1. who's	whose	5. who's	whose
2. who's	whose	6. who's	whose
3. who's	whose	7. who's	whose
4. who's	whose	8. who's	whose

❏ **Exercise 20. Let's talk: pairwork.** (Chart 13-4)
Work with a partner. Pretend you are in a room full of people. You and your partner are speaking. Together, you are identifying various people in the room. Begin each sentence with ***There is***. Alternate items, with Partner A doing item 1, Partner B doing item 2, Partner A doing item 3, etc.

1. That man's wife is your teacher.
   → PARTNER A: *There is the man whose wife is my teacher.*
2. That woman's husband is a football player.
   → PARTNER B: *There is the woman whose husband is a football player.*
3. That girl's mother is a dentist.
4. That person's picture was in the newspaper.
5. That woman's car was stolen.
6. That man's daughter won a gold medal at the Olympic Games.
7. You found that woman's keys.
8. You are in that teacher's class.
9. You read that author's book.
10. You borrowed that student's lecture notes.

Exercise 21. Listening. (Chart 13-4)

Listen to the sentences in normal, contracted speech. You will hear: *whose*, *who's* (meaning *who is*), or *who's* (meaning *who has*). Circle the correct meaning.

CD 2
Track 5

Example: You will hear: I know a woman who's a taxi driver.
You will choose: whose   (who is)   who has

1. whose	who is	who has		5. whose	who is	who has
2. whose	who is	who has		6. whose	who is	who has
3. whose	who is	who has		7. whose	who is	who has
4. whose	who is	who has		8. whose	who is	who has

❑ **Exercise 22. Let's talk: small groups.** (Chart 13-1 → 13-4)

Complete the sentences orally in small groups. Discuss each other's choices and opinions.

1. A famous person _____ life I admire is _____.
2. _____ is a famous person _____ has made the world a better place.
3. A person _____ is having a good influence on world affairs today is _____.
4. _____ is a country _____ is having a bad influence on world affairs today.
5. _____ is a country _____ leadership on issues of global warming is much admired throughout the world.

❑ **Exercise 23. Warm-up.** (Chart 13-5)

All of these sentences have the same meaning, and all of them are grammatically correct. The adjective clauses are in blue. What differences do you notice?

1. The **town** where I grew up is very small.
2. The **town** in which I grew up is very small.
3. The **town** which I grew up in is very small.
4. The **town** that I grew up in is very small.
5. The **town** I grew up in is very small.

13-5 Using *Where* in Adjective Clauses

		The building is very old. He lives **there** (**in that building**).		**Where** is used in an adjective clause to modify a place (*city, country, room, house, etc.*).	
(a)	The building	*where*	*he lives*	is very old.	If **where** is used, a preposition is NOT included in the adjective clause, as in (a).
(b)	The building	*in which*	*he lives*	is very old.	
	The building	*which*	*he lives in*	is very old.	If **where** is not used, the preposition must be included, as in (b).
	The building	*that*	*he lives in*	is very old.	
	The building	*Ø*	*he lives in*	is very old.	

Exercise 24. Looking at grammar. (Chart 13-5)
Combine the two sentences. Use the second sentence as an adjective clause.

1. The city was beautiful. We spent our vacation there (in that city).
2. That is the restaurant. I will meet you there (at that restaurant).
3. The office is busy. I work there (in that office).
4. That is the drawer. I keep my jewelry there (in that drawer).

❑ **Exercise 25. Warm-up.** (Chart 13-6)
All of these sentences have the same meaning, and all of them are grammatically correct. The adjective clauses are in blue. What differences do you notice?

1. I clearly remember the **day** when I rode a bike for the first time.
2. I clearly remember the **day** on which I rode a bike for the first time.
3. I clearly remember the **day** that I rode a bike for the first time.
4. I clearly remember the **day** I rode a bike for the first time.

13-6 Using *When* in Adjective Clauses

	I'll never forget the day. I met you **then** (**on that day**).		When is used in an adjective clause to modify a noun of time (*year, day, time, century,* etc.).	
(a)	I'll never forget the day	**when**	*I met you.*	The use of a preposition in an adjective clause that modifies a noun of time is somewhat different from that in other adjective clauses: a preposition is used preceding **which**, as in (b); otherwise, the preposition is omitted.
(b)	I'll never forget the day	**on which**	*I met you.*	
(c)	I'll never forget the day	**that**	*I met you.*	
(d)	I'll never forget the day	Ø	*I met you.*	

❑ **Exercise 26. Looking at grammar.** (Chart 13-6)
Combine the two sentences. Use the second sentence as an adjective clause.

1. Monday is the day. They will come then (on that day).

2. 7:05 is the time. My plane arrives then (at that time).

3. 1960 is the year. The revolution took place then (in that year).

4. July is the month. The weather is usually the hottest then (in that month).

❑ **Exercise 27. Looking at grammar.** (Charts 13-5 and 13-6)
Combine the two sentences. Use **where** or **when** to introduce an adjective clause.

1. That is the place. The accident occurred there.
→ *That is the place **where** the accident occurred.*
2. There was a time. Movies cost a dime then.
→ *There was a time **when** movies cost a dime.*
3. A café is a small restaurant. People can get a light meal there.
4. Every neighborhood in Brussels has small cafés. Customers drink coffee and eat pastries there.
5. There was a time. Dinosaurs dominated the earth then.
6. The house was destroyed in an earthquake ten years ago. I was born and grew up there.
7. The miser hid his money in a place. It was safe from robbers there.
8. There came a time. The miser had to spend his money then.

❑ **Exercise 28. Let's talk: interview.** (Charts 13-1 → 13-6)
Interview two classmates for each item. Encourage them to use adjective clauses that modify the nouns in **bold**. Share a few of their answers with the class.

Example: What kind of **food** don't you like?
→ *I don't like* **food** *that is too sugary.*

1. What kind of **people** do you like to spend time with?
2. What kind of **people** do you prefer to avoid?
3. What kind of **cities** do you like to visit?
4. What kind of **teachers** do you learn best from?
5. What kind of **place** would you like to live in?
6. What **time of day** do you feel most energetic?

❑ **Exercise 29. Listening.** (Charts 13-1 → 13-6)
Listen to the sentences. Choose the correct meanings for each sentence.

CD 2
Track 6

Example: You will hear: The nurse who gave the medicine to the patients seemed confused.
You will choose: a. The patients were confused.
b. The patients received medicine from the nurse.
c. The nurse was confused.

1. a. A man organized the dinner.
   b. The man is the speaker's friend.
   c. The speaker organized the dinner.

2. a. Two people were killed in an accident.
   b. Two people blocked all lanes of the highway for two hours.
   c. An accident blocked all lanes of the highway for two hours.

3. a. The speaker lives in a large city.
   b. The speaker was born in a small town.
   c. The speaker was born in a large city.

4. a. The music teacher and the students play in a rock band.
   b. The music teacher directs a rock band.
   c. The music teacher plays in a rock band.

5. a. The speaker gave Jack a camera for his birthday.
   b. The camera takes excellent pictures.
   c. Jack takes excellent pictures.

6. a. The speaker often invites the neighbor to dinner.
   b. The neighbor often visits at dinnertime.
   c. The speaker visits the neighbor at dinnertime.

❑ **Exercise 30. Let's talk.** (Charts 13-1 → 13-6)
Work in small groups or as a class. The leader will ask Speaker A a question. The leader will then ask Speaker B to summarize the information in Speaker A's response in one sentence beginning with *The*. Speaker B will use an adjective clause. Only the leader's book is open.

Example:
LEADER: Who got an email yesterday?
SPEAKER A (*Ali*): I did.
LEADER to A: Who was it from?
SPEAKER A: My brother.
LEADER to B: Summarize this information. Begin with *The*.
SPEAKER B: The email (*Ali*) got yesterday was from his brother.

1. Who lives in an apartment?
   Is it close to school?

2. Who is wearing earrings?
   What are they made of?

3. Pick up something that doesn't belong to you.
   What is it? Whose is it?

(Change leaders if working in groups.)

4. Who grew up in a small town?
   In what part of the country is it located?

5. Who has bought something recently?
   Was it expensive?

6. Who went to a restaurant yesterday?
   Was it crowded?

(Change leaders if working in groups.)

7. What did you have for dinner last night?
   Was it good?

8. Who watched a TV program last night?
   What was it about?

9. Who has borrowed something recently?
   What did you borrow?
   Who does it belong to?

(Change leaders if working in groups.)

10. Who shops for groceries?
    What is the name of the store?

11. Who eats lunch away from home?
    Where do you usually eat?
    Does it have good food?

12. Who took the bus to class today?
    Was it late or on time?

❑ **Exercise 31. Warm-up.** (Chart 13-7)
Underline each adjective clause. Draw an arrow to the word it modifies.

1. A: Is it okay if I come along on the picnic?
   B: Absolutely! Anyone who wants to come is more than welcome.

2. A: Should I apply for the opening in the sales department?
   B: I don't think so. They're looking for somebody who speaks Spanish.

3. A: Everything the Smiths do costs a lot of money.
   B: It's amazing, isn't it?

4. A: You're the only one who really understands me.
   B: Oh, that can't be true.

13-7 Using Adjective Clauses to Modify Pronouns

(a) There is **someone** *I want you to meet.* (b) **Everything** *he said* was pure nonsense. (c) **Anybody** *who wants to come* is welcome.	Adjective clauses can modify indefinite pronouns (e.g., *someone, everybody*). Object pronouns (e.g., *who(m), that, which*) are usually omitted in the adjective clause, as in (a) and (b).
(d) Paula was **the only one** *I knew at the party.* (e) Scholarships are available for *those* who need financial assistance.	Adjective clauses can modify **the one(s)** and **those**.*
(f) INCORRECT: ~~I who am a student at this school~~ come from a country in Asia. (g) It is **I** *who am responsible.* (h) **He** *who laughs last* laughs best.	Adjective clauses are almost never used to modify personal pronouns. Native English speakers would not write the sentence in (f). Example (g) is possible, but very formal and uncommon. Example (h) is a well-known saying in which **he** is used as an indefinite pronoun (meaning "anyone" or "any person").

*An adjective clause with **which** can also be used to modify the demonstrative pronoun **that**:
    *We sometimes fear **that which** we do not understand.*
    *The bread my mother makes is much better than **that which** you can buy at a store.*

❏ **Exercise 32. Looking at grammar.** (Chart 13-7)
Complete the sentences with adjective clauses.

1. Ask Jackie. She's the only one _____*who knows the answer.*_____

2. I have a question. There is something _____

3. He can't trust anyone. There's no one _____

4. I'm powerless to help her. There's nothing _____

5. I know someone _____

6. What was Mr. Wood talking about? I didn't understand anything _____
_____

7. I listen to everything _____

8. You shouldn't believe everything _____

9. All of the students are seated. The teacher is the only one _____
_____

10. The test we took yesterday was easier than the one _____

11. The courses I'm taking this term are more difficult than the ones _____
_____

12. The concert had already begun. Those _____
had to wait until intermission to be seated.

❏ **Exercise 33. Listening.** (Charts 13-1 → 13-7)

CD 2
Track 7

Listen to the entire conversation with your book closed. Then open your book and listen again. Complete the sentences with the words you hear. Write the uncontracted forms.

A: Do you see that guy _____ wearing the baseball cap?
1

B: I see two guys _____ wearing baseball caps. Do you mean the one
2

_____ T-shirt says "Be Happy"?
     3

A: Yeah, him. Do you remember him from high school? He looks a little different now,

doesn't he? Isn't he the one _____ joined the circus?
4

B: Nah, I heard that story too. That was just a rumor. When the circus was in town last

summer, his wife spent a lot of time there, so people started wondering why. Some people

started saying she was working there as a performer. But the truth is that she was only

visiting a cousin _____ a manager for the circus. She just wanted to spend
5

time with him while he was in town.

A: Well, you know, it was a story _____ pretty fishy* to me. But people
6

sure enjoyed talking about it. The last thing _____ was that
7

she'd learned how to eat fire and swallow swords!

B: Rumors really take on a life of their own, don't they?!

---

fishy = suspicious; hard to believe.

❑ **Exercise 34. Warm-up.** (Chart 13-8)
Listen to your teacher read the sentences aloud. Both are correct. Notice the use of pauses. Then answer these questions for both sentences:
- Which adjective clause can be omitted with no change in the meaning of the noun it modifies?
- What do you notice about the use of commas?

1. I just found out that Lara Johnson, who speaks Russian fluently, has applied for the job at the Russian embassy.
2. That's not the job for you. Only people who speak Russian fluently will be considered for the job at the Russian embassy.

13-8 Punctuating Adjective Clauses

General guidelines for the punctuation of adjective clauses:
(1) **DO NOT USE COMMAS IF** the adjective clause is necessary to identify the noun it modifies.*
(2) **USE COMMAS IF** the adjective clause simply gives additional information and is not necessary to identify the noun it modifies.**

(a) *The professor* who teaches Chemistry 101 is an excellent lecturer.	In (a): No commas are used. The adjective clause is necessary to identify which professor is meant.
(b) *Professor Wilson,* who teaches Chemistry 101, is an excellent lecturer.	In (b): Commas are used. The adjective clause is not necessary to identify Professor Wilson. We already know who he is: he has a name. The adjective clause simply gives additional information.
(c) *Hawaii,* which consists of eight principal islands, is a favorite vacation spot.	GUIDELINE: Use commas, as in (b), (c), and (d), if an adjective clause modifies a proper noun. (A proper noun begins with a capital letter.)
(d) *Mrs. Smith,* who is a retired teacher, does volunteer work at the hospital.	NOTE: A comma reflects a pause in speech.
(e) *The man* { who(m) / that / Ø } I met teaches chemistry.	In (e): If no commas are used, any possible pronoun may be used in the adjective clause. Object pronouns may be omitted.
(f) *Mr. Lee,* whom I met yesterday, teaches chemistry.	In (f): When commas are necessary, the pronoun *that* may not be used (only *who, whom, which, whose, where,* and *when* may be used), and object pronouns cannot be omitted.
COMPARE THE MEANING: (g) We took some children on a picnic. *The children, who wanted to play soccer,* ran to an open field as soon as we arrived at the park. (h) We took some children on a picnic. *The children who wanted to play soccer* ran to an open field as soon as we arrived at the park. The others played a different game.	In (g): The use of commas means that *all* of the children wanted to play soccer and *all* of the children ran to an open field. The adjective clause is used only to give additional information about the children. In (h): The lack of commas means that *only some* of the children wanted to play soccer. The adjective clause is used to identify which children ran to the open field.

*Adjective clauses that do not require commas are called *essential* or *restrictive* or *identifying*.

**Adjective clauses that require commas are called *nonessential* or *nonrestrictive* or *nonidentifying*. NOTE: Nonessential adjective clauses are more common in writing than in speaking.

❏ **Exercise 35. Looking at grammar.** (Chart 13-8)
Decide if the information in blue is necessary or additional. If it is additional, add commas. Read the sentences aloud, pausing where necessary.

1. The man who lives in the apartment next to mine has three cats and a dog. (*no commas, no pauses*)

2. Yes, Sandra Day is in my political science class. And Erica Nelson, [*pause*] who lives in the dorm room next to mine, [*pause*] is in my Greek Drama class.

3. Rice which is grown in many countries is a staple food throughout much of the world.

4. The rice which we had for dinner last night was very good.

5. The newspaper article was about a man who died two weeks ago of a rare tropical disease.

6. Paul O'Grady who died two weeks ago of a sudden heart attack was a kind and loving man.

7. I have fond memories of my hometown which is situated in a valley.

8. I live in a town which is situated in a valley.

9. People who live in glass houses shouldn't throw stones.

10. In a children's story, Little Red Riding Hood who went out one day to visit her grandmother found a wolf in her grandmother's bed when she got there.

❏ **Exercise 36. Listening and pronunciation.** (Chart 13-8)

Listen for pauses before and after adjective clauses in the given sentences. Add commas where you hear pauses. Practice pronouncing the sentences.

CD 2
Track 8

Examples: You will hear: Vegetables which are orange have a lot of vitamin A.
You will add: (*no commas*)

You will hear: Vegetables [*pause*] which come in many shapes and colors [*pause*] have lots of vitamins.
You will add: Vegetables, which come in many shapes and colors, have lots of vitamins.

1. Did you hear about the man who rowed a boat across the Atlantic Ocean? *0*

2. My uncle, who loves boating rows, his boat across the lake near his house nearly every day.

3. Tea, which is a common drink throughout the world is made by pouring boiling water onto the dried leaves of certain plants.

4. Tea which is made from herbs is called herbal tea. *0*

5. Toys which contain lead paint are unsafe for children.

6. Lead, which can be found in paint and plastics, is known to cause brain damage in children.

❑ **Exercise 37. Looking at grammar.** (Chart 13-8)
Add commas where necessary. Change the adjective clause pronoun to ***that*** if possible. Read the sentences aloud, pausing where necessary.

1. Mariko and Jackie**,** who didn't come to class yesterday**,** explained their absence to the teacher. (***Who*** *cannot be changed to* ***that***. *Pauses are used in speaking; add commas.*)

2. The students who did not come to class yesterday explained their absence to the teacher. (***Who*** *can be changed to* ***that***; *no commas.*)

3. The Mississippi River which flows south from Minnesota to the Gulf of Mexico is the major commercial river in the United States.

4. A river which is polluted is not safe for swimming.
   that.

5. Mr. Trang, whose son won the spelling contest is very proud of his son's achievement. The man whose daughter won the science contest is also very pleased and proud.
   that.

6. Goats, which were first tamed more than 9,000 years ago in Asia have provided people with milk, meat, and wool since prehistoric times.
   that

7. Mrs. Clark has two goats. She's furious at the goat which got on the wrong side of the fence and is eating her flowers.
   that.

☐ **Exercise 38. Pronunciation and grammar.** (Chart 13-8)
Read the sentences aloud. Choose the correct meaning (a. or b.) for each sentence.

1. The teacher thanked the students, who had given her some flowers.
   a. The flowers were from *only some* of the students.
   (b.) The flowers were from *all* of the students.

2. The teacher thanked the students who had given her some flowers.
   (a.) The flowers were from *only some* of the students.
   b. The flowers were from *all* of the students.

3. There was a terrible flood. The villagers who had received a warning of the impending flood escaped to safety.
   a. *Only some* of the villagers had been warned; only some escaped.
   b. *All* of the villagers had been warned; all escaped.

4. There was a terrible flood. The villagers, who had received a warning of the impending flood, escaped to safety.
   a. *Only some* of the villagers had been warned; only some escaped.
   b. *All* of the villagers had been warned; all escaped.

5. Natasha reached down and picked up the grammar book, which was lying upside down on the floor.
   a. There was *only one* grammar book near Natasha.
   b. There was *more than one* grammar book near Natasha.

6. Natasha reached down and picked up the grammar book which was lying upside down on the floor.
   a. There was *only one* grammar book near Natasha.
   b. There was *more than one* grammar book near Natasha.

☐ **Exercise 39. Listening.** (Chart 13-8)

CD 2
Track 9

Listen to the sentences. Choose the correct meaning (a. or b.) for each sentence.

1. a. She threw away all of the apples.
   b. She threw away only the rotten apples.

2. a. She threw away all of the apples.
   b. She threw away only the rotten apples.

3. a. Some of the students were excused from class early.
   b. All of the students were excused from class early.

4. a. Some of the students were excused from class early.
   b. All of the students were excused from class early.

☐ **Exercise 40. Looking at grammar.** (Chart 13-8)
Add commas where necessary. Read the sentences aloud, paying attention to pauses.

1. We enjoyed the city where we spent our vacation.

2. We enjoyed Mexico City, where we spent our vacation.

3. One of the elephants, which we saw at the zoo, had only one tusk.

4. One of the most useful materials in the world is glass which is made chiefly from sand, soda, and lime.

5. You don't need to take heavy clothes when you go to Bangkok, which has one of the highest average temperatures of any city in the world.

6. Child labor was a social problem in late eighteenth-century England, where employment in factories became virtual slavery for children.

7. We had to use a telephone, so we went to the nearest house. The woman who answered our knock listened cautiously to our request.

8. I watched a scientist conduct an experiment on bees. The research scientist who was wearing protective clothing before she stepped into the special chamber holding the bees was not stung. A person who was unprotected by the special clothing could have gotten 300 to 400 bee stings within a minute.

❏ **Exercise 41. Reading and grammar.** (Charts 13-1 → 13-8)
Part I. Answer these questions. Then read the article. Notice the adjective clauses in blue.

1. Do you have a computer?
2. Do you know the name of its operating system?

The History of DOS

As you know, a computer needs to have an operating system in order to run programs. When most people think about the first operating systems that were developed for the personal computer, Microsoft or Bill Gates may come to mind. Actually, the truth is somewhat different.

In the late 1970s, there was a man in Seattle named Tim Paterson who worked for a company that was called Seattle Computer. He was a computer programmer and needed an operating system for his computer. Paterson got tired of waiting for another company to create one and decided to develop his own program. He called it QDOS, which meant "quick and dirty operating system." It took him about four months to develop it.

At the same time, Microsoft was quietly looking for an operating system to run a personal computer that I.B.M. was developing. Microsoft saw the program that Tim had written and in 1980, paid him $25,000 for a license for DOS. A year later they paid another $50,000 to acquire the rights. It became known as the Microsoft disk operating system (MS-DOS), and the rest is history. Microsoft and Bill Gates became very successful using Paterson's operating system.

Part II. Complete the sentences with information from the article. Use adjective clauses in your completions.

1. Tim Paterson was the person who _____

2. Seattle Computer was the company that _____

3. The abbreviation for the program was QDOS, which _____

4. I.B.M. was a company that _____

5. Microsoft, which _____

6. Microsoft acquired rights to a program that _____

❑ **Exercise 42. Warm-up.** (Chart 13-9)
Choose the correct meaning (a. or b.) for each sentence.

1. The couple has thirteen children, only a few of whom live at home.
   a. Ten children live at home.
   b. A few of the couple's children live at home.

2. Victoria bought a dozen dresses, most of which she later returned to the store.
   a. Victoria returned a dozen dresses.
   b. Victoria kept a few of the dresses.

13-9 Using Expressions of Quantity in Adjective Clauses

In my class there are 20 students. *Most of **them** are from Asia.* (a) In my class there are 20 students, *most of **whom** are from Asia.* (b) He gave several reasons, *only a few of **which** were valid.* (c) The teachers discussed Jim, *one of **whose** problems* was poor study habits.	An adjective clause may contain an expression of quantity with ***of***: *some of, many of, most of, none of, two of, half of, both of,* etc.
	The expression of quantity precedes the pronoun. Only ***whom***, ***which***, and ***whose*** are used in this pattern. This pattern is more common in writing than speaking. Commas are used.

❑ **Exercise 43. Looking at grammar.** (Chart 13-9)
Combine the two sentences in each item. Use the second sentence as an adjective clause.

1. The city has sixteen schools. Two of them are junior colleges.
   → *The city has sixteen schools, two of which are junior colleges.*
2. Last night the orchestra played three symphonies. One of them was Beethoven's Seventh.
3. I tried on six pairs of shoes. I liked none of them.
4. The village has around 200 people. The majority of them are farmers.
5. That company currently has five employees. All of them are computer experts.
6. After the riot, over 100 people were taken to the hospital. Many of them had been innocent bystanders.

□ **Exercise 44. In your own words.** (Chart 13-9)
Complete the sentences with your own words. Use adjective clauses.

1. Al introduced me to his roommates, both of _____ *whom are from California.* _____

2. The Paulsons own four automobiles, one of _____ *which is ducaddi* _____

3. I have three brothers, all of _____ *whom are smart* _____

4. I am taking four courses, one of _____ *which is Math's 600WC.* _____

5. I have two roommates, neither of _____ *whom is* _____

6. This semester I had to buy fifteen books, most of _____ *wich are expensive* _____

7. The company hired ten new employees, some of _____ *whom are young people* _____

8. In my apartment building, there are twenty apartments, several of _____
which are empty. _____

□ **Exercise 45. Warm-up.** (Chart 13-10)
What does **which** refer to in each sentence?

1. The soccer team worked very hard to win**, which** made their coach very proud.
2. Some of the athletes in the class cheated on the final exam**, which** disappointed their coach.
3. Sam took the final exam**, which** he passed without cheating.

13-10 **Using *Which* to Modify a Whole Sentence**	
(a) Tom was late. ***That*** surprised me. (b) Tom was late**, *which surprised me.*** (c) The elevator is out of order. ***This*** is too bad. (d) The elevator is out of order**, *which is too bad.***	The pronouns ***that*** and ***this*** can refer to the idea of a whole sentence which comes before. In (a): The word ***that*** refers to the whole sentence ***Tom was late***. Similarly, an adjective clause with ***which*** may modify the idea of a whole sentence. In (b): The word ***which*** refers to the whole sentence ***Tom was late***. Using ***which*** to modify a whole sentence is informal and occurs most frequently in spoken English. This structure is generally not appropriate in formal writing. Whenever it is written, however, it is preceded by a comma to reflect a pause in speech.

❑ **Exercise 46. Looking at grammar.** (Chart 13-10)
Combine the two sentences. Use the second sentence as an adjective clause.

1. Sonya lost her job. That wasn't surprising.
   → *Sonya lost her job, which wasn't surprising.*
2. She usually came to work late. That upset her boss.
3. So her boss fired her. That made her angry.
4. She hadn't saved any money. That was unfortunate.
5. So she had to borrow some money from me. I didn't like that.
6. She has found a new job. That is lucky.
7. So she has repaid the money she borrowed from me. I appreciate that.
8. She has promised herself to be on time to work every day. That is a good idea.

❑ **Exercise 47. Looking at grammar.** (Charts 13-1 → 13-10)
Combine sentences a. and b. Use b. as an adjective clause. Use formal written English.
Punctuate carefully.

1. a. An antecedent is a word.
   b. A pronoun refers to this word.
      → *An antecedent is a word to which a pronoun refers.*

2. a. The blue whale is considered the largest animal that has ever lived.
   b. It can grow to 100 feet and 150 tons.

3. a. The plane was met by a crowd of 300 people.
   b. Some of them had been waiting for more than four hours.

4. a. In this paper, I will describe the basic process.
   b. Raw cotton becomes cotton thread by this process.

5. a. The researchers are doing case studies of people to determine the importance of heredity in health and longevity.
   b. These people's families have a history of high blood pressure and heart disease.

6. a. At the end of this month, scientists at the institute will conclude their AIDS research.
   b. The results of this research will be published within six months.

7. a. According to many education officials, "math phobia" (that is, a fear of mathematics) is a widespread problem.
   b. A solution to this problem can and must be found.

8. a. The art museum hopes to hire a new administrator.
   b. Under this person's direction, it will be able to purchase significant pieces of art.

9. a. The giant anteater licks up ants for its dinner.
   b. Its tongue is longer than 30 centimeters (12 inches).

10. a. The anteater's tongue is sticky.
    b. It can go in and out of its mouth 160 times a minute.

❑ **Exercise 48. Reading and grammar.** (Charts 13-1 → 13-10)
Read about Ellen and her commute to work. <u>Underline</u> what the words in blue refer to.

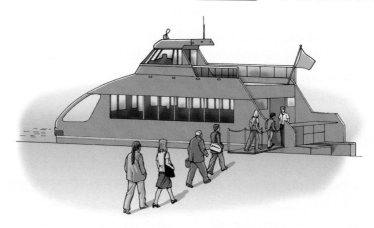

(1) Ellen lives on an island and <u>commutes to work by passenger ferry,</u> which means she takes a boat with other foot passengers to the city where they work.

(2) She leaves her house at 6:00, which is earlier than she'd like but necessary because the ferry ride takes 30 minutes. Ellen needs 20 minutes to drive to the parking lot where she leaves her car and boards the ferry. Once she's on the other side, she catches a bus which takes her to her office.

(3) Traffic is usually heavy at that hour, so she's on the bus for another 30 minutes. On the bus, she usually reads reports that she was too tired to finish the night before.

(4) The bus drops her off a few blocks from her office. Sometimes she stops at an espresso stand and picks up coffee for her co-workers, for which they reimburse her later.

(5) By the time she gets to her office, she has been commuting for an hour and a half, which she wishes she didn't have to do but isn't going to change because she enjoys her life on the island so much.

❑ **Exercise 49. Let's talk or write.** (Charts 13-1 → 13-10)
Discuss and/or write definitions for one or more of the given topics. Include an adjective clause in each definition. If you are writing, choose only one item and expand your definition to a paragraph.

The ideal . . .

1. friend	5. school	9. job
2. mother	6. vacation	10. doctor
3. father	7. teacher	11. lifestyle
4. spouse	8. student	12. (*your choice*)

Look at the words in blue. What differences do you notice between each pair of sentences?
NOTE: Sentences a. and b. have the same meaning.

1. a. I talked to the people who were sitting beside me at the ball game.
   b. I talked to the people sitting beside me at the ball game.

2. a. The notebooks that are on my desk are mine.
   b. The notebooks on my desk are mine.

3. a. I read an article about Marie Curie, who was a famous French scientist.
   b. I read an article about Marie Curie, a famous French scientist.

13-11 Reducing Adjective Clauses to Adjective Phrases

CLAUSE: *A clause* is a group of related words that contains a subject and a verb.
PHRASE: *A phrase* is a group of related words that does not contain a subject and a verb.

(a) CLAUSE: The girl *who is sitting next to me* is Mai. (b) PHRASE: The girl *sitting next to me* is Mai. (c) CLAUSE: The girl (*whom*) *I saw* was Mai. (d) PHRASE: (*none*)	An adjective phrase is a reduction of an adjective clause. It modifies a noun. It does not contain a subject and verb. Examples (a) and (b) have the same meaning. Only adjective clauses that have a subject pronoun — *who*, *which*, or *that* — are reduced to modifying adjective phrases. The adjective clause in (c) cannot be reduced to an adjective phrase.
(e) CLAUSE: The man *who is talking* to John is from Korea. 　　PHRASE: The man　Ø　Ø　*talking* to John is from Korea. (f) CLAUSE: The ideas *which are presented* in that book are good. 　　PHRASE: The ideas　Ø　　Ø　*presented* in that book are good. (g) CLAUSE: Ann is the woman *that is　　responsible* for the error. 　　PHRASE: Ann is the woman　Ø　Ø　*responsible* for the error.	There are two ways in which an adjective clause is changed to an adjective phrase. **1.** If the adjective clause contains the *be* form of a verb, omit the subject pronoun and the *be* form, as in (e), (f), and (g).*
(h) CLAUSE: English has an alphabet *that consists* of 26 letters. 　　PHRASE: English has an alphabet　Ø　*consisting* of 26 letters. (i) CLAUSE: Anyone *who wants　　* to come with us is welcome. 　　PHRASE: Anyone　Ø　*wanting* to come with us is welcome.	**2.** If there is no *be* form of a verb in the adjective clause, it is sometimes possible to omit the subject pronoun and change the verb to its *-ing* form, as in (h) and (i).
(j) *Paris,* which is the capital of France, is an exciting city. (k) *Paris,* the capital of France, is an exciting city.	If the adjective clause requires commas, as in (j), the adjective phrase also requires commas, as in (k). An adjective phrase in which a noun follows another noun, as in (k), is called an *appositive*.

*If an adjective clause that contains *be* + *a single adjective* is changed, the adjective is moved to its normal position in front of the noun it modifies.
　　CLAUSE: 　　　　　*Fruit that is fresh* tastes better than old, soft, mushy fruit.
　　CORRECT PHRASE: *Fresh fruit* tastes better than old, soft, mushy fruit.
　　INCORRECT PHRASE: Fruit fresh tastes better than old, soft, mushy fruit.

❑ **Exercise 51. Looking at grammar.** (Charts 13-10 and 13-11)
Change the adjective clauses to adjective phrases.

1. Do you know the woman who is coming toward us?
   → *Do you know the woman coming toward us?*
2. The scientists who are researching the causes of cancer are making progress.
3. We have an apartment which overlooks the park. (1)
4. The photographs which were published in the newspaper were extraordinary.
5. The rules that allow public access to wilderness areas need to be reconsidered.
6. The psychologists who study the nature of sleep have made important discoveries.
7. Antarctica is covered by a huge ice cap that contains 70 percent of the earth's fresh water.
8. When I went to Alex's house to drop off some paperwork, I met Jacob, who is his partner.
9. Many of the students who hope to enter this university will be disappointed because only one-tenth of those who apply for admission will be accepted.
10. Kuala Lumpur, which is the capital of Malaysia, is a major trade center in Southeast Asia.

❑ **Exercise 52. Listening.** (Charts 13-10 and 13-11)
CD 2
Track 10
Listen to the sentences. Choose the correct meaning (a. or b.) for each sentence. In some cases, both a. and b. are correct.

Example: You will hear: The experiment conducted by the students was successful.
You will choose: (a.) The students conducted an experiment.
(b.) The experiment was successful.

1. a. There is a fence around our house.
   b. Our house is made of wood.

2. a. All schoolchildren receive a good education.
   b. That school provides a good education.

3. a. The university president will give a speech.
   b. Dr. Stanton will give a speech.

4. a. There is a galaxy called the Milky Way.
   b. Our solar system is called the Milky Way.

❑ **Exercise 53. Looking at grammar.** (Charts 13-10 and 13-11)
Change the adjective phrases to adjective clauses.

1. We visited Barcelona, a city in northern Spain.
   → *We visited Barcelona, which is a city in northern Spain.*

2. Corn was one of the agricultural products introduced to the European settlers by the Indians. Some of the other products introduced by the Indians were potatoes, peanuts, and tobacco.

3. Mercury, the nearest planet to the sun, is also the smallest of the planets orbiting our sun.

4. The pyramids, the monumental tombs of ancient Egyptian pharaohs, were constructed more than 4,000 years ago.

5. Any student not wanting to go on the trip should inform the office.

6. Be sure to follow the instructions given at the top of the page.

❑ **Exercise 54. Looking at grammar.** (Charts 13-10 and 13-11)
Change the adjective clauses to adjective phrases.

Early Failures of Famous People

(1) Many famous people did not enjoy immediate success in their early lives. Abraham Lincoln, ~~who was~~ one of the truly great presidents of the United States, ran for public office 26 times and lost 23 of the elections.

(2) Walt Disney, who was the creator of Mickey Mouse and the founder of his own movie production company, once was fired by a newspaper editor because he had no good ideas.

(3) Thomas Edison, who was the inventor of the light bulb and the phonograph, was believed by his teachers to be too stupid to learn.

(4) Albert Einstein, who was one of the greatest scientists of all time, performed badly in almost all of his high school courses and failed his first college entrance exam.

❑ **Exercise 55. Looking at grammar.** (Charts 13-10 and 13-11)
Complete the sentences in Part II by turning the information in Part I into adjective phrases. Use commas as necessary.

Part I.
  a. It is the lowest place on the earth's surface.
✓b. It is the highest mountain in the world.
  c. It is the capital of Iraq.
  d. It is the capital of Argentina.
  e. It is the largest city in the Western Hemisphere.
  f. It is the largest city in the United States.
  g. It is the most populous country in Africa.
  h. It is the northernmost country in Latin America.
  i. They are sensitive instruments that measure the shaking of the ground.
  j. They are devices that produce a powerful beam of light.

Part II.
1. Mount Everest , *the highest mountain in the world,* _____ is in the Himalayas.

2. One of the largest cities in the Middle East is Baghdad _____

3. Earthquakes are recorded on seismographs _____

4. The Dead Sea _____
   is located in the Middle East between Jordan and Israel.

5. The newspaper reported an earthquake in Buenos Aires _____

6. Industry and medicine are continually finding new uses for lasers _____

_____

7. Mexico _____

lies just south of the United States.

8. The nation Nigeria _____ consists

of over 250 different cultural groups even though English is the official language.

9. Both Mexico City _____ and New York City

_____ face challenging futures.

❏ **Exercise 56. Listening.** (Chapters 12 and 13)

Part I. Listen to the lecture about animals and earthquake predictions with your book closed. Then open your book and read the statements. Circle "T" for true and "F" for false.

CD 2
Track 11

1. That animals can predict earthquakes is an indisputable fact.   T   F

2. Some animals exhibit unusual behavior before an earthquake.   T   F

3. According to the lecture, scientists are certain that the energy in the air
   changes before an earthquake.   T   F

4. Some scientists believe that animal behavior can be helpful in earthquake
   prediction.   T   F

Part II. Listen again. Complete the sentences with the words you hear.

Animals and Earthquakes

_____ animals can predict earthquakes has been widely debated for
1

hundreds of years. In fact, as far back as 373 B.C., villagers _____
2

hundreds of animals deserted the Greek town of Helice a few days before an earthquake

destroyed it. There are other interesting phenomena _____.
3

For example, before an earthquake, dogs may begin barking or howling for no reason; chickens

might stop laying eggs; and some pets will go into hiding.

In Asia in 2004, many animals _____ accustomed to being
4

on the beach in the early morning refused to go there the morning of the big tsunami. In

Thailand, a herd of buffalo on a beach noticed or heard _____
5

made them run to the top of a hill before the tsunami was anywhere in sight. The villagers

_____ them were saved.
6

What causes this strange behavior in animals? One theory _____
                                                                        7
can sense the earth move before people can. There are vibrations deep in the earth

_____ before an earthquake can be detected. Another idea
            8
_____ the energy in the air changes _____ animals are disturbed
            9   10
by these changes.

Some scientists dismiss these ideas, while others _____ they are worth
                                                                        11
researching further. Those scientists _____ witnessed this strange animal
                                                            12
behavior _____ animals are far more sensitive to subtle changes in the
                    13
earth than people are _____ studying their behavior can be useful in
                                14
the prediction of earthquakes.

❏ **Exercise 57. Looking at grammar.** (Chapter 13)
Combine each group of short, choppy sentences into one sentence. Use the underlined
sentence as the independent clause and build your sentence around it. Use adjective clauses
and adjective phrases wherever possible.

1. Chihuahua is divided into two regions. It is the largest Mexican state. One region is a
    mountainous area in the west. The other region is a desert basin in the north and east.

    Chihuahua, the largest Mexican state, is divided into two regions, a mountainous

    area in the west and a desert basin in the north and east.

2. Disney World covers a large area of land. It is an amusement park. It is located in
    Orlando, Florida. The land includes lakes, golf courses, campsites, hotels, and a wildlife
    preserve.

    Disney World, an amusement park, covers a large area of land,

    is located in Orlando, Florida, includes ————

3. Jamaica is one of the world's leading producers of bauxite. It is the third largest island in
    the Caribbean Sea. Bauxite is an ore. Aluminum is made from this ore.

    Jamaica, the third largest island in the Caribbean Sea, is one of

    the world's leading producers of bauxite, an ore of making Aluminum.

4. Robert Ballard made headlines in 1985. He is an oceanographer. In 1985 he discovered the remains of the *Titanic*. The *Titanic* was the "unsinkable" passenger ship. It has rested on the floor of the Atlantic Ocean since 1912. It struck an iceberg in 1912.

Robert Ballard, an oceangrapher, made headlines in 1985, discovered the remains of the Titanic in 1985, The unsinkable passenger ship rested on the floor of the Atlantic Ocean sinc 1912 and struck an iceberg in 1912.

5. The Republic of Yemen is an ancient land. It is located at the southwestern tip of the Arabian Peninsula. This land has been host to many prosperous civilizations. These civilizations include the Kingdom of Sheba and various Islamic empires.

_____

_____

_____

Exercise 58. Check your knowledge. (Chapter 13)

Correct the errors. All of the sentences are adapted from student writing.

1. Baseball is the only sport in which I am interested in it. *in which I am interested.*

2. My favorite teacher, Mr. Chu, ~~he~~ was always willing to help me after class.

3. It is important to be polite to people who lives in the same building. *are living* / *live*

4. My sister has two children, ~~who, their~~ names are Ali and Talal. *Whos*

5. He comes from Venezuela, ~~that is~~ a Spanish-speaking country.

6. There are some people in the government ~~who is~~ trying to improve the lives of the poor. *are*

7. My classroom is located on the second floor of Carver Hall ~~that is~~ a large brick building in the center of the campus.

8. A myth is a story expresses traditional beliefs. *that*

9. There is an old legend telling among people in my country about a man lived in the seventeenth century and saved a village from destruction. *ing* / *is told* / *s*

10. An old man ~~was~~ fishing next to me on the pier was muttering to himself.

11. The road that we took it through the forest it was narrow and steep. *AC* / *Adj C*

12. There are ten universities in Thailand, seven of them are located in Bangkok, is the capital city.

13. At the national park, ~~there is~~ a path leads to a spectacular waterfall.

14. At the airport, I was waiting for some relatives ~~which~~ I had never met ~~them~~ before.

15. It is almost impossible to find two ~~persons~~ *people* ~~who their~~ *whose* opinions are the same.

16. On the wall, there is a colorful poster ~~which it~~ consists of a group of young people (who ~~is~~ *are*) dancing.

17. The sixth member of our household is Pietro, ~~that is~~ (who is) my sister's son.

18. Before I came here, I didn't have the opportunity to speak with people who, *whose* English ~~is their~~ native tongue.

❏ **Exercise 59. Let's write.** (Chapter 13)
Write a paragraph on one or more of the given topics. Try to use adjective clauses and phrases.

Topics:
1. Write about three historical figures from your country. Give your reader information about their lives and accomplishments.
2. Write about your favorite TV shows. What are they? What are they about? Why do you enjoy them?
3. Who are some people in your country who are popular with young people (e.g., singers, movie stars, political figures, etc.)? Tell your readers about these people. Assume your readers are completely unfamiliar with them.
4. You are a tourist agent for your hometown/country. Write a descriptive brochure that would make your readers want to visit your hometown/country.

Chapter 14

Gerunds and Infinitives, Part 1

❑ **Exercise 1. Warm-up.** (Chart 14-1)
Complete the sentences with the words in the list. Give your own opinion. Then answer the questions.

baseball	golf	badminton
basketball	soccer	tennis

1. **Playing** _____ is fun.

2. My friends and I enjoy **playing** _____.

3. I don't know much about **playing** _____.

In which sentence is **playing**

   a. the object of the verb?

   b. the subject?

   c. the object of a preposition?

14-1 Gerunds: Introduction

S **V** (a) *Playing* tennis *is* fun.	A *gerund* is the *-ing* form of a verb used as a noun.* A gerund is used in the same ways as a noun, i.e., as a subject or as an object.
S **V** **O** (b) We enjoy *playing* tennis.	In (a): *playing* is a gerund. It is used as the subject of the sentence. *Playing tennis* is a *gerund phrase*.
PREP **O** (c) He's excited about *playing* tennis.	In (b): *playing* is a gerund used as the object of the verb *enjoy*. In (c): *playing* is a gerund used as the object of the preposition *about*.

*Compare the uses of the *-ing* form of verbs:
  (1) *Walking is good exercise.* → *walking* = a gerund used as the subject of the sentence.
  (2) *Bob and Ann are playing tennis.* → *playing* = a present participle used as part of the present progressive tense.
  (3) *I heard some surprising news.* → *surprising* = a present participle used as an adjective.

❏ **Exercise 2. Warm-up.** (Chart 14-2)
Each phrase in blue contains a preposition. What do you notice about the form of the verb that follows each preposition?

1. Sonya is excited about **moving** to a new city.
2. You'd better have a good excuse for **being** late.
3. I'm looking forward to **going** on vacation soon.

14-2 Using Gerunds as the Objects of Prepositions

(a) We talked *about going* to Canada for our vacation. (b) Sue is in charge *of organizing* the meeting. (c) I'm interested *in learning* more about your work.	A gerund is frequently used as the object of a preposition.
(d) I*'m used to sleeping* with the window open. (e) I*'m accustomed to sleeping** with the window open. (f) I *look forward to going* home next month.	In (d) through (f): *to* is a preposition, not part of an infinitive form, so a gerund follows.
(g) We *talked about not going* to the meeting, but finally decided we should go.	NEGATIVE FORM: *not* precedes a gerund.

Common preposition combinations followed by gerunds

be excited
be worried } *about doing* it

complain
dream
talk
think } *about/of doing* it

apologize
blame someone
forgive someone
have an excuse
have a reason
be responsible
thank someone } *for doing* it

keep someone
prevent someone
prohibit someone
stop someone } *from doing* it

be interested
believe
participate
succeed } *in doing* it

be accused
be capable
be guilty
instead
take advantage
take care } *of doing* it

be tired
insist *on doing* it } *of/from doing* it

be accustomed
in addition
be committed
be devoted
look forward
object
be opposed
be used } *to doing* it

*Possible in British English: *I'm accustomed to sleep with the window open.*

❏ **Exercise 3. Looking at grammar.** (Chart 14-2)
Complete each sentence with a preposition and a form of **go**.

1. We thought _____*about going*_____ to the beach.

2. We talked _____ there.

3. We're interested _____ there.

4. My family is excited _____ there.

5. The children insisted _____ there.

6. They're looking forward _____ there.

7. The rain prevented us _____ there.

8. A storm kept us _____ there.

❏ **Exercise 4. Looking at grammar.** (Chart 14-2)
Complete each sentence with a preposition and a form of the verb in parentheses.

SITUATION 1: An airplane flight.

1. Two children are excited (*take*) _____*about taking*_____ their first flight.

2. They have been looking forward (*be*) _____ above the clouds.

3. A first-time flyer is worried (*fly*) _____ in stormy weather.

4. One passenger is blaming another passenger (*spill*) _____
   his coffee.

5. A man is complaining (*have*) _____ an aisle seat rather than a
   window seat.

6. The pilot was late, but he had an excuse (*be*) _____ late.

7. The co-pilot will be responsible (*fly*) _____ the plane.

8. Security personnel are prohibiting a woman (*get*) _____ on
   the flight.

SITUATION 2: At a police station.

9. The teenager has been accused (*steal*) _____ a purse.

10. An elderly woman said he was responsible (*take*) _____ it.

11. The police are blaming him (*do*) _____ it.

12. The teenager said he was trying to prevent someone else (*take*) _____ it.

13. He is upset. The police are listening to the woman instead (*listen*) _____ to his version of the story.

14. He has not yet succeeded (*convince*) _____ the police of his innocence.

❏ **Exercise 5. Looking at grammar.** (Chart 14-2)
Complete each sentence with an appropriate preposition and the **-ing** form of the given verb.

1. look   Alice isn't interested ____*in looking*____ for a new job.

2. do   You are capable _____ better work.

3. have   I'm accustomed _____ a big breakfast.

4. help   Thank you _____ me carry my suitcases.

5. know   Mrs. Grant insisted _____ the whole truth.

6. be   I believe _____ honest at all times.

7. live   You should take advantage _____ here.

8. go, not   Fatima had a good reason _____ to class yesterday.

9. search   Everyone in the neighborhood participated _____ for the lost child.

10. make   I apologized to Yoko _____ her wait for me.

11. go   In addition _____ to school full-time, Spiro has a part-time job.

12. run   I stopped the child _____ into the street.

13. go   Where should we go for dinner tonight? Would you object _____ to an Italian restaurant?

14. clarify   The mayor made another public statement for the purpose _____ the new tax proposal.

15. wear   Larry isn't used _____ a suit and tie every day.

Exercise 6. Listening. (Chart 14-2)

Listen to each dialogue. Summarize it by completing each sentence with a preposition and a gerund phrase.

1. The man apologized _____ *for being late.* _____

2. The woman succeeded _____

3. Both speakers are complaining _____

4. The man thanked his friend _____

5. The man didn't have an excuse _____

6. The woman isn't used _____

7. The flu kept the man _____

Exercise 7. Let's talk: interview. (Chart 14-2)

Interview two classmates for each question. Share some of their answers with the class.

1. Where \ you \ think \ go \ today?
   → *Where are you thinking about going today?*

2. What \ you \ not accustomed \ do?

3. What \ you \ interested \ find out about?

4. Where \ you \ look forward \ go \ on your next trip?

5. What \ be \ a good reason \ not \ do \ your homework?

Exercise 8. Let's talk. (Chart 14-2)

Answer the questions in complete sentences. Use prepositions followed by gerunds in your answers. Work in pairs or small groups.

Example:
SPEAKER A (*book open*):   Your friend was rude. Did she apologize?
SPEAKER B (*book closed*):   Yes, she apologized *for being* rude. OR No, she didn't apologize *for being* rude.

1. Your neighbor helped you carry heavy boxes. Did you thank him/her?
2. You're going to visit your friends in another town this weekend. Are you looking forward to that?
3. You didn't come to class on time yesterday. Did you have a good excuse?
4. You're living in a cold/warm climate. Are you accustomed to that?
5. You're going to a tropical island for vacation. Are you excited?
6. A customer interrupted you while you were talking to the store manager. Did she apologize?
7. The students in the class did role-plays. Did all of them participate?

(Change roles if working in pairs.)

8. Someone broke the window. Do you know who was responsible?
9. People in some countries have their biggest meal at lunch. Are you used to doing that?
10. The weather is hot/cold. What does that prevent you from doing?
11. The advanced students have to do a lot of homework. Do they complain?
12. Your wallet was missing after your friend visited. Do you blame him?
13. You didn't study grammar last night. What did you do instead?
14. You studied last weekend. What did you do in addition?

❑ **Exercise 9. Let's talk.** (Chart 14-2)
Answer the questions with **by** + *a gerund or gerund phrase* to express how something is done.
Work in pairs, in small groups, or as a class.

1. How do you turn off a cell phone? → *By pushing a button.*
2. How can students improve their listening comprehension?
3. How do people satisfy their hunger?
4. How do people quench their thirst?
5. How did you find out what *quench* means?
6. What are some ways employees get in trouble with their manager?
7. How do dogs show they are happy?
8. In a restaurant, how do you catch the server's attention?

❑ **Exercise 10. Let's talk: interview.** (Chart 14-2)
Part I. Interview your classmates about the different ways people express emotions. Answers
can include descriptions of facial expressions, actions, what people say, etc. Try to use
by + *gerund* in your answers. Share some of the answers with the class.

Example: excitement
SPEAKER A: How do people show excitement at a sports event?
SPEAKER B: People show excitement at a sports event by clapping their hands, jumping up
and down, and yelling.

1. happiness	3. anger	5. confusion	7. agreement
2. sadness	4. frustration	6. disagreement	8. surprise

Part II. Draw a face that shows an emotion. Ask a classmate to guess which emotion you've
tried to show.

❑ **Exercise 11. Warm-up.** (Chart 14-3)
Complete the sentences with phrases in the list that are true for you. What do you notice about the form of the verbs in these phrases?

buying things online	surfing the internet
going online to get news	talking about politics
reading newspapers	watching commercials on TV
spending hours at a computer	watching the news on TV

1. I enjoy _____ .

2. I don't enjoy _____ .

3. I avoid _____ .

14-3 Common Verbs Followed by Gerunds

verb + gerund	
(a) I *enjoy* *playing* tennis.	Gerunds are used as the objects of certain verbs. In (a): *enjoy* is followed by a gerund (*playing*). *Enjoy* is not followed by an infinitive. INCORRECT: I enjoy ~~to play~~ tennis. Common verbs that are followed by gerunds are listed below.
(b) Joe *quit smoking*. (c) Joe *gave up smoking*.	Examples (b) and (c) have the same meaning. Some phrasal verbs,* e.g., *give up*, are followed by gerunds. See these phrasal verbs in parentheses below.

Verb + gerund

enjoy	quit (give up)	avoid	consider
appreciate	finish (get through)	postpone (put off)	discuss
mind	stop**	delay	mention
		keep (keep on)	suggest

*A *phrasal verb* consists of a verb and a particle (a small word such as a preposition) that together have a special meaning. For example, *put off* means "postpone."

Stop can also be followed by an infinitive of purpose. *He **stopped** at the station (**in order) to get** some gas.* See *infinitives of purpose*, Charts 14-7, p. 317, and 15-1, p. 331.

❑ **Exercise 12. Looking at grammar.** (Chart 14-3)
Make sentences with the given words. Use any tense and subject. Work in pairs, in small groups, or as a class.

Example: enjoy \ drink tea
SPEAKER A: enjoy [*pause*] drink tea
SPEAKER B: I enjoy drinking tea with breakfast.

(Change roles if working in pairs.)

1. mind \ open the window
2. finish \ eat dinner
3. get through \ eat dinner
4. stop \ rain
5. keep \ work
6. keep on \ work

7. postpone \ do my work
8. put off \ do my work
9. delay \ leave on vacation
10. consider \ get a job
11. talk about \ go to a movie
12. mention \ go out of town

❏ **Exercise 13. Listening.** (Chart 14-3)

CD 2
Track 13

Listen to the conversations. Complete the sentences with appropriate verbs.

1. The speakers enjoy _____watching_____ movies on weekends.

2. The speakers have given up _____ for better weather.

3. The speakers are going to keep on _____.

4. The speakers are discussing _____ to a concert in the city.

5. The speakers have put off _____ their homework.

6. The speakers are going to delay _____ the office.

❏ **Exercise 14. Looking at grammar.** (Chart 14-3)

Complete the sentences with appropriate gerunds.

1. When Beth got tired, she stopped _____working / studying_____.

2. Would you mind _____ the door? Thanks.

3. I have a lot of homework tonight, but I'd still like to go with you later on. I'll call you when I get through _____.

4. Where are you considering _____ for your break?

5. Sometimes I put off _____ my apartment.

6. You have to decide where you want to go to school next year. You can't postpone _____ that decision much longer.

7. I wanted to go to Mexico. Sally suggested _____ to Hawaii.

8. Tony mentioned _____ the bus to school instead of walking.

9. I appreciate _____ able to study in peace and quiet.

❏ **Exercise 15. Warm-up.** (Chart 14-4)

Complete the sentences by circling all the activities that are true for you. All the choices end in **-ing**. What do you notice about the verbs in blue?

1. Last week I went *shopping   running   biking   dancing*.

2. I like to go *hiking   swimming   camping   sightseeing*.

3. I've never gone *fishing   bowling   skiing   diving*.

14-4 *Go* + Gerund

(a) Did you *go shopping*? (b) We *went fishing* yesterday.	*Go* is followed by a gerund in certain idiomatic expressions to express, for the most part, recreational activities.

Go + gerund

go biking	go dancing	go running	go skiing
go birdwatching	go fishing*	go sailing	go skinnydipping
go boating	go hiking	go shopping	go sledding
go bowling	go hunting	go sightseeing	go snorkeling
go camping	go jogging	go skating	go swimming
go canoeing/kayaking	go mountain climbing	go skateboarding	go window shopping

*Also, in British English: *go angling*.

❑ **Exercise 16. Let's talk.** (Chart 14-4)
Discuss the activities listed in Chart 14-4. Work in pairs, in small groups, or as a class.

1. Which ones have you done? When? Briefly describe your experiences.
2. Which ones do you like to do?
3. Which ones do you never want to do?
4. Which ones have you not done but would like to do?

❑ **Exercise 17. Listening.** (Chart 14-4)
Listen to the story with your book closed. Then open your book and listen again. Complete the sentences with a form of *go* and any verb that makes sense.

CD 2
Track 14

1. The first thing Saturday morning, Ron ____went canoeing____.

2. He brought a fishing rod so he could _____.

3. He saw some friends on a sailboat but didn't _____ with them.

4. He _____ instead.

5. After lunch, he _____.

6. He finished the day by _____ with some of his friends.

❑ **Exercise 18. Let's talk.** (Chart 14-4)
Make a sentence that is true for you using the words in parentheses. Then ask a classmate, "How about you?"

Example: I (*enjoy, don't enjoy*) \ go \ shop \ for clothes
SPEAKER A: I don't enjoy going shopping for clothes. How about you?
SPEAKER B: No, I don't enjoy it either. OR Actually, I enjoy it.

1. I (*go, never go*) \ dance \ on weekends
2. I (*like to go, don't like to go*) \ bowl
3. I (*sometimes postpone, never postpone*) \ do \ my homework
4. I (*really appreciate, don't appreciate*) \ get \ emails from advertisers
5. I (*am considering, am not considering*) \ look \ for a new place to live
6. I (*enjoy, don't enjoy*) \ play \ card games
7. I (*used to go, never went*) \ fish \ as a child
8. I (*go, never go*) \ jog \ for exercise

❑ **Exercise 19. Warm-up.** (Chart 14-5)
Read the story. Look at the phrases in blue. <u>Underline</u> the verb that follows each phrase. What form do these verbs take?

Ms. Jones, the teacher, is new and inexperienced. She speaks very quickly, so students have a hard time <u>following</u> her. Because they have difficulty understanding her, they spend a lot of class time asking questions. In response, Ms. Jones gives long, wordy explanations and wastes a lot of class time trying to make herself understood. The students sit at their desks looking confused, and Ms. Jones stands in front of the class feeling frustrated.

14-5 Special Expressions Followed by *-ing*

(a) We *had fun* / We *had a good time* } *playing* volleyball.	*-ing* forms follow certain special expressions: **have fun/a good time + -ing** **have trouble/difficulty + -ing** **have a hard time/difficult time + -ing**
(b) I *had trouble* / I *had difficulty* / I *had a hard time* / I *had a difficult time* } *finding* his house.	
(c) Sam *spends most of his time studying*.	**spend** + expression of time or money + **-ing**
(d) I *waste a lot of time watching* TV.	**waste** + expression of time or money + **-ing**
(e) She *sat at her desk writing* a letter.	**sit** + expression of place + **-ing**
(f) I *stood there wondering* what to do next.	**stand** + expression of place + **-ing**
(g) He *is lying in bed reading* a novel.	**lie** + expression of place + **-ing**
(h) When I walked into my office, I *found George using* my telephone.	**find** + (pro)noun + **-ing** **catch** + (pro)noun + **-ing**
(i) When I walked into my office, I *caught a thief looking* through my desk drawers.	In (h) and (i): Both **find** and **catch** mean "discover." **Catch** often expresses anger or displeasure.

Exercise 20. Looking at grammar. (Chart 14-5)
Complete the sentences with appropriate **-ing** verbs.

1. We had a lot of fun _____playing_____ games at the picnic.

2. I have trouble _____ Mrs. Maxwell when she speaks. She talks too fast.

3. I spent five hours _____ my homework last night.

4. Olga is standing at the corner _____ for the bus.

5. Ricardo is sitting in class _____ notes.

6. It was a beautiful spring day. Dorothy was lying under a tree _____ to the birds sing.

7. We wasted our money _____ to that movie. It was very boring.

8. Ted is an indecisive person. He has a hard time _____ up his mind about anything.

9. I wondered what the children were doing while I was gone. When I got home, I found them _____ TV.

10. When Mr. Chan walked into the kitchen, he caught the children _____ some candy even though he'd told them not to spoil their dinners.

□ **Exercise 21. Let's talk: pairwork.** (Chart 14-5)
Work with a partner. Complete a sentence about yourself using an **-ing** verb. Ask your partner, "How about you?"

Example: Sometimes I have trouble . . . .
SPEAKER A: Sometimes I have trouble understanding spoken English. How about you?
SPEAKER B: Yeah. Me too. I have a lot of trouble understanding people in TV shows especially.

1. Every week I spend at least an hour . . . .
2. In my free time, I have fun . . . .
3. Sometimes I sit in class . . . .
4. Sometimes I waste money . . . .
5. If you come to my home at midnight, you will find me . . . .

Change roles.
6. I think it's fun to spend all day . . . .
7. Sometimes I have trouble . . . .
8. You will never catch me . . . .
9. I *am/am not* a decisive person. I have a *hard/easy* time . . . .
10. When I'm on a picnic, I always have a good time . . . .

❑ **Exercise 22. Listening.** (Chart 14-5)

Listen to the sentences. Complete the sentences, orally or in writing, using **-ing** verbs.

CD 2
Track 15

Example: You will hear: I play soccer every day. I love it!

You will write (or say): The speaker has fun _____*playing soccer*_____.

1. The speaker has trouble _____.

2. The speaker caught his son _____.

3. The speaker stands at the kitchen counter in the mornings _____.

4. The speaker has a hard time _____.

5. The speaker wasted two hours _____.

6. The speaker had a good time _____.

7. The speaker found Tom _____.

8. The speaker spent an hour _____.

❑ **Exercise 23. Let's talk: interview.** (Chart 14-5)

Make questions with the given words. Interview two people for each item. Share some of the answers with the class.

1. What \ you \ have difficulty \ remember?
2. What \ you \ have a hard time \ learn?
3. What \ you \ have a good time \ play?
4. What English sounds \ you \ have a hard time \ pronounce?
5. What \ people \ waste money \ do?
6. What \ people \ waste time \ do?

❑ **Exercise 24. Warm-up.** (Chart 14-6)

Check (✓) all the correct sentences.

1. a. ____ We hope visiting them soon.
   b. ____ We hope to visit them soon.
   c. ____ We hope you to visit them soon.

2. a. ____ We told you to call us.
   b. ____ We told to call us.
   c. ____ We told calling us.

3. a. ____ I invited to go to the party.
   b. ____ I invited Ella to go to the party.
   c. ____ Ella was invited to go to the party.

14-6 Common Verbs Followed by Infinitives

Verb + Infinitive

(a) I *hope to see* you again soon.	An *infinitive* = **to** + the simple form of a verb (*to see, to be, to go,* etc.).
(b) He *promised to be* here by ten.	
(c) He *promised not to be* late.	Some verbs are followed immediately by an infinitive, as in (a) and (b).
	Negative form: **not** precedes the infinitive, as in (c).

Common verbs followed by infinitives

hope to (do something)	promise to	seem to	expect to
plan to	agree to	appear to	would like to
intend to*	offer to	pretend to	want to
decide to	refuse to	ask to	need to

Verb + Object + Infinitive

(d) Mr. Lee *told me to be* here at ten o'clock.	Some verbs are followed by a (pro)noun object and then an infinitive, as in (d) and (e).
(e) The police *ordered the driver to stop*.	
(f) I *was told to be* here at ten o'clock.	These verbs are followed immediately by an infinitive when they are used in the passive, as in (f) and (g).
(g) The driver *was ordered* to stop.	

Common verbs followed by (pro)nouns and infinitives

tell someone to	invite someone to	require someone to	expect someone to
advise someone to**	permit someone to	order someone to	would like someone to
encourage someone to	allow someone to	force someone to	want someone to
remind someone to	warn someone to	ask someone to	need someone to

Verb + Infinitive/Verb + Object + Infinitive

(h) I *expect to pass* the test.	Some verbs have two patterns:
(i) I *expect Mary to pass* the test.	• *verb + infinitive*, as in (h)
	• *verb + object* + infinitive, as in (i)
	COMPARE:
	In (h): I think I will pass the test.
	In (i): I think Mary will pass the test.

Common verbs followed by infinitives or by objects and then infinitives

ask to / ask someone to	want to / want someone to
expect to / expect someone to	would like to / would like someone to
need to / need someone to	

Intend is usually followed by an infinitive (*I intend to go to the meeting.*) but sometimes may be followed by a gerund (*I intend going to the meeting.*) with no change in meaning.

**A gerund is used after *advise* (active) if there is no noun or pronoun object.
  COMPARE:
    (1) *He advised buying a Fiat.*
    (2) *He advised me to buy a Fiat. I was advised to buy a Fiat.*

❑ **Exercise 25. Looking at grammar.** (Chart 14-6)
Complete the sentences with **to leave** or **me to leave**. In some cases, both completions are possible.

1. He told ____*me to leave*____ .

2. He decided ____*to leave*____ .

3. He asked ____*to leave / me to leave*____ .

4. He offered _____ .

5. She wanted _____ .

6. He agreed _____ .

7. She would like _____ .

8. He warned _____ .

9. She refused _____ .

10. He promised _____ .

11. She hoped _____ .

12. He permitted _____ .

13. She expected _____ .

14. He forced _____ .

15. She allowed _____ .

16. He reminded _____ .

17. She planned _____ .

18. He pretended _____ .

❑ **Exercise 26. Looking at grammar.** (Chart 14-6)
Report what was said by using the verbs in the list to introduce an infinitive phrase.

advise	encourage	order	require
allow	expect	permit	tell
ask	force	remind	warn

1. The professor said to Alan, "You may leave early."

   → *The professor allowed Alan to leave early.* OR

   → *Alan was allowed to leave early.*

2. Roberto said to me, "Don't forget to take your book back to the library."

3. Mr. Chang thinks I have a good voice, so he said to me, "You should take singing lessons."

4. Mrs. Alvarez was very stern and a little angry. She shook her finger at the children and said to them, "Don't play with matches!"

5. I am very relieved because the Dean of Admissions said to me, "You may register for school late."

6. The law says, "Every driver must have a valid driver's license."

7. My friend said to me, "You should get some automobile insurance."

8. The robber had a gun. He said to me, "Give me all of your money."

9. My boss said to me, "Come to the meeting ten minutes early."

❑ **Exercise 27. Let's talk.** (Chart 14-6)
Work in small groups. Speaker A forms the question, and Speaker B gives the answer.
Speaker C changes the sentence to passive (the *by*-phrase can be omitted).

Example: What \ someone \ remind \ you \ do \ recently?
SPEAKER A: What did someone remind you to do recently, Mario?
SPEAKER B: My roommate reminded me to recharge my cell phone.
SPEAKER C: Mario was reminded to recharge his cell phone.

1. What \ a family member \ remind \ you \ do \ recently?

2. Where \ a friend \ ask \ you \ go \ recently?

3. What \ the government \ require \ people \ do?

4. What \ doctors \ advise \ patients \ do?

5. What \ teachers \ expect \ students \ do?

6. What \ our teacher \ tell \ you \ do \ recently?

7. What \ the laws \ not permit \ you \ do?

8. Where \ parents \ warn \ their kids \ not \ go?

9. What \ our teacher \ encourage \ us \ do to practice our English?

❑ **Exercise 28. Looking at grammar.** (Charts 14-3 and 14-6)
Complete each sentence with a gerund or an infinitive.

1. We're going out for dinner. Would you like _____*to join*_____ us?

2. Jack avoided _____*looking at*_____ me.

3. I was broke, so Jenny offered _____ me a little money.

4. Would you mind _____ the door for me?

5. Even though I asked the people in front of me at the movie _____ quiet,
   they kept _____.

6. Lucy pretended _____ the answer to my question.

7. The teacher seems _____ in a good mood today, don't you think?

8. I don't mind _____ alone.

9. Mrs. Jackson warned her young son not
   _____ the hot stove.

10. Residents are not allowed _____
    pets in my apartment building.

11. All applicants are required _____
    an entrance examination.

12. My boss expects me _____ the work ASAP.*

13. Joan and David were considering _____ married in June, but they finally decided _____ until August.

14. Jack advised me _____ a new apartment.

15. I was advised _____ a new apartment.

16. Jack advised _____ a new apartment.

17. Jack suggested _____ a new apartment.

18. When we were in New York, we had a really good time _____ in Central Park on sunny days.

19. This is my first term at this school. I haven't really had any problems, but sometimes I have trouble _____ the lectures. Some professors speak too fast.

20. Ms. Gray is a commuter. Every workday, she spends almost two hours _____ to and from work.

❑ **Exercise 29. Warm-up.** (Chart 14-7)
Which pairs (a. and b.) have basically the same meaning? Which pairs have different meanings?

1. a. It began to snow.
   b. It began snowing.

2. a. I remembered to call my parents.
   b. I remembered calling my parents.

3. a. We love to listen to music.
   b. We love listening to music.

4. a. He forgot to buy a gift.
   b. He forgot buying a gift.

5. a. I stopped to talk to my friend.
   b. I stopped talking to my friend.

---

*ASAP = *as soon as possible.*

14-7 Common Verbs Followed by Either Infinitives or Gerunds

Some verbs can be followed by either an infinitive or a gerund, sometimes with no difference in meaning, as in Group A below, and sometimes with a difference in meaning, as in Group B below.

Group A: Verb + Infinitive or Gerund, with No Difference in Meaning

begin start continue	like love prefer*	hate can't stand can't bear	The verbs in Group A may be followed by either an infinitive or a gerund with little or no difference in meaning.

(a) It *began to rain.* / It *began raining.* (b) I *started to work.* / I *started working.*	In (a): There is no difference between *began to rain* and *began raining*.
(c) It *was beginning to rain.*	If the main verb is progressive, an infinitive (not a gerund) is usually used, as in (c).

Group B: Verb + Infinitive or Gerund, with a Difference in Meaning

remember forget	regret try	stop	The verbs in Group B may be followed by either an infinitive or a gerund, but the meaning is different.

(d) Judy always *remembers to lock* the door.	*Remember* + *infinitive* = remember to perform responsibility, duty, or task, as in (d).
(e) Sam often *forgets to lock* the door.	*Forget* + *infinitive* = forget to perform a responsibility, duty, or task, as in (e).
(f) I *remember seeing* the Alps for the first time. The sight was impressive.	*Remember* + *gerund* = remember (recall) something that happened in the past, as in (f).
(g) I'*ll never forget seeing* the Alps for the first time.	*Forget* + *gerund* = forget something that happened in the past, as in (g).**
(h) I *regret to tell* you that you failed the test.	*Regret* + *infinitive* = regret to say, to tell someone, to inform someone of some bad news, as in (h).
(i) I *regret lending* him some money. He never paid me back.	*Regret* + *gerund* = regret something that happened in the past, as in (i).
(j) I'*m trying to learn* English.	*Try* + *infinitive* = make an effort, as in (j).
(k) The room was hot. I *tried opening* the window, but that didn't help. So I *tried turning* on the fan, but I was still hot. Finally, I turned on the air conditioner.	*Try* + *gerund* = experiment with a new or different approach to see if it works, as in (k).
(l) The students *stopped talking* when the professor entered the room. The room became quiet.	*Stop* + *gerund* = stop an activity.
(m) When Ann saw her professor in the hallway, she *stopped* (*in order*) *to talk* to him.	*Stop* can also be followed immediately by an infinitive of purpose, as in (m): Ann stopped walking in order to talk to her professor. (See Chart 15-1, p. 331.)

*Notice the patterns with **prefer:***
  prefer + *gerund:* I ***prefer staying*** home ***to going*** to the concert.
  prefer + *infinitive:* I'd ***prefer to stay*** home (rather) ***than*** (***to***) go to the concert.
****Forget** followed by a gerund usually occurs in a negative sentence or in a question: e.g., *I'll never forget, I can't forget, Have you ever forgotten,* and *Can you ever forget* are often followed by a gerund phrase.

❑ **Exercise 30. Looking at grammar.** (Chart 14-7)
Complete each sentence with the correct form of the verb in parentheses.

1. I always remember (*turn*) _____ *to turn* _____ off all the lights before I leave my house.

2. I remember (*play*) _____ with dolls when I was a child.

3. What do you remember (*do*) _____ when you were a child?

4. What do you remember (*do*) _____ before you leave for class every day?

5. What did you forget (*do*) _____ before you left for class this morning?

6. I won't ever forget (*watch*) _____ our team score the winning goal in the last seconds of the championship game.

7. Don't forget (*do*) _____ your homework tonight.

8. Please stop (*bite*) _____ your fingernails.

9. I stopped (*get*) _____ gas yesterday and was shocked at the high price.

10. I stopped (*drive*) _____ so much because of the high price of gas.

❑ **Exercise 31. Listening.** (Chart 14-7)

CD 2
Track 16

Listen to each sentence and choose the sentence (a. or b.) with the same meaning.

1. a. Joan thought about her phone call with her husband.
   b. Joan didn't forget to call her husband.

2. a. Rita was thinking about the times she went to the farmers' market with her grandmother.
   b. Rita didn't forget to go to the farmers' market with her grandmother.

3. a. Roger got a cigarette and began to smoke.
   b. Roger quit smoking.

4. a. Mr. and Mrs. Olson finished eating.
   b. Mr. and Mrs. Olson got something to eat before the movie.

5. a. The speaker is sorry about something he did.
   b. The speaker is delivering some bad news.

❑ **Exercise 32. Looking at grammar.** (Charts 14-3 → 14-7)
Complete each sentence with the correct form of the verb in parentheses.

1. Maria loves (*swim*) _____ *swimming / to swim* _____ in the ocean.

2. After a brief interruption, the professor continued (*lecture*) _____.

3. I hate (*see*) _____ any living being suffer. I can't bear (*watch*)

   _____ news reports of children who are starving. I can't stand (*read*)

   _____ about animals that have been cruelly abused by people.

4. I'm afraid of flying. When a plane begins (*move*) _____ down the runway, my heart starts (*race*) _____. Uh-oh! The plane is beginning (*move*★) _____, and my heart is starting (*race*) _____.

5. When I travel, I prefer (*drive*) _____ to (*take*) _____ a plane.

6. I prefer (*drive*) _____ rather than (*take*) _____ a plane.

7. I regret (*inform*) _____ you that your loan application has not been approved.

8. I regret (*listen, not*) _____ to my father's advice. He was right.

9. When a student asks a question, the teacher always tries (*explain*) _____ the problem as clearly as possible.

10. I tried everything, but the baby still wouldn't stop (*cry*) _____.

I tried (*hold*) _____ him, but that didn't help.
I tried (*feed*) _____ him, but he
refused the food and continued (*cry*) _____.
I tried (*burp*) _____ him.
I tried (*change*) _____ his diaper.
Nothing worked. The baby wouldn't stop crying.

★If possible, native speakers usually prefer to use an infinitive following a progressive verb instead of using two *-ing* verbs in a row.
   Usual: *The baby is starting **to walk**.* (instead of *walking*)
If the main verb is not progressive, either form is used:
   *Babies **start to walk** around one.* OR *Babies **start walking** around one.*

❑ **Exercise 33. Let's talk.** (Charts 14-3 → 14-7)

Speaker A gives the cues. Speaker B makes sentences from the verb combinations. Any name, verb tense, or modal can be used. Work in pairs or small groups.

Examples:
SPEAKER A (*book open*): like \ go
SPEAKER B (*book closed*): I like to go (OR going) to the park.

SPEAKER A (*book open*): ask \ open
SPEAKER B (*book closed*): Kostas asked me to open the window.

1. advise \ go		11. continue \ walk
2. offer \ lend		12. finish \ do
3. start \ laugh		13. encourage \ go
4. remind \ take		14. can't stand \ have to wait
5. be allowed \ have		15. regret \ take

Change roles.

Change roles.

6. postpone \ go		16. decide \ ask \ come
7. look forward to \ see		17. stop \ walk
8. forget \ bring		18. consider \ not go
9. remember \ go		19. keep \ put off \ do
10. suggest \ go		20. intend \ finish

❑ **Exercise 34. Let's talk: interview.** (Charts 14-3 → 14-7)

Make true sentences about yourself using the words in parentheses. Ask other students about themselves using the given question word. Share some of the answers with the class.

Example: (like \ go \ on weekends) Where?
→ *I like to go to Central Park on weekends. How about you? Where do you like to go on weekends?*

1. (enjoy \ listen to) What?
2. (be interested in \ learn) What?
3. (be used to \ have \ for breakfast) What?
4. (prefer \ go to bed) What time?
5. (can't stand \ watch) What?
6. (decide \ study English) Why?

❑ **Exercise 35. Looking at grammar.** (Charts 14-3 → 14-7)

Complete each sentence with an appropriate form of the verb in parentheses.

1. Mary reminded me (*be, not*) _____*not to be*_____ late for the meeting.

2. I've volunteered (*help*) _____ at the local school during my time off and
(*paint*) _____ the lunchroom.

3. We discussed (*quit*) _____ our jobs and (*open*) _____ our
own business.

4. I'm getting tired. I need (*take*) _____ a break.

5. Sometimes students avoid (*look*) _____ at the teacher if they don't want (*answer*) _____ a question.

6. Most children prefer (*watch*) _____ television to (*listen*) _____ to the radio.

7. The taxi driver refused (*take*) _____ a check. He wanted the passenger (*pay*) _____ cash.

8. The travel agent advised us (*wait, not*) _____ until August (*make*) _____ a reservation.

9. Keep (*talk*) _____. I'm listening to you.

10. Linda offered (*water*) _____ my plants while I was out of town.

11. Igor suggested (*go*) _____ (*ski*) _____ in the mountains this weekend. How does that sound to you?

12. The doctor ordered Mr. Gray (*smoke, not*) _____.

13. Don't tell me his secret. I prefer (*know, not*) _____.

14. Toshi was allowed (*renew*) _____ his student visa.

15. Don't forget (*tell*) _____ Jane (*call*) _____ me about (*go*) _____ (*swim*) _____ tomorrow.

16. Sally reminded me (*ask*) _____ you (*tell*) _____ Bob (*remember*) _____ (*bring*) _____ his soccer ball to the picnic.

17. Recently, Jo has been spending most of her time (*do*) _____ research for a book on pioneer women.

18. The little boy had a lot of trouble (*convince*) _____ anyone he had seen a mermaid.

WHERE?

❏ **Exercise 36. Warm-up.** (Chart 14-8)
All of the sentences are correct. What differences do you notice in their grammatical structure?
Do you agree or disagree with the statements? Why or why not?

1. Speaking a second language without an accent is nearly impossible for adult language learners.

2. To speak a second language without an accent is nearly impossible for adult language learners.

3. It is nearly impossible for adult language learners to speak a second language without an accent.

14-8 *It* + Infinitive; Gerunds and Infinitives as Subjects

(a) *It* is difficult *to learn* a second language.	Often an infinitive phrase is used with *it* as the subject of a sentence. The word *it* refers to and has the same meaning as the infinitive phrase at the end of the sentence.
	In (a): *It* means "to learn a second language."
(b) *Learning* a second language is difficult.	A gerund phrase is frequently used as the subject of a sentence, as in (b).
(c) *To learn* a second language is difficult.	An infinitive can also be used as the subject of a sentence, as in (c), but far more commonly an infinitive phrase is used with *it*, as in (a).
(d) It is easy *for young children* to learn a second language.	The phrase *for* (*someone*) may be used to specify exactly who the speaker is talking about, as in (d).
Learning a second language is easy *for young children*.	
To learn a second language is easy *for young children*.	

❏ **Exercise 37. Looking at grammar.** (Chart 14-8)
Make sentences beginning with *it*. Use a form of the given word followed by an infinitive phrase for each sentence.

1. be dangerous → *It's dangerous to ride a motorcycle without wearing a helmet.*
2. be important
3. not be easy
4. be silly
5. must be interesting
6. be always a pleasure
7. be smart
8. not cost much money
9. be necessary
10. take time

❏ **Exercise 38. Looking at grammar.** (Chart 14-8)
Add *for* (***someone***) and any other words to give a more specific and accurate meaning to each sentence.

1. It isn't possible to be on time.
   → *It isn't possible for me to be on time for class if the bus drivers are on strike and I have to walk to class in a rainstorm.*
2. It's easy to speak Spanish.
3. It's important to learn English.
4. It is essential to get a visa.
5. It's important to take advanced math courses.
6. It's difficult to communicate.
7. It was impossible to come to class.
8. It is a good idea to study gerunds and infinitives.

❏ **Exercise 39. Let's talk: pairwork.** (Chart 14-8)
Work with a partner. Speaker A gives the cue. Speaker B completes the sentence with an infinitive phrase. Speaker A restates the sentence using a gerund phrase as the subject.

Example:
SPEAKER A (*book open*): It's fun . . .
SPEAKER B (*book closed*): . . . to ride a horse.
SPEAKER A (*book open*): Riding a horse is fun.

1. It's dangerous . . .
2. It's easy . . .
3. It's impolite . . .
4. It is important . . .

Change roles.

5. It is wrong . . .
6. It takes a lot of time . . .
7. It's a good idea . . .
8. Is it difficult . . . ?

❏ **Exercise 40. Let's talk: interview.** (Chart 14-8)
Interview two different students for each item. Ask the students to answer each question using a gerund phrase as the subject.

1. What is easy for you?
2. What is hard for you?
3. What is or isn't interesting for you?
4. What has been a good experience for you?
5. What sounds like fun to you?
6. What is considered impolite in your country?
7. What is a complicated process?
8. What demands patience and a sense of humor?

14-9 Reference List of Verbs Followed by Gerunds

Verbs with a bullet (•) can also be followed by infinitives. See Chart 14-10.

1.	admit	He *admitted stealing* the money.
2.	advise•	She *advised waiting* until tomorrow.
3.	anticipate	I *anticipate having* a good time on vacation.
4.	appreciate	I *appreciated hearing* from them.
5.	avoid	He *avoided answering* my question.
6.	can't bear•	I *can't bear waiting* in long lines.
7.	begin•	It *began raining*.
8.	complete	I finally *completed writing* my term paper.
9.	consider	I *will consider going* with you.
10.	continue•	He *continued speaking*.
11.	delay	He *delayed leaving* for school.
12.	deny	She *denied committing* the crime.
13.	discuss	They *discussed opening* a new business.
14.	dislike	I *dislike driving* long distances.
15.	enjoy	We *enjoyed visiting* them.
16.	finish	She *finished studying* about ten.
17.	forget•	I*'ll never forget visiting* Napoleon's tomb.
18.	hate•	I *hate making* silly mistakes.
19.	can't help	I *can't help worrying* about it.
20.	keep	I *keep hoping* he will come.
21.	like•	I *like going* to movies.
22.	love•	I *love going* to operas.
23.	mention	She *mentioned going* to a movie.
24.	mind	*Would* you *mind helping* me with this?
25.	miss	I *miss being* with my family.
26.	postpone	Let's *postpone leaving* until tomorrow.
27.	practice	The athlete *practiced throwing* the ball.
28.	prefer•	Ann *prefers walking* to driving to work.
29.	quit	He *quit trying* to solve the problem.
30.	recall	I *don't recall meeting* him before.
31.	recollect	I *don't recollect meeting* him before.
32.	recommend	She *recommended seeing* the show.
33.	regret•	I *regret telling* him my secret.
34.	remember•	I *can remember meeting* him when I was a child.
35.	resent	I *resent her interfering* in my business.
36.	resist	I *couldn't resist eating* the dessert.
37.	risk	She *risks losing* all of her money.
38.	can't stand•	I *can't stand waiting* in long lines.
39.	start•	It *started raining*.
40.	stop	She *stopped going* to classes when she got sick.
41.	suggest	She *suggested going* to a movie.
42.	tolerate	She *won't tolerate cheating* during an examination.
43.	try•	I *tried changing* the light bulb, but the lamp still didn't work.
44.	understand	I *don't understand his leaving* school.

14-10 Reference List of Verbs Followed by Infinitives

Verbs with a bullet (•) can also be followed by gerunds. See Chart 14-9.

Verbs Followed Immediately by an Infinitive

1.	afford	I *can't afford to buy* it.
2.	agree	They *agreed to help* us.
3.	appear	She *appears to be* tired.
4.	arrange	I'*ll arrange to meet* you at the airport.
5.	ask	He *asked to come* with us.
6.	can't bear•	I *can't bear to wait* in long lines.
7.	beg	He *begged to come* with us.
8.	begin•	It *began to rain.*
9.	care	I *don't care to see* that show.
10.	claim	She *claims to know* a famous movie star.
11.	consent	She finally *consented to marry* him.
12.	continue•	He *continued to speak.*
13.	decide	I *have decided to leave* on Monday.
14.	demand	I *demand to know* who is responsible.
15.	deserve	She *deserves to win* the prize.
16.	expect	I *expect to enter* graduate school in the fall.
17.	fail	She *failed to return* the book to the library on time.
18.	forget•	I *forgot to mail* the letter.
19.	hate•	I *hate to make* silly mistakes.
20.	hesitate	*Don't hesitate to ask* for my help.
21.	hope	Jack *hopes to arrive* next week.
22.	intend	He *intends to be* a firefighter.
23.	learn	He *learned to play* the piano.
24.	like•	I *like to go* to the movies.
25.	love•	I *love to go* to operas.
26.	manage	She *managed to finish* her work early.
27.	mean	I *didn't mean to hurt* your feelings.
28.	need	I *need to have* your opinion.
29.	offer	They *offered to help* us.
30.	plan	I'*m planning to have* a party.
31.	prefer•	Ann *prefers to walk* to work.
32.	prepare	We *prepared to welcome* them.
33.	pretend	He *pretends not to understand.*
34.	promise	I *promise not to be* late.
35.	refuse	I *refuse to believe* his story.
36.	regret•	I *regret to tell* you that you failed.
37.	remember•	I *remembered to lock* the door.
38.	seem	That cat *seems to be* friendly.
39.	can't stand•	I *can't stand to wait* in long lines.
40.	start•	It *started to rain.*
41.	struggle	I *struggled to stay* awake.
42.	swear	She *swore to tell* the truth.
43.	talk	He *tends to talk* too much.
44.	threaten	She *threatened to tell* my parents.
45.	try•	I'*m trying to learn* English.
46.	volunteer	He *volunteered to help* us.
47.	wait	I'*ll wait to hear* from you.
48.	want	I *want to tell* you something.
49.	wish	She *wishes to come* with us.

Verbs Followed by a (Pro)noun + an Infinitive

50.	advise•	She *advised me to wait* until tomorrow.
51.	allow	She *allowed me to use* her car.
52.	ask	I *asked John to help* us.
53.	beg	They *begged us to come.*
54.	cause	Her laziness *caused her to fail.*
55.	challenge	She *challenged me to race* her to the corner.
56.	convince	I couldn't *convince him to accept* our help.
57.	dare	He *dared me to do* better than he had done.
58.	encourage	He *encouraged me to try* again.
59.	expect	I *expect you to be* on time.
60.	forbid	I *forbid you to tell* him.
61.	force	They *forced him to tell* the truth.
62.	hire	She *hired a boy to mow* the lawn.
63.	instruct	He *instructed them to be* careful.
64.	invite	Harry *invited the Johnsons to come* to his party.
65.	need	We *needed Chris to help* us figure out the solution.
66.	order	The judge *ordered me to pay* a fine.
67.	permit	He *permitted the children to stay* up late.
68.	persuade	I *persuaded him to come* for a visit.
69.	remind	She *reminded me to lock* the door.
70.	require	Our teacher *requires us to be* on time.
71.	teach	My brother *taught me to swim.*
72.	tell	The doctor *told me to take* these pills.
73.	urge	I *urged her to apply* for the job.
74.	want	I *want you to be* happy.
75.	warn	I *warned you not to drive* too fast.

Work with a partner. Partner A gives the cue. Partner B completes the sentence with **doing it** or **to do it**. Check Charts 14-9 and 14-10 for the correct verb form if necessary.

Example: I promise
PARTNER A (*book open*): I promise . . .
PARTNER B (*book closed*): . . . to do it.

1. We plan . . .
2. I can't afford . . .
3. She didn't allow me . . .
4. I don't care . . .
5. Please remind me . . .
6. I am considering . . .
7. Our director postponed . . .
8. He persuaded me . . .
9. I don't mind . . .
10. Everyone avoided . . .

Change roles.
11. I refused . . .
12. I hope . . .
13. She convinced me . . .
14. He mentioned . . .
15. I expect . . .
16. I encouraged him . . .
17. I warned him not . . .
18. We prepared . . .
19. I don't recall . . .
20. We decided . . .

Change roles.
21. He resented . . .
22. When will you finish . . . ?
23. Did you practice . . .
24. She agreed . . .
25. They consented . . .

26. Stop . . .
27. I didn't force him . . .
28. I couldn't resist . . .
29. Somehow, the cat managed . . .
30. Did the little boy admit . . . ?

Change roles.
31. He denied . . .
32. I didn't mean . . .
33. She swore . . .
34. I volunteered . . .
35. He suggested . . .
36. He advised me . . .
37. He struggled . . .
38. I don't want to risk . . .
39. Do you recommend . . . ?
40. I miss . . .

Change roles.
41. I can't imagine . . .
42. She threatened . . .
43. He seems to dislike . . .
44. The children begged . . .
45. She challenged me . . .
46. Did he deny . . . ?
47. She taught me . . .
48. Do you anticipate . . . ?
49. I don't recollect . . .
50. I'll arrange . . .

❏ **Exercise 42. Game.** (Charts 14-9 and 14-10)
Divide into teams. Your teacher will begin a sentence by using any of the verbs in Charts 14-9 and 14-10. Complete the sentence with **to do it** or **doing it**, or with your own words. Each correct completion scores one point.

Example:
TEACHER: I reminded Mario . . .
STUDENT A: . . . to do it. OR . . . to be on time.
TEACHER: Yes. One point!

❏ **Exercise 43. Looking at grammar.** (Charts 14-9 and 14-10)
Choose the correct form of the verbs in *italics*. In some sentences, both verbs are correct.

1. Hassan volunteered *bringing / to bring* some food to the reception.

2. The students practiced *pronouncing / to pronounce* the "th" sound in the phrase "these thirty-three dirty trees."

3. In the fairy tale, the wolf threatened *eating / to eat* a girl named Little Red Riding Hood.

4. The movers struggled *lifting / to lift* the piano up the stairs.

5. Anita demanded *knowing / to know* why she had been fired.

6. My skin can't tolerate *being / to be* in the sun all day. I get sunburned easily.

7. Mr. Kwan broke the antique vase. I'm sure he didn't mean *doing / to do* it.

8. Fred Washington claims *being / to be* a descendant of George Washington.

9. Linda failed *passing / to pass* the entrance exam.

10. I hate *getting / to get* to work late.

11. I can't bear *seeing / to see* animals suffer.

12. Ming Wan just started a new business. He risks *losing / to lose* everything if it doesn't succeed.

❏ **Exercise 44. Looking at grammar.** (Charts 14-9 and 14-10)
Complete each sentence with an appropriate form of the verb in parentheses.

1. How did you manage (*find*) _____to find_____ out about the surprise party?

2. I think Sam deserves (*have*) _____ another chance.

3. Olga finally admitted (*be*) _____ responsible for the problem.

4. Mrs. Freeman can't help (*worry*) _____ about her children.

5. Children, I forbid you (*play*) _____ in the street. There's too much traffic.

6. Lori suggested (*leave*) _____ around six. Is that too early for you?

7. I urged Omar (*return*) _____ to school and (*finish*) _____ his education.

8. Oscar keeps (*hope*) _____ and (*pray*) _____ that things will get better.

9. Nadia keeps (*promise*) _____ (*visit*) _____ us, but she never does.

10. My little cousin is a blabbermouth! He can't resist (*tell*) _____ everyone my secrets!

11. I finally managed (*persuade*) _____ Yoko (*stay*) _____ in school and (*finish*) _____ her degree.

12. Margaret challenged me (*race*) _____ her across the pool.

❏   **Exercise 45. Let's talk.** (Chapter 14)
Work in groups of three to five. Choose one of the story beginnings or make up your own. Each group member continues the story by adding a sentence or two. At least one of the sentences should contain words from the list on page 329, plus a gerund or infinitive phrase (but it is okay to continue the story without using a gerund or infinitive if it works out that way). As a group, use as many of the words in the list as you can.

Example: Yoko had a bad night last night. First, when she got home, she discovered that . . .
SPEAKER A: . . . her door was unlocked. She didn't ***recall leaving*** her door unlocked. She always ***remembers to lock*** her door and in fact specifically ***remembered locking*** it that morning. So she became afraid that someone had broken into her apartment.
SPEAKER B: She ***thought about going*** inside, but then decided ***it*** would be better ***not to go*** into her apartment alone. What if there was a burglar inside?
SPEAKER C: ***Instead of going*** into her apartment alone, Yoko walked to her next-door neighbor's door and knocked.
SPEAKER D: Her neighbor answered the door. He could see that something was the matter. "Are you all right?" he asked her.
Etc.

Story beginnings:

1. (_____) is having trouble with (her/his) roommate, whose name is (_____). (Her/His) roommate keeps many pets even though the lease they signed forbids residents to keep animals in their apartments. Yesterday, one of these pets, a/an . . . .

2. It was a dark and stormy night. (_____) was all alone at home. Suddenly . . . .

3. Not long ago, (_____) and (_____) were walking home together after dark. They heard a strange whooshing sound. When they looked up in the night sky, they saw a huge hovering aircraft. It glowed! It was round and green! (_____) was frightened and curious at the same time. (She/He) wanted to . . . , but . . . .

4. Once upon a time, (_____) lived in a faraway village in a remote mountainous region. All of the villagers were terrified because of the dragon that lived nearby. At least once a week, the dragon would descend on the village and . . . .

5. (_____) had a bad day yesterday. First of all, when (she/he) got up in the morning, (she/he) discovered that . . . .

List of words and phrases to use in your story:

Prepositional expressions followed by gerunds	Verbs followed by gerunds or infinitives		*It* + an infinitive or a gerund subject
be accused of	admit	mind	be a bad experience
be accustomed to	advise	need	be a bad idea
in addition to	afford	offer	be better
be afraid of	agree	permit	be clever
apologize (to someone) for	ask	persuade	be dangerous
believe in	avoid	plan	be difficult
blame (someone) for	beg	postpone	be easy
be capable of	begin	prefer	be essential
be committed to	consider	prepare	be foolish
complain about	continue	pretend	be a good experience
dream of	convince	promise	be a good idea
be excited about	decide	quit	be fun
forgive (someone) for	demand	recall	be hard
be guilty of	deny	refuse	be important
instead of	discuss	regret	be impossible
be interested in	dislike	remember	be interesting
look forward to	encourage	remind	be necessary
be opposed to	enjoy	risk	be a pleasure
prevent (someone) from	expect	seem	be possible
be scared of	fail	start	be relaxing
stop (someone) from	force	stop	take effort
succeed in	forget	struggle	take energy
take advantage of	hesitate	suggest	take money
be terrified of	hope	threaten	take patience
thank (someone) for	invite	wait	take time
think of	learn	want	
be tired of	like	warn	
be worried about	manage		

Correct the errors.

1. I don't mind to have a roommate.

2. Most students want return home as soon as possible.

3. Learning about another country it is very interesting.

4. I tried very hard to don't make any mistakes.

5. The task of find a person who could tutor me in English wasn't difficult.

6. All of us needed to went to the ticket office before the game yesterday.

7. I'm looking forward to go to swimming in the ocean.

8. Ski in the Alps it was a big thrill for me.

9. Don't keep to be asking me the same questions over and over.

10. During a fire drill, everyone is required leaving the building.

11. I don't enjoy to play card games. I prefer to spend my time for read or watch movies.

12. Is hard for me understand people who speak very fast.

13. When I entered the room, I found my young son stand on the kitchen table.

14. When I got home, Irene was lying in bed think about what a wonderful time she'd had.

Chapter 15
Gerunds and Infinitives, Part 2

❑ **Exercise 1. Warm-up.** (Chart 15-1)
Which sentences answer the question "Why"?

   1. Joe went to the library to study last night.
      → *Why did Joe go to the library last night? To study.*
   2. Lucy wants to leave now.
      → *(The sentence doesn't answer the question "Why?")*
   3. Eva opened the window to let in some fresh air.
   4. Oscar came to this school in order to learn English.
   5. Rick needs to call his mother.
   6. Rick needs to call his mother to tell her the good news.

15-1 Infinitive of Purpose: *In Order To*	
(a) He came here *in order to study* English. (b) He came here *to study* English.	*In order to* is used to express *purpose*. It answers the question "Why?" *In order* is often omitted, as in (b).
(c) INCORRECT: He came here ~~for studying~~ English. (d) INCORRECT: He came here ~~for to study~~ English. (e) INCORRECT: He came here ~~for study~~ English.	To express purpose, use (*in order*) *to*, not *for*, with a verb.*
(f) I went to the store *for* some bread. (g) I went to the store *to buy* some bread.	*For* can be used to express purpose, but it is a preposition and is followed by a noun object, as in (f).

*Exception: The phrase *be used for* expresses the typical or general purpose of a thing. In this case, the preposition *for* is followed by a gerund: *A saw is used for cutting* wood. Also possible: *A saw is used to cut* wood.

However, to talk about a particular thing and a particular situation, *be used* + *an infinitive* is used: *A chain saw was used to cut* (NOT *for cutting*) *down the old oak tree.*

❑ **Exercise 2. Looking at grammar.** (Chart 15-1)
Complete the sentences with *to* or *for*.

Isabella spent a month in Miami. She went there . . .

   1. ___to___ see her cousins.

   2. ___for___ a vacation.

   3. _____ business.

   4. _____ meet with company executives.

5. _____ discuss long-term plans for the company.

6. _____ spend time with her parents.

7. _____ a visit with childhood friends.

❏ **Exercise 3. In your own words.** (Chart 15-1)
Complete the sentences with your own words. Express the purpose of the action.

1. I went to Chicago to _____ *visit my grandparents.* _____

2. Ron went to Chicago for _____ *a medical conference.* _____

3. I went to the grocery store for _____

4. Reisa went to the grocery store to _____

5. I went to the doctor to _____

6. My son went to the doctor for _____

7. I swim every day to _____

8. Kevin swims every day for _____

❏ **Exercise 4. Looking at grammar.** (Chart 15-1)
Add *in order* wherever possible. If nothing should be added, write **Ø**.

1. I went to the garden center _____ *in order* _____ to get some fertilizer for my flowers.

2. When the teacher asked him a question, Scott pretended _____ *Ø* _____ to understand what she was saying.

3. My roommate asked me _____ to clean up the dishes after dinner.

4. Mustafa climbed onto a chair _____ to change a light bulb in the ceiling.

5. Rita has to work at two jobs _____ to support herself and her three children.

6. I really want _____ to learn Italian before I visit Venice next year.

7. I jog three times a week _____ to stay healthy.

8. Karen finally went to the dentist _____ to get some relief from her toothache.

9. It's easier for me _____ to understand written English than it is to understand spoken English.

10. Is it important _____ to speak English without an accent as long as people understand what you're saying?

□ **Exercise 5. Check your knowledge.** (Chart 15-1)
Correct the errors.

1. I went to the library ~~for~~ ^{to} study last night.

2. Helen borrowed my dictionary for to look up the spelling of *occurred*.

3. The teacher opened the window for letting some fresh air into the room.

4. I came to this school for learn English.

5. I traveled to Osaka for to visit my sister.

□ **Exercise 6. Let's talk: interview.** (Chart 15-1)
Ask two classmates each question. Share some of their responses with the class.

What are two reasons why some people . . .

1. go to Hawaii for vacation?	3. cheat on exams?	5. tell white lies?*
2. exercise?	4. meditate?	6. become actors?

□ **Exercise 7. Warm-up.** (Chart 15-2)
Look at the adjectives in blue. What do you notice about the words that come after them? about the words that come before them?

1. Anya *was* sorry *to hear* that her favorite restaurant closed.
2. Nate *is* certain *to pass* his test.
3. Timmy *was* sad *to learn* his pet goldfish had died.
4. I would *be* happy *to help* you.

15-2 Adjectives Followed by Infinitives

(a) We *were **sorry to** hear* the bad news.	Certain adjectives can be immediately followed by infinitives, as in (a) and (b).
(b) I *was **surprised to** see* Ted at the meeting.	In general, these adjectives describe a person (or persons), not a thing. Many of these adjectives describe a person's feelings or attitudes.

Common adjectives followed by infinitives

glad to (do it)	sorry to*	ready to	careful to	surprised to*
happy to	sad to*	prepared to	hesitant to	amazed to*
pleased to	upset to*	anxious to	reluctant to	astonished to*
delighted to	disappointed to*	eager to	afraid to	shocked to*
content to		willing to		stunned to*
relieved to	embarrassed to	motivated to	certain to	
lucky to	proud to	determined to	likely to	
fortunate to	ashamed to		unlikely to	

*The expressions with asterisks are usually followed by infinitive phrases with verbs such as *see, learn, discover, find out, hear.*

---

white lies = lies that aren't considered serious, e.g., telling a friend her dress looks nice when you don't think it does.

❏ **Exercise 8. In your own words.** (Chart 15-2)
Complete the sentences using the expressions listed in Chart 15-2 and your own words. Use infinitive phrases in your completions.

1. Nicole always speeds on the expressway. She's . . . .
   → *She's certain to get stopped by the police.*
   → *She's likely to get a ticket.*

2. I've worked hard all day long. Enough's enough! I'm . . . .

3. Next month, I'm going to a family reunion — the first one in 25 years. I'm very much looking forward to it. I'm . . . .

4. Some children grow up in unhappy homes. My family, however, has always been loving and supportive. I'm . . . .

5. Ivan's run out of money again, but he doesn't want anyone to know his situation. He needs money desperately, but he's . . . .

6. Rosalyn wants to become an astronaut. That has been her dream since she was a little girl. She has been working hard toward her goal and is . . . .

7. Our neighbors had extra tickets to the ballet, so they invited us to go with them. Since both of us love the ballet, we were . . . .

8. Andrea recently told me what my wayward brother is up to these days. I couldn't believe my ears! I was . . . .

❏ **Exercise 9. Let's talk.** (Chart 15-2)
Work in small groups. Complete the sentences with adjectives from Chart 15-2 that make sense. Discuss your answers.

SITUATION 1: Mr. Wah was offered an excellent job in another country. He sees advantages and disadvantages to moving.

He is . . .

1. _____*sad to / prepared to / reluctant to*_____ leave his country.

2. _____ move away from his parents.

3. _____ take his wife and children away from family and friends.

4. _____ try a new job.

5. _____ learn a new language.

SITUATION 2: There have been a lot of nighttime burglaries in the town of Viewmont.

The residents have been . . .

6. _____ leave their homes overnight.

7. _____ lock their doors and windows at night.

8. _____ watch for strangers on the streets.

9. _____ have weekly meetings with the police

for updates on their progress.

10. _____ hear that the police suspect

neighborhood teenagers.

❏ **Exercise 10. Let's talk: interview.** (Chart 15-2)
Make questions using the words in parentheses. Ask two classmates each question. Share some of their answers with the class.

1. What are children sometimes (afraid \ do)?
2. When you're tired in the evening, what are you (content \ do)?
3. What should drivers be (careful \ do) in traffic?
4. If one of your friends has a problem, what are you (willing \ do)?
5. What are people who don't speak English well (reluctant \ do)?
6. What are you (determined \ do) before you are too old?
7. What are some things people are (ashamed \ do)?
8. Can you tell me something you were (shocked \ find out)?
9. Can you tell me something you were (sad \ hear)?
10. What are you (eager \ do) in the near future?

❏ **Exercise 11. Warm-up.** (Chart 15-3)
In which sentences are the speakers expressing a negative idea (in other words, expressing the idea that there's something wrong or that there's a bad result)?

1. The soup is too spicy. I can't eat it.
2. The soup is very spicy, but I like it.
3. It's very late, but the restaurant is still open.
4. We're too late. The restaurant has closed.

15-3 Using Infinitives with *Too* and *Enough*	
COMPARE: (a) That box is *too heavy* for Bob to lift. (b) That box is *very heavy*, but Bob can lift it.	In the speaker's mind, the use of *too* implies a negative result. In (a): *too heavy* = It is *impossible* for Bob to lift that box. In (b): *very heavy* = It is *possible but difficult* for Bob to lift that box.
(c) I am *strong enough to lift* that box. I can lift it. (d) I have *enough strength to lift* that box. (e) I have *strength enough to lift* that box.	*Enough* follows an adjective, as in (c). Usually *enough* precedes a noun, as in (d). In formal English, it may follow a noun, as in (e).

❑ **Exercise 12. Let's talk.** (Chart 15-3)
Work in pairs, in small groups, or as a class.

Part I. Think of a negative result for each sentence. Make negative statements using infinitive phrases.

1. That ring is too expensive.
   → Negative result: *I can't buy it. That ring is too expensive for me to buy.*
2. I'm too tired.
   → Negative result: *I don't want to go to the meeting. I'm too tired to go to the meeting.*
3. It's too late.
4. It's too cold.
5. Physics is too difficult.
6. I'm too busy.
7. My son is too young.
8. The mountain cliff is too steep.

Part II. Now think of a positive result for each sentence. Make positive statements using infinitive phrases.

9. That ring is very expensive, but it isn't too expensive.
   → Positive result: *I can buy it. That ring isn't too expensive for me to buy.*
10. I'm very tired, but I'm not too tired.
11. My suitcase is very heavy, but it's not too heavy.
12. I'm very busy, but I'm not too busy.

❑ **Exercise 13. Let's talk.** (Chart 15-3)
Discuss possible answers to the given questions. Work in pairs, in small groups, or as a class.

1. What is a child too young to do but an adult old enough to do?
2. What is your pocket big enough to hold? What is it too small to hold?
3. What do you have enough time to do after class today? Are you too busy to do something you'd like to do or should do?
4. Is there enough space in this classroom for 100 people? Or is it too small to hold that many people? How many people is this room big enough to hold comfortably?
5. Here's an English saying: "Too many cooks spoil the soup." What do you think it means?
6. Do you think it is very important to practice your English? Do you get enough practice? In your opinion, how much practice is enough?
7. Is it very difficult or too difficult to learn English?

❑ **Exercise 14. Listening.** (Chart 15-3)
Listen to Speaker A. Choose the response that you expect Speaker B to give.

CD 2
Track 17

Example: You will hear: Oh, no. I spilled the coffee!
          You will choose: a. I'm sorry. I didn't fill your cup full enough.
                           (b.) I'm sorry. I filled your cup too full.

SPEAKER B:

1. a. Yes. It was too good to eat.
    b. Yes. It was very good.

2. a. No. She's old enough to stay home alone.
    b. Never. She's too young to stay home alone.

3. a. I agree. It can be very difficult at times.
    b. I agree. It's too difficult.

4. a. Really well. They're too clean. Thanks.
    b. Really well. They're very clean. Thanks.

5. a. I know. He shouldn't be driving.
    b. I know he's very old, but it's okay for him to keep driving.

6. a. I guess we don't have enough big envelopes.
    b. I guess we don't have big enough envelopes.

❏ **Exercise 15. Grammar and speaking.** (Charts 14-7, 14-8, 14-11, and 15-1 → 15-3)
Complete the sentences with your own words. Try to use a gerund or infinitive in each statement. Then work with a partner. Ask him/her to agree or disagree with your statements (and to explain why). Share some of their answers with the class.

		PARTNER AGREES?	
1.	It's important for _____	yes	no
2.	A person should never forget to _____	yes	no
3.	Teachers often advise their students to _____	yes	no
4.	I'm not willing to _____	yes	no
5.	It's too difficult for most people to _____	yes	no
6.	In order to _____, employees should _____	yes	no
	_____		
7.	It's easy to _____	yes	no
8.	It's hard to get accustomed to _____	yes	no

❏ **Exercise 16. Warm-up.** (Chart 15-4)
Choose the correct form of the passive verbs. Reminder: A passive verb is *a form of* ***be*** + *the past participle.*★ For example, *the patient **was seen** by a specialist.*

1. The patient appreciated (*to be seen / being seen*) by a specialist.
2. It was important for him (*to be seen / being seen*) by a specialist.

★See Chart 11-2, p. 213.

15-4 Passive Infinitives and Gerunds

(a) I didn't *expect to be asked* to his party.	PASSIVE INFINITIVE: ***to be*** + *past participle* In (a): ***to be asked*** is a passive infinitive. The understood *by*-phrase is *by him: I didn't expect to be asked to his party (by him).*
(b) I *enjoyed being asked* to his party.	PASSIVE GERUND: ***being*** + *past participle* In (b): ***being asked*** is a passive gerund. The understood *by*-phrase is *by him: I enjoyed being asked to his party (by him).*

❏ **Exercise 17. Looking at grammar.** (Chart 15-4)
Complete the sentences with the passive form of ***invite***.

1. Sam would like _____*to be invited*_____ to Ann's birthday party.

2. Mark also hopes _____.

3. Maria has no doubts. She expects _____ to it.

4. Omar is looking forward to _____ too.

5. I would enjoy _____ to it, but I probably won't be.

6. Everyone I know wants _____ to Ann's birthday party.

❏ **Exercise 18. Looking at grammar.** (Chart 15-4)
Complete each sentence with the correct form of the verb in parentheses.

1. I don't enjoy (*laugh*) _____*being laughed*_____ at by other people.

2. Ryan is a convincing liar. It's easy (*fool*) _____*to be fooled*_____ by his lies.

3. Sometimes adolescents complain about not (*understand*) _____ by their parents.

4. Your compositions are supposed (*write*) _____ in ink.

5. Ms. Thompson is always willing to help if there is a problem in the office, but she doesn't want (*call*) _____ at home unless there is an emergency.

6. Despite his name, Freddie Frankenstein has a good chance of (*elect*) _____ _____ to the local school board.

7. You must tell me the truth. I insist on your (*tell*) _____ the truth.

8. Don't all of us want (*love*) _____ and (*need*) _____ by other people?

Exercise 19. Let's talk. (Chart 15-4)
Agree or disagree with the following statements and explain your reasons why. Work in pairs, in small groups, or as a class.

1. I appreciate *being given* advice by my family and friends.
2. I didn't like *being given* advice by my family when I was young.
3. I always expect *to be told* the absolute and complete truth by everyone at all times.
4. I would like *to be invited* to an event where there are a lot of famous people.

❏ **Exercise 20. Warm-up.** (Chart 15-5)
Make statements that are true for you. Use the same noun to complete each sentence. Do the sentences have the same or different meanings?

1. I need to clean my _____.

2. My _____ needs cleaning.

3. My _____ needs to be cleaned.

15-5 Using Gerunds or Passive Infinitives Following *Need*

(a) I *need to paint* my house.	Usually an infinitive follows *need*, as in (a) and (b).
(b) John *needs to be told* the truth.	
(c) My house *needs painting*.	In certain circumstances, a gerund may follow *need*, as in (c). In this case, the gerund carries a passive meaning. Usually the situations involve fixing or improving something.
(d) My house *needs to be painted*.	Examples (c) and (d) have the same meaning.

❏ **Exercise 21. Looking at grammar.** (Chart 15-5)
Complete each sentence with an appropriate form of the verb in parentheses.

1. The chair is broken. I need (*fix*) _____*to fix*_____ it. The chair needs (*fix*) _____*fixing / to be fixed*_____.

2. The baby's diaper is wet. It needs (*change*) _____.

3. What a mess! This room needs (*clean*) _____ up. We need (*clean*) _____ it up before the company arrives.

4. My shirt is wrinkled. It needs (*iron*) _____.

5. There is a hole in our roof. The roof needs (*repair*) _____.

6. I have books and papers all over my desk. I need (*take*) _____ some time to straighten up my desk. It needs (*straighten*) _____ up.

7. The apples on the tree are ripe. They need (*pick*) _____.

8. The dog's been digging in the mud. He needs (*wash*) _____.

❏ **Exercise 22. Let's talk.** (Chart 15-5)
Look at the picture. What needs doing/to be done?

❏ **Exercise 23. Let's talk or write.** (Chart 15-5)
Choose a situation. Think about what needs to be done and make a list of all the tasks. Then talk or write about your list.

Situations:

1. a student applying to a university

2. a parent trying to get young children off to school in the morning

3. a group of students planning for an end-of-the-year party

4. a person going on vacation to another country for a month

5. an engaged couple making plans for a wedding

6. a farmer on a large farm in the early morning

7. a restaurant owner preparing to open for dinner

❏ **Exercise 24. Warm-up.** (Chart 15-6)
See and *hear* are called "verbs of perception." In other words, they express things that we can perceive (become aware of) through our physical senses. What do you notice about the verb forms following *see* and *hear?*

1. a. CORRECT: I **saw** Mr. Reed give something to the boss.
   b. CORRECT: I **saw** Mr. Reed giving something to the boss.
   c. *INCORRECT:* I **saw** Mr. Reed ~~to~~ give something to the boss.

2. a. CORRECT: I **heard** Mr. Reed say something to the boss.
   b. CORRECT: I **heard** Mr. Reed saying something to the boss.
   c. *INCORRECT:* I **heard** Mr. Reed ~~to~~ say something to the boss.

15-6 Using Verbs of Perception

(a) I *saw* my friend *run* down the street. (b) I *saw* my friend *running* down the street. (c) I *heard* the rain *fall* on the roof. (d) I *heard* the rain *falling* on the roof.	Certain verbs of perception are followed by either *the simple form** or the *-ing* form** of a verb. Examples (a) and (b) have essentially the same meaning, except that the *-ing* form emphasizes the idea of "while." In (b): I saw my friend while she was running down the street.
(e) When I walked into the apartment, I *heard* my roommate *singing* in the shower. (f) I *heard* a famous opera star *sing* at the concert last night.	Sometimes (not always) there is a clear difference between using the simple form or the *-ing* form. The use of the *-ing* form gives the idea that an activity is already in progress when it is perceived, as in (e): The singing was in progress when I first heard it. In (f): I heard the singing from beginning to end. It was not in progress when I first heard it.

Verbs of perception followed by the simple form or the *-ing* form

see	look at	hear	feel	smell
notice	observe	listen to		
watch				

**The simple form of a verb* = the infinitive form without *to*. INCORRECT: I saw my friend ~~to~~ run down the street.

**The -ing form refers to the present participle.

❏ **Exercise 25. Let's talk.** (Chart 15-6)
Describe what you see and hear.

1. Ask a classmate to stand up and sit back down. What did you just see him/her do?
2. Close your eyes. What do you hear happening right now?
3. Ask a classmate to do something. As he/she continues to do this, describe what you see and hear him/her doing.

❏ **Exercise 26. Looking at grammar.** (Chart 15-6)
Part I. Complete the sentences with any appropriate verbs. Both the simple form and the *-ing* form are possible with little or no difference in meaning.

1. Polly was working in her garden, so she didn't hear the phone _____*ring / ringing*_____ .

2. I like to listen to the birds _____ when I get up early in the morning.

3. The guard observed a suspicious-looking person _____ into the bank.

4. There was an earthquake in my hometown last year. It was just a small one, but I could feel the ground _____ .

5. I was almost asleep last night when I suddenly heard someone _____ on the door.

6. While I was waiting for my plane, I watched other planes _____ and _____ .

Part II. Read each situation. Complete the sentence below it with the verb form that seems better to you. Remember that the *-ing* form gives the idea that an activity is in progress when it is perceived.

Both the simple form and the *-ing* form of a verb are grammatically correct, so you can't make a grammar mistake. But a speaker might choose one instead of the other.

SITUATION 1: *I smell smoke. Something must be burning.*

Do you smell something _____*burning*_____? I do.

SITUATION 2: *The front door slammed. I got up to see if someone had come in.*

When I heard the front door _____, I got up to see if someone had come in.

SITUATION 3: *Uncle Ben is in the bedroom. He is snoring.*

I know Uncle Ben is in the bedroom because

I can hear him _____.

SITUATION 4: *When I walked past the park, some children were playing softball.*

When I walked past the park, I saw some children _____ softball.

SITUATION 5: *It was graduation day in the auditorium. When the school principal called my name, I walked to the front of the room.*

When I heard the school principal _____ my name, I walked to the front of the auditorium to receive my diploma.

SITUATION 6: *I glanced out the window. Adam was walking toward the house. I was surprised.*

I was surprised when I saw Adam _____ toward the house.

SITUATION 7: *A fly landed on the table. I swatted it with a rolled-up newspaper.*

As soon as I saw the fly _____ on the table, I swatted it with a rolled-up newspaper.

SITUATION 8: *Someone is calling for help in the distance. I suddenly hear that.*

Listen! Do you hear someone _____ for help? I do.

❑ **Exercise 27. Warm-up.** (Chart 15-7)
Check (✓) the sentences that are correct.

   1. ____ My parents let me sleep late on weekends.

   2. ____ My parents let me to sleep late on weekends.

   3. ____ After I wake up, I help them do the chores.

   4. ____ After I wake up, I help them to do the chores.

15-7 Using the Simple Form after *Let* and *Help*

(a) My father *lets* me *drive* his car. (b) I *let* my friend *borrow* my bicycle. (c) *Let's go* to a movie.	**Let** is followed by the simple form of a verb, not an infinitive. *INCORRECT:* My father lets me ~~to~~ drive his car.
(d) My brother *helped* me *wash* my car. (e) My brother *helped* me *to wash* my car.	**Help** is often followed by the simple form of a verb, as in (d). Although less common, an infinitive is also possible, as in (e). Both (d) and (e) are correct.

❑ **Exercise 28. In your own words.** (Chart 15-7)
Complete the sentences with your own words. Use verb phrases.

1. Don't let me _____*forget to take my house keys with me.*_____

2. The teacher usually lets us _____

3. Why did you let your roommate _____

4. You shouldn't let other people _____

5. A stranger helped the lost child _____

6. It was very kind of my friend to help me _____

7. Keep working. Don't let me _____

8. Could you help me _____

❑ **Exercise 29. Warm-up.** (Chart 15-8)
Match the conversations with the descriptions that follow them.

1. ADAM: Mom, can I go out and play?
   MRS. LEE: No, Adam, you cannot go out and play until you clean up your room. I don't know how many times I have to say this. Go clean up your room, and I mean now!
   ADAM: Okay, okay!

2. ADAM: Mom, can I go out and play?
   MRS. LEE: Well, let's make a deal. First you clean up your room. Then you can go out and play. How does that sound? It needs to be clean before Grandma comes for a visit this evening. And if you do it now, you can stay out and play until dark. You won't have to come home early to clean your room. Okay?
   ADAM: Okay.

3. ADAM: Mom, can I go out and play?
   MRS. LEE: Sure, but first you need to clean up your room. Okay?
   ADAM: Okay.

Descriptions of conversations:
a. Mrs. Lee got Adam to clean up his room. _____
b. Mrs. Lee made Adam clean up his room. _____
c. Mrs. Lee had Adam clean up his room. _____

15-8 Using Causative Verbs: *Make, Have, Get*

(a) I *made* my brother *carry* my suitcase.	*Make*, *have*, and *get* can be used to express the idea that "X" causes "Y" to do something. When they are used as causative verbs, their meanings are similar but not identical.
(b) I *had* my brother *carry* my suitcase.	
(c) I *got* my brother *to carry* my suitcase.	In (a): My brother had no choice. I insisted that he carry my suitcase.
Forms	In (b): My brother carried my suitcase because I asked him to.
X *makes* Y *do* something. (*simple form*) X *has* Y *do* something. (*simple form*) X *gets* Y *to do* something. (*infinitive*)	In (c): I managed to persuade my brother to carry my suitcase.

Causative *Make*

(d) Mrs. Lee *made* her son *clean* his room.	Causative *make* is followed by the simple form of a verb, not an infinitive.
(e) Sad movies *make* me *cry*.	*INCORRECT*: She made him ~~to~~ clean his room.
	Make gives the idea that "X" **gives** "Y" **no choice**.
	In (d): Mrs. Lee's son had no choice.

Causative *Have*

(f) I *had* the plumber *repair* the leak.	Causative *have* is followed by the simple form of a verb, not an infinitive.
(g) Jane *had* the waiter *bring* her some tea.	*INCORRECT*: I had him ~~to~~ repair the leak.
	Have gives the idea that "X" **requests** "Y" to do something.
	In (f): The plumber repaired the leak because I asked him to.

Causative *Get*

(h) The students *got* the teacher *to dismiss* class early.	Causative *get* is followed by an infinitive.
(i) Jack *got* his friends *to play* soccer with him after school.	*Get* gives the idea that "X" **persuades** "Y" to do something.
	In (h): The students managed to persuade the teacher to let them leave early.

Passive Causatives

(j) I *had* my watch *repaired* (by someone).	The past participle is used after *have* and *get* to give a passive meaning. In this case, there is usually little or no difference in meaning between *have* and *get*.
(k) I *got* my watch *repaired* (by someone).	In (j) and (k): I caused my watch to be repaired by someone.

❏ **Exercise 30. Looking at grammar.** (Chart 15-8)
Choose the meaning that is closest to the meaning of the verb in **boldface**.

1. The teacher **had** her class write a composition.
    a. gave them no choice   b. persuaded them   c. requested them to do this

2. Mrs. Wilson **made** the children wash their hands before dinner.
    a. gave them no choice   b. persuaded them   c. requested them to do this

3. Kostas **got** some neighborhood kids to help him clean out his garage.
    a. gave them no choice   b. persuaded them   c. requested them to do this

4. My boss **made** me redo my report because he wasn't satisfied with it.
   a. gave me no choice   b. persuaded me   c. requested me to do this

5. I **got** Rosa to lend me some lunch money.
   a. gave her no choice   b. persuaded her   c. requested her to do this

6. The police officer **had** the driver get out of his car.
   a. gave him no choice   b. persuaded him   c. requested him to do this

❑ **Exercise 31. Looking at grammar.** (Chart 15-8)
Complete the sentences with the correct form of the verbs in parentheses.

1. I made my son (*wash*) _____*wash*_____ the windows before he could go outside to play.

2. Mrs. Crane had her house (*paint*) _____*painted*_____.

3. I went to the bank to have a check (*cash*) _____.

4. Tom had a bad headache yesterday, so he got his twin brother, Tim, (*go*)

   _____ to class for him. The teacher didn't know the difference.

5. When Scott went shopping, he found a jacket that he

   really liked. After he had the sleeves (*shorten*)

   _____, it fit him perfectly.

6. When my laptop stopped working, I took it to the

   computer store to have it (*fix*) _____.

7. Peeling onions always makes me (*cry*) _____.

8. Tom Sawyer was supposed to paint the fence, but he

   didn't want to do it. He was a very clever boy. Somehow he got his friends (*do*)

   _____ it for him.

9. We had a professional photographer (*take*) _____ pictures of everyone at

   the wedding. We had over 500 pictures (*take*) _____.

❑ **Exercise 32. Let's talk or write.** (Chart 15-8)
Think about the shopping area nearest your home. What can people do there? Make
sentences with **can** and **can't**.

At the shopping area nearest my home, people can/can't get . . .

1. car \ fix	4. laundry \ do	7. shoes \ repair
2. hair \ cut	5. picture \ take	8. clothes \ dry-clean
3. checks \ cash	6. blood pressure \ check	9. money \ exchange

Exercise 33. Let's talk or write. (Chart 15-8)
Ask and answer the questions. Work in pairs, in small groups, or as a class.

1. What do children sometimes try to **get** their parents **to do** (perhaps at a toy store or grocery store)?
2. What do bosses sometimes **make** their employees **do**?
3. What does our teacher sometimes **have** us **do**?
4. Do teachers usually **let** their students **leave** the classroom whenever they want to? What kinds of things do teacher usually not **let** their students **do** inside a classroom?
5. What do your classmates (or friends) sometimes **help** you **do**?

(Change roles if working in pairs.)
6. What didn't your parents **let** you **do** when you were a child?
7. Will you **let** your children **do** those things? (Or, if you're a parent, do you **let** your children **do** those things?)
8. Did your parents **make** you **do** certain things when you were a child?
9. What do you sometimes **have** the server at a restaurant **do**?
10. What do you sometimes **get** your friends **to do**?

□ **Exercise 34. Check your knowledge.** (Chapter 15)
Correct the errors.

1. My parents made me ~~to~~ promise to write them once a week.

2. I asked my roommate to let me to use his shoe polish.

3. I heard a car door to open and closing.

4. I had my friend to lend me his car.

5. You should visit my country. It is too beautiful.

6. I went to the college bookstore for getting my books for the new term.

7. One of our fights ended up with me having to sent to the hospital for getting stitches.

8. Lilly deserves to be tell the truth about what happened last night.

9. Barbara always makes me laughing. She has a great sense of humor.

10. Stop telling me what to do! Let me to make up my own mind.

11. I went to the pharmacy for having my prescription to be filled.

12. You shouldn't let children playing with matches.

13. When Shelley needed a passport photo, she had her picture taking by a professional photographer.

14. I've finally assembled enough information for beginning writing my research paper.

15. Omar is at the park right now. He is sit on a park bench watch the ducks swimming in the pond. The sad expression on his face makes me to feel sorry for him.

16. The music director tapped his baton for beginning the rehearsal.

❑ **Exercise 35. Looking at grammar.** (Chapters 14 and 15)
Choose the correct completions.

1. My cousins helped me _____ into my new apartment.
   (a.) move   (b.) to move   c. moving   d. being moved

2. It was a hot day, and the work was hard. I could feel sweat _____ down my back.
   a. trickle   b. to trickle   c. trickling   d. trickled

3. You can lead a horse to water, but you can't make him _____.
   a. drink   b. to drink   c. drinking   d. to be drunk

4. As he contemplated the meaning of life, Edward stood on the beach _____ out over the ocean.
   a. look   b. to look   c. looking   d. looked

5. He's a terrific soccer player! Did you see him _____ that goal?
   a. make   b. to make   c. making   d. made

6. We spent the entire class period _____ about the revolution.
   a. talk   b. to talk   c. talking   d. being talked

7. Only seven people applied for the sales job, so Maleek has a good chance of _____ for an interview.
   a. chosen   b. being chosen   c. to be chosen   d. to choose

8. If you hear any news, I want _____ immediately.
   a. told　　　　　b. being told　　　　　c. to be told　　　　　d. telling

9. I was getting sleepy, so I had my friend _____ the car.
   a. drive　　　　　b. being driven　　　　　c. to be driven　　　　　d. to drive

10. The witness to the murder wanted her name kept secret. She asked not _____ in the newspaper.
    a. identify　　　　　b. being identified　　　　　c. to be identified　　　　　d. to identify

❏ **Exercise 36. Reading and listening.** (Chapters 14 and 15)

First, read the paragraph and try to complete the sentences using the words in the list. Second, listen to the paragraph and check your answers.

CD 2
Track 18

to be understood	to solve	to read
able to read	using	being

An Issue in Health Care: Illiteracy

According to some estimates, well over half of the people in the world are functionally illiterate. This means they are unable to perform everyday tasks because they can't read, understand, and respond appropriately to information. One of the problems this creates in health care is that millions of people are not _____ directions on
1

medicine bottles or packages. Imagine _____ a parent with a sick
2

child and being unable _____ the directions on a medicine bottle. We
3

all know that it is important for medical directions _____ clearly.
4

One solution is pictures. Many medical professionals are working today

_____ this problem by _____ pictures to
5　　　　　　　　　　　　　　　　　　　6

convey health-care information.

❏ **Exercise 37. Looking at grammar.** (Chapters 14 and 15)

Complete each sentence with an appropriate form of the verb in parentheses.

1. My children enjoy (*allow*) ___*being allowed*___ to stay up late when there's something special on TV.

2. I couldn't get to sleep last night, so for a long time I just lay in bed (*think*)
   _____ about my career and my future.

3. Jacob's at an awkward age. He's old enough (*have*) _____ adult problems but too young (*know*) _____ how (*handle*) _____ them.

4. I don't anticipate (*have*) _____ any difficulties (*adjust*) _____ to a different culture when I go abroad.

5. We sat in his kitchen (*sip*) _____ very hot, strong tea and (*eat*) _____ pastries from the bakery.

6. I don't like (*force*) _____ (*leave*) _____ the room (*study*) _____ whenever my roommate feels like (*have*) _____ a party.

7. Let's (*have*) _____ Ron and Maureen (*join*) _____ us for dinner tonight, okay?

8. Do you know that your co-workers complain about your* (*come*) _____ late to work and (*leave*) _____ early?

9. Fish don't use their teeth for (*chew*) _____. They use them for (*grab*) _____, (*hold*) _____, or (*tear*) _____. Most fish (*swallow*) _____ their prey whole.

10. It is the ancient task of the best artists among us (*force*) _____ us (*use*) _____ our ability (*feel*) _____ and (*share*) _____ emotions.

11. Traffic has become too heavy for the Steinbergs (*commute*) _____ easily to their jobs in the city from their suburban apartment. They're considering (*move*) _____ to an apartment in the city (*be*) _____ closer to their work. Both of them hate the long commute. They want (*spend*) _____ more time (*do*) _____ things they really enjoy (*do*) _____ in their free time rather than being tied up on the highway during rush hour.

---

*In formal English, a possessive adjective (e.g., *your coming*) is used to modify a gerund. In informal English, the object form of a pronoun is frequently used (*you coming*).

Complete each sentence with the correct form of the verb in parentheses.

1. I was tired, so I just watched them (*play*) _____ volleyball instead of
   (*join*) _____ them.

2. Emily stopped her car (*let*) _____ a black cat (*run*) _____ across the
   street.

3. I'm tired. I wouldn't mind just (*stay*) _____ home tonight and (*get*)
   _____ to bed early.

4. I can't seem (*get*) _____ rid of the cockroaches in my apartment. Every night I
   see them (*run*) _____ all over my kitchen counters. It drives me crazy. I'm
   considering (*have*) _____ the whole apartment (*spray*)
   _____ by a professional pest control expert.

5. Last week I was sick with the flu. It made me (*feel*) _____ awful. I didn't have
   enough energy (*get*) _____ out of bed. I just lay there (*feel*) _____
   sorry for myself. When my father heard me (*sneeze*) _____ and
   (*cough*) _____, he opened my bedroom door (*ask*) _____ me if
   I needed anything. I was really happy to see his kind and caring face, but there wasn't
   anything he could do to make the flu (*go*) _____ away.

❏ **Exercise 39. Let's talk and listen.** (Chapters 14 and 15)
Part I. Answer these questions. Then listen to the lecture on lightning storms with your
book closed.

CD 2
Track 19

1. Have you ever been in a lightning storm?
2. How did you protect yourself?

Part II. Open your book and read the statements. Circle "T" for true and "F" for false.

1. It's important to hide under a tree during a lightning storm.   T   F
2. It's advisable to make yourself as small as possible when a storm is nearby.   T   F
3. If you are lucky enough to be near a car during a storm, get inside it.   T   F
4. Few lightning deaths occur after a storm has passed.   T   F

Part III. Listen to the lecture again. Complete the sentences with the words you hear.

Protecting Yourself in a Lightning Storm

Lightning storms can occur suddenly and without warning. It's important

_____ safe if you're outside when a storm begins. Some people
₁

stand under trees or in open shelters like picnic areas _____ themselves.
₂

They are _____ that this can be a fatal mistake. Tall objects are
₃

_____ lightning, so when you are out in the open, you should try
₄

_____ yourself as small as possible. _____
₅ ₆

into a ball lessens the chance that a lightning bolt will strike you. _____
₇

a depression in the ground to hide in, like a hole or a ditch, is even better.

_____ a building is safer than _____, but it's not
₈ ₉

without dangers. _____ away from doors and windows. If
₁₀

you're talking on a phone with a cord, hang up. Lightning has been known to travel along a

phone cord and strike the person holding the phone. Even TVs can conduct lightning through

the cable or antenna, so it's a good idea _____ away from the television. It's also
₁₁

inadvisable _____ a shower or bath since plumbing can conduct electricity
₁₂

from lightning. How safe are cars? Surprisingly, the inside of a car is safe as long as it has a

metal roof, but _____ any part of the car that leads to the outside.
₁₃

There's a 30/30 rule regarding lightning. As soon as you see lightning, _____
₁₄

the seconds until you hear thunder. If you hear thunder before you reach 30, this means you

_____ shelter immediately. Additionally, even if the storm
₁₅

_____, you want _____ in a protected place for 30 minutes
₁₆ ₁₇

after you hear the last sounds of thunder or have seen the last flashes of lightning. Many

lightning deaths, in fact more than half in the United States, occur after a storm has passed.

❑ **Exercise 1. Warm-up.** (Chart 16-1)
Identify the parts of speech of the words in blue and the word that connects them. What do you notice about the words in blue?

	Part of speech	Connective
1. The old man is extremely kind and generous.	*adjective*	*and*
2. He received a book and a sweater for his birthday.	none noun	
3. She spoke angrily and bitterly about the war.	adj	
4. In my spare time, I enjoy reading novels or watching television.	gerund (noun) verb-ing	
5. He will leave early but arrive late.	adv	

16-1 Parallel Structure

One use of a conjunction is to connect words or phrases that have the same grammatical function in a sentence. This use of conjunctions is called "parallel structure." The conjunctions used in this pattern are **and**, **but**, **or**, and **nor**. These words are called "coordinating conjunctions."

(a) *Steve **and** his friend* are coming to dinner.	In (a): *noun* + **and** + *noun*
(b) Susan *raised* her hand **and** *snapped* her fingers.	In (b): *verb* + **and** + *verb*
(c) He *is waving* his arms **and** *(is) shouting* at us.	In (c): *verb* + **and** + *verb* (The second auxiliary may be omitted if it is the same as the first auxiliary.)
(d) These shoes are *old* **but** *comfortable*.	In (d): *adjective* + **but** + *adjective*
(e) He wants *to watch* TV **or** *(to) listen* to some music.	In (e): *infinitive* + **or** + *infinitive* (The second *to* is usually omitted.)

❑ **Exercise 2. Looking at grammar.** (Chart 16-1)
Choose the correct completions.

1. My roommate is friendly and _____.

    a. helpful   b. kind   c. kindness

2. Jack opened the window and _____.

    a. turn on the fan   b. turning on the fan   c. turned on the fan

3. Honesty and _____ are admirable qualities in a person.
   a. generous   b. generosity   c. intelligence

4. Kate was listening to the radio and _____ at the same time.
   a. study   b. studying   c. studies

5. I was tired and _____ after our long hike.
   a. hungry   b. hunger   c. thirsty

6. Everyone had a good time at the party and _____ home happy.
   a. go   b. went   c. going

7. No one wanted to stay after the party and _____ up.
   a. clean   b. cleaning   c. cleaned

8. No one enjoys staying and _____ up at the end of a party.
   a. clean   b. cleaning   c. cleaned

❑ **Exercise 3. Looking at grammar.** (Chart 16-1)
Complete each sentence with <u>one</u> word that gives the same idea as the words in parentheses.

1. Lisa was saddened and _____*upset*_____ by the news.
   (*her feelings were upset*)

2. We enjoy fish and _____ for dinner.
   (*we eat vegetables*)

3. The clerk spoke impatiently and _____ when I asked for help.
   (*her words were rude*)

4. Mr. Evans is very old but _____.
   (*has a lot of strength*)

5. The driver ran a stop sign and _____ down the street.
   (*he was driving at a high speed*)

❑ **Exercise 4. Warm-up.** (Chart 16-2)
Check (✓) the sentences that are correctly punctuated. Notice the use of commas.

1. ___ Oranges, and strawberries are high in vitamin C. (*not correct*)

2. ✓ Oranges and strawberries are high in vitamin C.

3. ___ Oranges, strawberries, and broccoli are high in vitamin C.

4. ___ Oranges, strawberries and broccoli are high in vitamin C.

5. ___ Oranges strawberries and broccoli are high in vitamin C.

6. ___ Oranges, strawberries, and broccoli, are high in vitamin C.

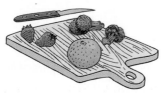

16-2 Parallel Structure: Using Commas

(a) **Steve** and **Joe** are in class.	No commas are used when *and* connects **two** parts of a parallel structure, as in (a).
(b) INCORRECT PUNCTUATION: Steve, and Joe are in class.	
(c) **Steve,** **Joe** *and* **Rita** are in class.	When *and* connects **three or more** parts of a parallel structure, a comma is used between the first items in the series.
(d) **Steve,** **Joe,** *and* **Rita** are in class.	A comma may also be used before *and,* as in (d) and (f). The use of this comma is optional (i.e., the writer can choose).*
(e) **Steve,** **Joe,** **Rita,** **Jan** *and* **Kim** are in class.	
(f) **Steve,** **Joe,** **Rita,** **Jan,** *and* **Kim** are in class.	NOTE: A comma often represents a pause in speech.

*The purpose of punctuation is to make writing clear for readers. This chart and others in this chapter describe the usual use of commas in parallel structures. Sometimes commas are required according to convention (i.e., the expected use by educated language users). Sometimes use of commas is a stylistic choice made by the experienced writer.

❏ **Exercise 5. Listening and punctuation.** (Chart 16-2)

CD 2
Track 20

Listen to the sentences and add commas as necessary. Practice pronouncing the sentences.

1. My bedroom has a bed, a desk (*optional comma*), and a lamp.
2. The price of the meal includes a salad a main dish and dessert.
3. The price of the meal includes a salad and a main dish.
4. Elias waited for his son wife and daughter.
5. Elias waited for his son's wife and daughter.
6. Susan raised her hand snapped her fingers and asked a question.
7. Red yellow gold and olive green are the main colors in the fabric.
8. I love films full of action adventure and suspense.
9. I love action and adventure films.
10. "Travel is fatal to prejudice bigotry and narrow-mindedness." —*Mark Twain**

❏ **Exercise 6. Looking at grammar.** (Charts 16-1 and 16-2)

Parallel structure makes repeating the same words unnecessary. Cross out the words that are unnecessary, and then combine the two given sentences into one concise sentence that contains parallel structure.

1. Molly opened the door. ~~Molly~~ greeted her guests.
   → *Molly opened the door **and** greeted her guests.*
2. Molly is opening the door. Molly is greeting her guests.
3. Molly will open the door. Molly will greet her guests.
4. Linda is kind. Linda is generous. Linda is trustworthy.
5. Please try to speak more loudly. Please try to speak more clearly.

---

*Mark Twain (1835–1910) is a well-known American writer and humorist. His most famous novel is *The Adventures of Huckleberry Finn.* He is also famous for his witty quotations.

6. He gave her flowers on Sunday. He gave her candy on Monday. He gave her a ring on Tuesday.

7. He decided to quit school. He decided to go to California. He decided to find a job.

8. I am looking forward to going to Italy. I am looking forward to eating wonderful pasta every day.

9. The boy was old enough to work. The boy was old enough to earn some money.

10. I should have finished my homework. Or I should have cleaned up my room.

11. I like coffee. I do not like tea.
    → *I like coffee **but** not tea.*

12. I have met his mother. I have not met his father.

13. Jake would like to live in Puerto Rico. He would not like to live in Iceland.

❑ **Exercise 7. Looking at grammar.** (Charts 16-1 and 16-2)
First, complete the unfinished sentence in each group. Second, combine the sentences into one concise sentence that contains parallel structure.

1. The country lane was narrow.
    The country lane was steep.

    The country lane was _____*muddy*_____.

    The country lane was narrow, ____*steep, and muddy*____.

2. I dislike living in a city because of the air pollution.
    I dislike living in a city because of the crime.

    I dislike living in a city because of _____.

    I dislike living in a city because of the air pollution, _____

    _____.

3. Hawaii has a warm climate.
    Hawaii has beautiful beaches.
    Hawaii has many interesting tropical trees.

    Hawaii has many interesting tropical _____.

    Hawaii has a warm climate, beautiful beaches, _____

    _____.

4. Mary Hart would make a good president because she works effectively with others.
    Mary Hart would make a good president because she has a reputation for integrity.
    Mary Hart would make a good president because she has a reputation for independent thinking.

    Mary Hart would make a good president because she _____.

    Mary Hart would make a good president because she works effectively with others,

    _____.

□ **Exercise 8. Looking at grammar.** (Charts 16-1 and 16-2)
Complete the sentences with your own words. Use parallel structure.

1. Judge Holmes served the people of this country with fairness, ability, and _____honesty_____.

2. Ms. Garcia has proven herself to be a hard-working, responsible, and _____

manager.

3. The professor walked through the door and ____sayed said hellow_____.

4. I was listening to music and ____reading the book_____

when I heard a knock at the door.

5. I get up at seven every morning, eat a light breakfast, and ____drink a cup of coffee___.

6. ____Going beachs_____ and attending concerts in the park

are two of the things my wife and I like to do on summer weekends.

7. Our whole family enjoys camping. We especially enjoy fishing in mountain streams and

____hiking in mounthins._____.

□ **Exercise 9. Let's talk.** (Charts 16-1 and 16-2)
Complete the sentences in pairs or small groups. Share some of your completions with the class.

1. A good friend needs to be ____honesty honest____ and ____pacent_____.

2. English teachers should have these qualities: ____wise_____,

____pnident_____, and ____effecent._____.

3. Parents need to ____Edncateing thier children____ and ____protactiny them_____.

4. Doctors should _____ or _____.

5. _____, _____, and _____

are three easy ways for me to relax at the end of the day.

6. In my free time, I like to _____, _____, and

_____.

7. Three activities I don't enjoy are _____, _____, and

_____.

8. _____, _____, and _____ are difficult

subjects for me.

❏ **Exercise 10. Check your knowledge.** (Charts 16-1 and 16-2)
Correct the errors. All of the sentences are adapted from student writing.

1. By obeying the speed limit, we can save energy, lives, and ~~it costs us less.~~ *money*

2. My home offers me a feeling of security, ~~warm~~, and love. *warmth*

3. The pioneers hoped to clear away the forest and planting crops.

4. When I refused to help Alice, she became very angry and ~~shout~~ at me. *shouted,*

5. When Nadia moved, she had to rent an apartment, make new friends, and ~~to~~ find a job.

6. All plants need light, ~~to have~~ a suitable climate, ~~and~~ an ample supply of water and minerals from the soil.

7. Slowly and ~~being cautious~~, the firefighter climbed the burned staircase. *cautiously*

8. On my vacation, I lost a suitcase, broke my glasses, and ~~I~~ missed my flight home.

9. With their keen sight, fine hearing, ~~and~~ *and* they have a refined sense of smell, wolves hunt elk, deer, moose, and caribou.

10. When Anna moved, she had to rent an apartment, make new friends, and to find a job.

11. The Indian cobra snake and the king cobra use poison from their fangs in two ways: by injecting it directly into their prey or they spit it into the eyes of the victim.

❏ **Exercise 11. Warm-up.** (Chart 16-3)
What do you notice about the subject-verb agreement in each pair of sentences?

1. a. Either my brother or my sister is going to tutor me in science.
   b. Either my brother or my sisters are going to tutor me in science.

2. a. Neither my brother nor my sister is a teacher.
   b. Neither my brother nor my sisters are teachers.

3. a. Not only my brother but also my sister has a doctorate in science.
   b. Not only my brother but also my sisters have doctorates in science.

16-3 Paired Conjunctions: *Both . . . And; Not Only . . . But Also; Either . . . Or; Neither . . . Nor*

(a) **Both** my mother **and** my sister **are** here.	Two subjects connected by **both . . . and** take a plural verb, as in (a).
(b) **Not only** my mother **but also** my sister **is** here. (c) **Not only** my sister **but also** my parents **are** here. (d) **Neither** my mother **nor** my sister **is** here. (e) **Neither** my sister **nor** my parents **are** here.	When two subjects are connected by **not only . . . but also, either . . . or**, or **neither . . . nor**, the subject that is closer to the verb determines whether the verb is singular or plural.
(f) The research project will take **both** time **and** money. (g) Sue saw **not only** a fox in the woods **but (also)** a bear. (h) I'll take **either** chemistry **or** physics next quarter. (i) That book is **neither** interesting **nor** accurate.	Notice the parallel structure in the examples. The same grammatical form should follow each part of the paired conjunctions.*
	In (f): **both** + noun + **and** + noun In (g): **not only** + noun + **but also** + noun In (h): **either** + noun + **or** + noun In (i): **neither** + adjective + **nor** + adjective NOTE: Paired conjuctions are usually used for emphasis; they draw attention to both parts of the parallel structure.

*Paired conjunctions are also called "correlative conjunctions."

□ **Exercise 12. Looking at grammar.** (Chart 16-3)
Complete the sentences with *is/are*.

1. Both the teacher and the student _____ are _____ here.

2. Neither the teacher nor the student _____ *is* _____ here.

3. Not only the teacher but also the student _____ *is* _____ here.

4. Not only the teacher but also the students _____ *are* _____ here.

5. Either the students or the teacher _____ *is* _____ planning to come.

6. Either the teacher or the students _____ *are* _____ planning to come.

7. Both the students and the teachers _____ *are* _____ planning to come.

8. Both the students and the teacher _____ *are* _____ planning to come.

□ **Exercise 13. Looking at grammar.** (Chart 16-3)
Answer the questions. Use paired conjunctions. Work in pairs, in small groups, or as a class.

Part I. Use *both . . . and*.

1. You've met his father. Have you met his mother?
   → Yes. I've met both his father and his mother.
2. The driver was injured in the accident. Was the passenger injured in the accident? Both the ~ and~ were
3. Wheat is grown in Kansas. Is corn grown in Kansas? Yes. Both wheat and corn are ose
4. The city suffers from air pollution. Does it suffer from water pollution?

Part II. Use ***not only ... but also***.

5. I know you are studying math. Are you studying chemistry too?

    → *Yes. I'm studying not only math but also chemistry.*

6. I know his cousin is living with him. Is his mother-in-law living with him too? *Yes, he is not ...*

7. I know you lost your wallet. Did you lose your keys too?

8. I know she goes to school. Does she have a full-time job too?
    Yes, she not only goes to school but also has a full-time job.

Part III. Use ***either ... or***.

9. Omar has your book, or Rosa has your book. Is that right?

    → *Yes. Either Omar or Rosa has my book.*

10. You're going to give your friend a book for her birthday, or you're going to give her some jewelry. Is that right? *Yes. Either I am going to give my friend either...*

11. Your sister will meet you at the airport, or your brother will meet you there. Right?

12. They can go swimming, or they can play tennis. Is that right?

Part IV. Use ***neither ... nor***.

13. He doesn't like coffee. Does he like tea?

    → *No. He likes neither coffee nor tea.*

14. Her husband doesn't speak English. Do her children speak English?

15. They don't have a refrigerator for their new apartment. Do they have a stove?

16. The result wasn't good. Was the result bad?

❑ **Exercise 14. Listening.** (Chart 16-3)

CD 2
Track 21

Choose the sentence (a. or b.) that has the same meaning as the sentence you hear.

Example: You will hear: Sarah is working on both a degree in biology and a degree in chemistry.

You will choose: a. Sarah is working on only one degree.
                           (b.) Sarah is working on two degrees.

1. a. Ben will call Mary and Bob.
   b. Ben will call one of them but not both.

2. a. My mother and my father talked to my teacher.
   b. Either my mother or my father talked to my teacher.

3. a. Simon saw both a whale and a dolphin.
   b. Simon didn't see a whale, but he did see a dolphin.

4. a. Our neighborhood had electricity but not water.
   b. Our neighborhood didn't have electricity or water.

5. a. We will have two teachers today.
   b. We will have one teacher today.

❏ **Exercise 15. Looking at grammar.** (Chart 16-3)

Combine each pair of sentences into one new sentence with parallel structure. Use *both . . . and; not only . . . but also; either . . . or; neither . . . nor*.

1. He does not have a pen. He does not have paper.
    → *He has neither a pen nor paper.*
2. You can have tea, or you can have coffee.
    → *You can have tea or coffee.*
3. Tanya enjoys horseback riding. Beth enjoys horseback riding.
4. Arthur is not in class today. Ricardo is not in class today.
5. Arthur is absent. Ricardo is absent.
6. We can fix dinner for them here, or we can take them to a restaurant.
7. The leopard faces extinction. The tiger faces extinction.
8. The library doesn't have the book I need. The bookstore doesn't have the book I need.
9. We could fly, or we could take the train.
10. The hospital will not confirm the story. The hospital will not deny the story.
11. Coal is an irreplaceable natural resource. Oil is an irreplaceable natural resource.
12. Her roommates don't know where she is. Her brother doesn't know where she is.

❏ **Exercise 16. Listening.** (Charts 16-1 → 16-3)

CD 2
Track 22

Part I. Answer these questions. Then listen to the short lecture on bats with your book closed.

1. Do you ever see bats?
2. Are you afraid of them?

Part II. Open your book. Choose the correct completions. Then listen again and check your answers.

Bats

(1) What do people in your country think of bats? Are they mean and scary creatures, or are they symbols of both happiness and ((luck), *lucky*)?

(2) In Western countries, many people have an unreasoned fear of bats. According to scientist Dr. Sharon Horowitz, bats are not only (*harm, harmless*) but also (*benefit, beneficial*) mammals. "When I was a child, I believed that a bat would attack me and (*tangle, tangled*) itself in my hair. Now I know better," said Dr. Horowitz.

(3) Contrary to popular Western myths, bats do not (*attack, attacking*) humans. Although a few bats may have diseases, they are not major carriers of rabies or other frightening diseases. Bats help natural plant life by pollinating plants, spreading seeds, and (*to eat, eating*) insects. If you get rid of bats that eat overripe fruit, then fruit flies can flourish and (*destroy, destruction*) the fruit industry.

(4) According to Dr. Horowitz, bats are both gentle and (*train, trainable*) pets. Not many people, however, own or train bats, and bats themselves prefer to avoid people.

Check (✓) the items with correct punctuation. NOTE: Only one of the items has incorrect punctuation.

1. ___ Thunder clouds rolled by. Flashes of lightning lit the sky.

2. ___ Thunder clouds rolled by, flashes of lightning lit the sky.

3. ___ Thunder clouds rolled by, and flashes of lightning lit the sky.

4. ___ Thunder clouds rolled by. And flashes of lightning lit the sky.

16-4	Separating Independent Clauses with Periods; Connecting Them with *And* and *But*
(a) It was raining hard. There was a strong wind.	Example (a) contains two *independent clauses* (i.e., two complete sentences).
(b) *INCORRECT PUNCTUATION:* It was raining hard, there was a strong wind.	PUNCTUATION: A period,* NOT A COMMA, is used to separate two independent clauses. The punctuation error in (b) is called a "run-on sentence." In spoken English, a pause, slightly longer than a pause for a comma, separates the two sentences.
(c) It was raining hard, *and* there was a strong wind. (d) It was raining hard. *And* there was a strong wind. (e) It was raining hard *and* there was a strong wind. (f) It was late, *but* he didn't care. (g) It was late. *But* he didn't care.	*And* and *but* (coordinating conjunctions) are often used to connect two independent clauses. PUNCTUATION: Usually a comma immediately precedes the conjunction, as in (c) and (f). In informal writing, a writer might choose to begin a sentence with a conjunction, as in (d) and (g). In a very short sentence, a writer might choose to omit the comma in front of *and*, as in (e). (Omitting the comma in front of *but* is rare.)

*In British English, a period is called a "full stop."

❏ **Exercise 18. Looking at grammar.** (Chart 16-4)
Punctuate the sentences by adding commas and periods. Do not add any words. Add capitalization as necessary.

1. The boys walked the girls ran.
   → *The boys walked. The girls ran.*

2. The boys walked and the girls ran.

3. The teacher lectured the students took notes.

4. The teacher lectured and the students took notes.

5. Elena came to the meeting but Pedro stayed home.

6. Elena came to the meeting her brother stayed home.

Listen to the sentences, paying special attention to pauses. Add periods and commas where you hear pauses. Add capitalization as necessary.

1. Both Jamal and I had many errands to do yesterday. Jamal had to go to the post office and the bookstore I had to go to the post office the travel agency and the bank.

2. Roberto slapped his hand on his desk in frustration he had failed another examination and had ruined his chances for a passing grade in the course.

3. When Alex got home he took off his coat and tie threw his briefcase on the kitchen table and opened the refrigerator looking for something to eat Ann found him sitting at the kitchen table when she got home.*

4. When Tara went downtown yesterday she bought birthday presents for her children shopped for clothes and saw a movie at the theater it was a busy day but she felt fine because it ended on a relaxing note.

5. It was a wonderful picnic the children waded in the stream collected rocks and insects and flew kites the teenagers played an enthusiastic game of baseball the adults busied themselves preparing the food supervising the children and playing some volleyball.

◻ **Exercise 20. Looking at grammar.** (Charts 16-2 and 16-4)

Punctuate the sentences by adding commas and periods. Do not add any words. Add capitalization as necessary.

1. Janice entered the room and looked around she knew no one.

2. A thermometer is used to measure temperature a barometer measures air pressure.

3. Derek made many promises but he had no intention of keeping them.

4. The earthquake was devastating tall buildings crumbled and fell to the ground.

5. Birds have certain characteristics in common they have feathers wings and a beak with no teeth birds lay hard-shelled eggs and their offspring are dependent on parental care for an extended period after birth.

6. The ancient Egyptians had good dentists archeologists have found mummies that had gold fillings in their teeth.

---

* See Chart 17-1, p. 365, for the punctuation of adverb clauses. Commas are used when the adverb clause comes before the main clause but not when it comes after the main clause.
  Examples: ***When the phone rang,*** *I answered it.* (comma used)
  I answered the phone ***when it rang****.* (no comma used)

❑ **Exercise 21. Listening and grammar.** (Chart 16-4)

Part I. Read the passage on butterflies quickly. How does the lack of punctuation and capitalization make a difference in how easily you can read the passage?

Butterflies

A butterfly is a marvel it begins as an ugly caterpillar and turns into a work of art the sight of a butterfly floating from flower to flower on a warm, sunny day brightens anyone's heart a butterfly is a charming and gentle creature caterpillars eat plants and cause damage to some crops but adult butterflies feed principally on nectar from flowers and do not cause any harm when cold weather comes some butterflies travel great distances to reach tropical climates they can be found on every continent except Antarctica because they are so colorful and beautiful butterflies are admired throughout the world.

Part II. Listen to the passage with your book open. Listen for pauses and add periods, commas, and capital letters as necessary. Then read the passage again and make sure it is punctuated the way you think is best.

Part III. Listen to the passage one more time to see if your punctuation reflects the spoken pauses.

❑ **Exercise 22. Let's read and talk.** (Chapter 16)

Part I. Read the paragraph about Dr. Martin Luther King, Jr.

Martin Luther King, Jr., was the leader of the 1960s civil rights movement in the United States that sought to end segregation and racial discrimination against African-Americans. In 1964, Dr. King became the youngest person to receive the Nobel Peace Prize. He was assassinated in 1968, but his powerful and inspiring words still live.

Part II. Underline the parallel structures that you find in these quotes from the speeches and writings of Dr. Martin Luther King, Jr. Discuss the ideas. Work in pairs, in small groups, or as a class.

1. "The hope of a <u>secure and livable</u> world lies with disciplined nonconformists who are dedicated to justice, peace and brotherhood."

2. "The ultimate measure of a man is not where he stands in moments of comfort and convenience, but where he stands at times of challenge and controversy."

3. "In the end, we will remember not the words of our enemies, but the silence of our friends."

4. "Nonviolence is the answer to the crucial political and moral question of our time: the need for mankind to overcome oppression and violence without resorting to oppression and violence. Mankind must evolve for all human conflict a method which rejects revenge, aggression, and retaliation. The foundation of such a method is love."

❏ **Exercise 23. Let's write.** (Chapter 16)
Choose one of the given topics. Write two versions of the same paragraph. The first version should be a draft in which you get your ideas on paper. Then the second version should be a "tightened" revision of the first. Look for places where two or three sentences can be combined into one by using parallel structure. In the second version, use as few words as possible and still communicate your meaning.

Topics:
1. Give a physical description of your place of residence (apartment, dorm room, etc.)
2. Describe the characteristics and activities of a successful student.
3. Give your reader directions for making a particular food dish.

Example:

First Draft: You'll need several ingredients to make spaghetti sauce. You'll need some ground beef. Probably about one pound of ground beef is enough. You should also have an onion. If the onions are small, you should use two. Also, find a green pepper and put it in the sauce. Of course, you will also need some tomato sauce or tomatoes.

Revision: To make spaghetti sauce, you will need one pound of ground beef, one large or two small onions, a green pepper, and some tomato sauce or tomatoes.

Chapter 17
Adverb Clauses

❑ **Exercise 1. Warm-up.** (Chart 17-1)
The words in blue are adverb clauses. What do you notice about their sentence placement and punctuation?

1. He closed the window when it got windy.
2. Because it got windy, he closed the window.
3. Even though it was windy, he opened the window.
4. Would you please close the window if it gets windy?

17-1 Introduction

Adverb clauses are used to show relationships between ideas. They show relationships of *time, cause and effect, contrast,* and *condition.*

adverb clause — main clause (a) *When the phone rang,* the baby woke up. (b) The baby woke up *when the phone rang.*	In (a) and (b): ***when the phone rang*** is an adverb clause of time. Examples (a) and (b) have the same meaning. PUNCTUATION: When an adverb clause precedes a main clause, as in (a), a comma is used to separate the clauses. When the adverb clause follows, as in (b), usually no comma is used.
(c) *Because he was sleepy,* he went to bed. (d) He went to bed *because he was sleepy.*	In (c) and (d), ***because*** introduces an adverb clause that shows a cause-and-effect relationship.
(e) INCORRECT PUNCTUATION: When we were in New York. We saw several plays. (f) INCORRECT PUNCTUATION: He went to bed. Because he was sleepy.	Adverb clauses are dependent clauses. They cannot stand alone as a sentence in written English. They must be connected to a main (or independent) clause.*

Summary list of words used to introduce adverb clauses**

TIME		CAUSE AND EFFECT	CONTRAST	CONDITION
after	by the time (that)	because	even though	if
before	once	now that	although	unless
when	as/so long as	since	though	only if
while	whenever			whether or not
as	every time (that)		DIRECT CONTRAST	even if
as soon as	the first time (that)		while	in case
since	the last time (that)			
until	the next time (that)			

*See Chart 13-1, p. 270, for the definition of dependent and independent clauses.

**Words that introduce adverb clauses are called "subordinating conjunctions."

❑ **Exercise 2. Looking at grammar.** (Chart 17-1)
Check (✓) the sentences that are grammatically complete and contain the correct punctuation.

1. _✓_ I woke up.
2. ___ When the door slammed.
3. ___ I woke up. When the door slammed.
4. ___ I woke up when the door slammed.
5. ___ When the door slammed, I woke up.
6. ___ The door slammed. I woke up.
7. ___ As soon as you finish dinner, you will need to pick up Andy at work.
8. ___ The first time I saw you at the school dance last February.
9. ___ Every time the phone rings and I answer it.
10. ___ We won't know the results until the doctor calls.
11. ___ We got something to eat. After we went to the movie.

❑ **Exercise 3. Looking at grammar.** (Chart 17-1)
Underline the adverb clauses. Add punctuation and capitalization as necessary. Do not add or delete any words.

       W
1. when Abder was in New York, he stayed with his cousins.

2. we went inside when it began to rain

3. it began to rain we went inside

4. when it began to rain we went inside

5. when the mail comes my assistant opens it

6. my assistant opens the mail when it comes

7. the mail comes around ten o'clock every morning my assistant opens it

❑ **Exercise 4. Looking at grammar.** (Charts 16-2, 16-4, and 17-1)
Add punctuation and capitalization as necessary. Do not add or delete any words.

1. As soon as the rain began the children wanted to go outdoors they love to play outside in the warm summer rain I used to do the same thing when I was a child.

2. I had a cup of tea before I left for work this morning but I didn't have anything to eat I rarely eat breakfast.

3. When Jack and his wife go on vacation they have to drive or take the train because his wife is afraid of flying.

4. After Ellen gets home from work she likes to read the newspaper she follows the same routine every day after work as soon as she gets home she changes her clothes gets a snack and a drink and sits down in her favorite chair to read the newspaper in peace and quiet she usually has about half an hour to read the paper before her husband arrives home.

5. When you speak to someone who is hard of hearing you do not have to shout it is important to face the person directly and speak clearly my elderly father is hard of hearing but he can understand me when I look directly at him and say each word clearly.

6. Jane wears contact lenses because she is near-sighted without them, she can't see from one end of a basketball court to the other when one of her contacts popped out during a recent game both teams stopped playing and searched the floor for the lens.

❑ **Exercise 5. Warm-up.** (Chart 17-2)
Add the word(s) in parentheses to the correct place in each sentence. Add commas and capitalization as necessary.

1. Anya listened to some music ∧ *while* she was working at her computer. (*while*)

2. I go to bed I always brush my teeth. (*before*)

3. I was a child I've been interested in butterflies. (*ever since*)

4. I'm going to meet some friends I leave class today. (*after*)

5. People speak English too fast Oscar can't catch the meaning. (*when*)

6. The teacher speaks too fast Oscar is going to ask her to slow down. (*the next time*)

17-2 Using Adverb Clauses to Show Time Relationships

after*	(a) **After** she graduates, she will get a job. (b) **After** she (had) graduated, she got a job.	A present tense, NOT a future tense, is used in an adverb clause of time, as in (a) and (c) (See Chart 4-3, p. 67, for tense usage in future time clauses.)
before*	(c) I will leave **before** he comes. (d) I (had) left **before** he came.	
when	(e) **When** I arrived, he *was talking* on the phone. (f) **When** I got there, he *had* already *left*. (g) **When** it began to rain, I *stood* under a tree. (h) **When** I was in Chicago, I *visited* the museums. (i) **When** I see him tomorrow, I *will ask* him.	**when** = at that time Notice the different time relationships expressed by the tenses.
while as	(j) **While** I was walking home, it began to rain. (k) **As** I was walking home, it began to rain.	**while, as** = during that time
by the time	(l) **By the time** he arrived, we *had* already *left*. (m) **By the time** he comes, we *will have* already *left*.	**by the time** = one event is completed before another event Notice the use of the past perfect and future perfect in the main clause.
since	(n) I *haven't seen* him **since** he left this morning. (o) I've *known* her **ever since** I was a child.	**since** = from that time to the present In (o): **ever** adds emphasis. NOTE: The present perfect is used in the main clause.
until till	(p) We stayed there **until** we finished our work. (q) We stayed there **till** we finished our work.	**until, till** = to that time and then no longer (**Till** is used more in speaking than in writing; it is generally not used in formal English.)
as soon as once	(r) **As soon as** it stops raining, we will leave. (s) **Once** it stops raining, we will leave.	**as soon as, once** = when one event happens, another event happens soon afterward
as long as so long as	(t) I will never speak to him again **as long as** I live. (u) I will never speak to him again **so long as** I live.	**as long as, so long as** = during all that time, from beginning to end
whenever every time	(v) **Whenever** I see her, I say hello. (w) **Every time** I see her, I say hello.	**whenever** = every time
the first time the last time the next time	(x) **The first time** (that) I went to New York, I went to an opera. (y) I saw two plays **the last time** (that) I went to New York. (z) **The next time** (that) I go to New York, I'm going to see a ballet.	Adverb clauses can be introduced by: the { first / second / third, etc. / last / next / etc. } time (that)

After and *before* are commonly used in the following expressions:

    shortly after   **shortly** before
    a short time after   **a short time** before
    a little while after   **a little while** before
    not long after   **not long** before
    soon after

□ **Exercise 6. Looking at grammar.** (Charts 17-1 and 17-2)
Complete the sentences with your own words. Add brackets around the adverb clause in each sentence.

1. I will call you [before I _____ *come over* _____.]

2. Last night I went to bed after I _____ my homework.

3. Tonight I will go to bed after I _____ my homework.

4. Ever since I was a child, I _____ afraid of dogs.

5. Be sure to reread your composition for errors before you _____ it to the teacher tomorrow.

6. By the time I left my apartment this morning, the mail carrier _____ the mail.

7. I have known Jim Bates since he _____ ten years old.

8. A black cat ran across the road as I _____ my car to work this morning.

9. By the time I leave this city, I _____ here for four months.

10. Whenever Mark _____ angry, his nose gets red.

11. I _____ to the beach whenever the weather was nice, but now I don't have time to do that because I have to study.

12. We will have a big party when _____.

13. The next time I _____ to Hawaii, I'm going to visit Mauna Loa, the world's largest active volcano.

14. I had fried chicken the last time I _____ at that restaurant.

□ **Exercise 7. Looking at grammar.** (Charts 17-1 and 17-2)
Combine each pair of sentences with the words in parentheses. Add commas as necessary.

1. The other passengers will get on the bus soon. We'll leave. (*as soon as*)
   → *As soon as the other passengers get on the bus, we'll leave.*
2. I left the room. I turned off the lights. (*after*)
3. I left the room. I turned off the lights. (*before*)
4. Suki feels nervous. She bites her nails. (*whenever*)
5. The frying pan caught on fire. I was making dinner. (*while*)
6. We were sitting down to eat. Someone knocked on the door. (*just as*★)

★*Just* adds the idea of "immediately":
   just as = at that immediate or same moment.
   just before = immediately before.
   just after = immediately after.

7. The audience burst into applause. The singer finished her song. (*as soon as*)
8. We have to wait here. Nancy will come. (*until*)
9. Julia will come. We can leave for the theater. (*as soon as*)
10. My roommate walked into the room. I knew something was wrong. (*just as soon as*)
11. I stood up to give my speech. I got butterflies in my stomach. (*just before*)
12. I saw the great pyramids of Egypt in the moonlight. I was speechless. (*the first time*)
13. Lori started working at this company six months ago. Lori has gotten three promotions in the last six months. (*since*)
14. The weather will get warmer soon. We can start spending more time outside. (*once*)
15. Shakespeare died in 1616. He had written more than 37 plays. (*by the time*)
16. Sam will go to get his driver's license. He'll remember to take his glasses. (*the next time*)

❏ **Exercise 8. Looking at grammar.** (Chart 17-2)
Choose the best completions.

1. As soon as Martina saw the fire, she _____ the fire department.
   - a. was telephoning
   - b. telephoned
   - c. had telephoned
   - d. has telephoned

2. Before Jennifer won the lottery, she _____ any kind of contest.
   - a. hasn't entered
   - b. doesn't enter
   - c. wasn't entering
   - d. hadn't entered

3. Every time Prakash sees a movie made in India, he _____ homesick.
   - a. will have felt
   - b. felt
   - c. feels
   - d. is feeling

4. Since I left Venezuela six years ago, I _____ to visit friends and family several times.
   - a. return
   - b. will have returned
   - c. am returning
   - d. have returned

5. While he was washing his new car, Mr. De Rosa _____ a small dent in the rear fender.
   - a. has discovered
   - b. was discovering
   - c. is discovering
   - d. discovered

6. Yesterday while I was attending a sales meeting, Matthew _____ on the company's annual report.
   - a. was working
   - b. had been working
   - c. has worked
   - d. works

7. Tony _____ to have children until his little daughter was born. After she won his heart, he decided he wanted a big family.
   - a. doesn't want
   - b. hadn't wanted
   - c. wasn't wanting
   - d. hasn't wanted

8. After the horse threw her to the ground for the third time, Jennifer picked herself up and said, "I _____ on another horse as long as I live."
   a. never ride
   b. have never ridden
   c. will never ride
   d. do not ride

9. The next time Paul _____ to New York, he will visit the Metropolitan Museum of Art's famous collection of international musical instruments.
   a. will fly
   b. flies
   c. has flown
   d. will have flown

10. Ever since Maurice arrived, he _____ quietly in the corner. Is something wrong?
    a. sat
    b. has been sitting
    c. had been sitting
    d. will have sat

11. After Nela _____ for twenty minutes, she began to feel tired.
    a. jogging
    b. had been jogging
    c. has been jogging
    d. has jogged

12. Peter, _____ since you got home from football practice?
    a. have you eaten
    b. will you eat
    c. are you eating
    d. do you eat

13. By the time the young birds _____ the nest for good, they will have learned how to fly.
    a. will leave
    b. will have left
    c. are leaving
    d. leave

14. The last time I _____ in Athens, the weather was hot and humid.
    a. had been
    b. was
    c. am
    d. will have been

❑ **Exercise 9. Looking at grammar.** (Charts 17-1 and 17-2)
Read the description of events. Make sentences using the words below the example.

Events:
   4:00   Judy parked her car at the mall and went to buy some jeans.
   4:03   A thief broke into her car and stole her radio.
   4:30   Judy returned to her car.
   4:31   Judy called the police.
   4:35   The police arrived.
   4:35   Judy began crying in frustration.

Example: just after
   → Just after Judy parked her car, a thief broke into it.

1. just after
2. just as
3. when
4. while
5. by the time
6. as soon as

❑ **Exercise 10. Let's talk.** (Charts 17-1 and 17-2)
Work in small groups. Complete the sentences with your own words. Each member of the group should finish each sentence.

Example: After I left class yesterday, ...
→ *After I left class yesterday, I met my cousin for tea.*

1. After I leave class today, ...
2. Before I go to bed tonight, ...
3. As soon as I get up tomorrow, ...
4. Whenever I feel nervous, ...
5. The first time I came to this class, ...
6. Ever since I was a child, ...
7. As long as I live, ...
8. Just as I was falling asleep last night, ...

❑ **Exercise 11. Listening and grammar.** (Charts 17-1 and 17-2)
Listen to the story about Marco's and Anya's cultural misunderstandings with your book closed. Then open your book and complete the sentences.

CD 2
Track 25

1. The first time Marco was asked "How's it going?", _____

   _____

2. At first, every time someone asked Anya how she was, _____

   _____

3. The next time Marco wants to get the server's attention at a restaurant, _____

   _____

4. Since Marco and Anya have come to this country, _____

   _____

5. Whenever they have a cultural misunderstanding, _____

   _____

❑ **Exercise 12. Warm-up.** (Chart 17-3)
Which adverb clauses give the idea of "because"?

1. Now that I've finished art school, I can focus on finding work as an illustrator.
2. Since I was young, I have been artistic.
3. Since you're artistic, you can illustrate the story.

17-3 Using Adverb Clauses to Show Cause and Effect

because	(a) **Because** *he was sleepy,* he went to bed. (b) He went to bed **because** *he was sleepy.*	An adverb clause may precede or follow the independent clause. Notice the punctuation in (a) and (b).
now that	(c) **Now that** *I've finished the semester,* I'm going to rest a few days and then take a trip. (d) Jack lost his job. **Now that** *he's unemployed,* he can't pay his bills.	**Now that** means "because now." In (c): **Now that I've finished the semester** means "because the semester is now over." **Now that** is used for present causes of present or future situations.
since	(e) **Since** *Monday is a holiday,* we don't have to go to work. (f) **Since** *you're a good cook and I'm not,* you should cook the dinner.	When **since** is used to mean "because," it expresses a known cause; it means "because it is a fact that" or "given that it is true that." Cause-and-effect sentences with **since** say, "Given the fact that X is true, Y is the result." In (e): "Given the fact that Monday is a holiday, we don't have to go to work."
	(g) **Since** *I came here,* I have met many people.	NOTE: **Since** has two meanings. One is "because." It is also used in time clauses, as in (g). See Chart 17-2.

❏ **Exercise 13. Looking at grammar.** (Chart 17-3)
Combine each pair of sentences with the words in parentheses. Add commas as necessary.

1. We can go swimming every day. The weather is warm. (*now that*)
   → *We can go swimming every day now that the weather is warm.*
2. The students had done poorly on the test. The teacher decided to give it again. (*since*)
   → *Since the students had done poorly on the test, the teacher decided to give it again.*
3. Cold air hovers near the earth. It is heavier than hot air. (*because*)
4. You paid for the theater tickets. Please let me pay for our dinner. (*since*)
5. Do you want to go for a walk? The rain has stopped. (*now that*)
6. Our TV set was broken. We listened to the news on the radio. (*because*)
7. Many young people move to the cities in search of employment. There are few jobs available in the rural areas. (*since*)
8. The civil war has ended. A new government is being formed. (*now that*)
9. Ninety-two thousand people already have reservations with an airline company for a trip to the moon. I doubt that I'll get the chance to go on one of the first tourist flights. (*since*)

❏ **Exercise 14. Looking at grammar.** (Chart 17-3)
Complete the sentences with your own words. Punctuate carefully.

1. Now that I've finally finished _____

2. The teacher didn't _____
   because _____

3. Since it's too expensive to _____

4. Gary can't stay out all night with his friends now that _____
   _____
   _____

5. Since we don't have class tomorrow _____
   _____

❏ **Exercise 15. Warm-up.** (Chart 17-4)
Which sentence expresses an unexpected result?

1. Because I was very tired, I went to bed early.
2. Even though I was very tired, I stayed up late.

17-4	**Expressing Contrast (Unexpected Result): Using** *Even Though*	
(a)	***Because*** the weather was cold, I *didn't go* swimming.	***Because*** is used to express expected results.
(b)	***Even though*** the weather was cold, I *went* swimming.	***Even though*** is used to express unexpected results.*
(c)	***Because*** I wasn't tired, I *didn't go* to bed.	NOTE: Like ***because***, ***even though*** introduces an adverb clause.
(d)	***Even though*** I wasn't tired, I *went* to bed.	

*Although and though have basically the same meaning and use as even though. See Chart 19-6, p. 406, for information on the use of although and though.

❏ **Exercise 16. Looking at grammar.** (Chart 17-4)
Choose the correct completions.

1. Because it was a dark, cloudy day, _____.
   a. I didn't put on my sunglasses   b. I put on my sunglasses

2. Even though it was a dark, cloudy day, _____.
   a. I put on my sunglasses   b. I didn't put on my sunglasses

3. Even though Mira has a cold, _____.
   a. she feels okay   b. she feels tired

4. Because gas is so expensive, _____.
   a. I drive my car a lot   b. I avoid driving my car a lot

❏ **Exercise 17. Looking at grammar.** (Chart 17-4)
Complete the sentences with *even though* or *because*.

1. Tim's in good shape physically _____*even though*_____ he doesn't get much exercise.

2. Barry's in good shape physically _____*because*_____ he gets a lot of exercise.

3. _____ Melissa has a job, she doesn't make enough money to support her four children.

4. _____ Yoko has a job, she is able to pay her rent and feed her family.

5. Sherry didn't learn Spanish _____ she lived in Mexico for a year.

6. Joe speaks Spanish well _____ he lived in Mexico for a year.

7. Jing-Won jumped into the river to rescue a little girl who was drowning

   _____ he wasn't a good swimmer.

8. A newborn kangaroo can find its mother's pouch _____ its eyes are not yet open.

9. Some people protest certain commercial fishing operations _____ dolphins, considered to be highly intelligent and social mammals, are killed unnecessarily.

10. _____ the earthquake damaged the bridge across Skunk River, the

    Smiths were able to cross the river _____ they had a boat.

❏ **Exercise 18. Let's talk.** (Chart 17-4)
Work in pairs, in small groups, or as a class. Speaker A asks the question. Speaker B answers the question beginning with *Yes/No* and followed by *Even though*.

Examples:
SPEAKER A (*book open*): It was raining. Did you go to the zoo anyway?
SPEAKER B (*book closed*): Yes. Even though it was raining, I went to the zoo.

SPEAKER A (*book open*): You studied hard. Did you pass the test?
SPEAKER B (*book closed*): No. Even though I studied hard, I didn't pass the test.

1. You weren't tired. Did you go to bed anyway?
2. The phone rang many times, but did you wake up?
3. The food was terrible. Did you eat it anyway?
4. You didn't study. Did you pass the test anyway?
5. The weather is terrible today. Did you stay home?
6. You fell down the stairs. Did you get hurt?

(Change roles if working in pairs.)
7. You told the truth, but did anyone believe you?
8. You turned on the air conditioner. Is it still hot in here?
9. You mailed the letter a week ago. Has it arrived yet?
10. You have a lot of money. Can you afford to buy an airplane?
11. Your grandmother is ninety years old. Is she still young at heart?
12. (. . .) told a joke. You didn't understand it. Did you laugh anyway?

□ **Exercise 19. Warm-up.** (Chart 17-5)
Check (✓) the sentences that show contrast (i.e., show that "this" is the opposite of "that").

1. ＿＿ I am a vegetarian, while my husband is a meat-eater.

2. ＿＿ While I was shopping, I ran into some friends from high school.

3. ＿＿ While some people prefer hot weather, I prefer cooler climates.

17-5 Showing Direct Contrast: *While*

(a) Mary is rich, *while John is poor.* (b) John is poor, *while Mary is rich.* (c) *While John is poor,* Mary is rich. (d) *While Mary is rich,* John is poor.	*While* is used to show direct contrast: "this" is exactly the opposite of "that."* Examples (a), (b), (c), and (d) all have the same meaning. Note the use of the comma in (a) and (b): In using *while* for direct contrast, a comma is often used even if the *while*-clause comes second (unlike the punctuation of most other adverb clauses).
COMPARE: (e) The phone rang *while I was studying.*	REMINDER: *While* is also used in time clauses and means "during that time," as in (e). See Chart 17-2.

*Whereas can have the same meaning and use as *while*, but it occurs mostly in formal written English and occurs with considerably less frequency than *while*: *Mary is rich, whereas John is poor.*

□ **Exercise 20. Looking at grammar.** (Chart 17-5)
Choose the best completion for each sentence.

1. Some people are tall, while others are ＿＿＿.
   a. intelligent
   b. thin
   c.) short
   d. large

2. A box is square, while ＿＿＿.
   a. a rectangle has four sides
   b. my village has a town square in the center
   c. we use envelopes for letters
   d. a circle is round

3. While some parts of the world get an abundance of rain, others ＿＿＿.
   a. are warm and humid
   b. are cold and wet
   c. get little or none
   d. get a lot

4. In some nations the favorite beverage is coffee, while ＿＿＿.
   a. I like tea
   b. it has caffeine
   c. in others it is tea
   d. they drink tea

5. Some people like cream and sugar in their coffee, while ＿＿＿.
   a. others like it black
   b. others drink hot coffee
   c. milk is good in coffee too
   d. sugar can cause cavities

6. Steve is an interesting storyteller and conversationalist, while his brother ＿＿＿.
   a. is a newspaper reporter
   b. bores other people by talking about himself all the time
   c. has four children
   d. knows a lot of stories too

□ **Exercise 21. Let's talk.** (Chart 17-5)
Ask two classmates to complete each sentence. Share some of their completions with the class.

Example: Some people are talkative, while . . . .
→ *Some people are talkative, while others are quiet.*
→ *While some people are talkative, others are quiet.*

1. Some people have curly hair, while . . . .
2. Some people prefer to live in the country, while . . . .
3. While some people know only their native language, ...
4. The climate at sea level at the equator is always hot, while the climate at the North and South poles . . . .
5. Some people . . . , while . . . .
6. Some countries . . . , while . . . .

□ **Exercise 22. Warm-up.** (Chart 17-6)
Check (✓) the sentence with *if* that is grammatically correct.

1. ____ If I will need help, I will ask you.
2. ____ If I need help, I will ask you.
3. ____ If I will need help, I ask you.

17-6 Expressing Conditions in Adverb Clauses: *If*-Clauses

(a) *If it **rains** tomorrow, I **will take** my umbrella.*	*If*-clauses (also called "adverb clauses of condition") present possible conditions. The main clause expresses RESULTS. In (a): POSSIBLE CONDITION = *it may rain tomorrow* RESULT = *I will take my umbrella* A present tense, not a future tense, is used in an *if*-clause even though the verb in the *if*-clause may refer to a future event or situation, as in (a).*

Words that introduce adverb clauses of condition (*if*-clauses)		
if	even if	unless
whether or not	in case	only if

*See Chapter 20 for uses of other verb forms in sentences with *if*-clauses.

□ **Exercise 23. Looking at grammar.** (Chart 17-6)
Make sentences with *if* using the given conditions.

Example: It may be cold tomorrow.
→ *If it's cold tomorrow, I'm going to stay home.*
→ *We can't go on a picnic if it's cold tomorrow.*

1. The teacher may not be in class tomorrow.
2. You will stay up until two in the morning.
3. Maybe the sun will be shining when you get up tomorrow morning.
4. Predictions about global warming may be correct.
5. Think of something that may happen this year in world politics.

❏ **Exercise 24. Warm-up.** (Chart 17-7)
Check (✓) the sentences that logically follow the question and are grammatically correct.

Do you have your cell phone with you?

   1. ____ If you do, could I use it?

   2. ____ If so, could I use it?

   3. ____ If not, I can use the pay phone.

   4. ____ If you don't, I can use the pay phone.

   5. ____ If you are, could I use it?

17-7 Shortened *If*-Clauses

(a) Are you a student? *If so / If you are*, the ticket is half-price. *If not / If you aren't*, the ticket is full price.	When an *if*-clause refers to the idea in the sentence immediately before it, it is sometimes shortened.

(b) It's a popular concert. Do you have a ticket?
If so / If you do, you're lucky.
If not / If you don't, you're out of luck.
	In (a): *If so / If you are* = If you are a student
	       If not / If you aren't = If you aren't a student
	
	In (b): *If so / If you do* = If you have a ticket
	       If not / If you don't = If you don't have a ticket

❏ **Exercise 25. Looking at grammar.** (Chart 17-7)
First, complete the sentences in two ways:

    a. Use **so** or **not**.
    b. Use a helping verb or main verb **be**.

Second, give the full meaning of the shortened *if*-clause.

  1. Does Lisa want to go out to dinner with us?

    a. If _____*so*_____, tell her to meet us at 8:00.

    b. If she _____*does*___, tell her to meet us at 8:00.

      → *Meaning: if Lisa wants to go out to dinner with us*

  2. Are you free this weekend?

    a. If _____, do you want to go to a movie?

    b. If you _____, do you want to go to a movie?

  3. Do you have a ride to the theater?

    a. If _____, would you like to ride with us?

    b. If you _____, would you like to ride with us?

4. Are you coming to the meeting?

    a. If _____, I'll see you there.

    b. If you _____, I'll see you there.

5. Did you use a spellcheck on your email to me?

    a. If _____, it didn't catch all the spelling errors.

    b. If you _____, it didn't catch all the spelling errors.

6. We need some rice. Can you stop at the store on your way home today?

    a. If _____, I'll do it.

    b. If you _____, I'll do it.

❑ **Exercise 26. Warm-up.** (Chart 17-8)
Check (✓) all the sentences that are true for David.

SITUATION: If David gets married, he will be happy. If he doesn't get married, he will be happy.

1. ____ David will be happy if he doesn't get married.

2. ____ If he gets married, David won't be happy.

3. ____ Even if David gets married, he won't be happy.

4. ____ Even if David doesn't get married, he will be happy.

5. ____ David will be happy whether or not he gets married.

6. ____ Whether or not David gets married, he will be happy.

17-8 Adverb Clauses of Condition: Using *Whether Or Not* and *Even If*

Whether or not

(a) I'm going to go swimming tomorrow *whether or not it is cold.* OR *whether it is cold or not.*	***Whether or not*** expresses the idea that neither this condition nor that condition matters; the result will be the same. In (a): "If it is cold, I'm going swimming. If it is not cold, I'm going swimming. I don't care about the temperature. It doesn't matter."

Even if

(b) I have decided to go swimming tomorrow. *Even if the weather is cold,* I'm going to go swimming.	Sentences with ***even if*** are close in meaning to those with ***whether or not***. ***Even if*** gives the idea that a particular condition does not matter. The result will not change.

❑ **Exercise 27. Looking at grammar.** (Chart 17-8)
Choose the sentence (a. or b.) that has the same meaning as the given sentence.

1. Even if I get an invitation to the reception, I'm not going to go.
   a. I won't go to the reception without an invitation.
   (b.) I don't care if I get an invitation. I'm not going.

2. Even if the weather improves, I won't go to the beach.
   a. I'm going to the beach if the weather improves.
   b. I don't care if the weather improves. I'm not going to the beach.

3. Whether or not you want help, I plan to be at your house at 9:00.
   a. I'm going to help you because I think you need help.
   b. I'm going to help you because you want me to.

4. I won't tell even if someone pays me.
   a. I won't tell whether or not someone gives me money.
   b. If someone pays me enough money, I will tell.

5. Even if John apologizes, I won't forgive him!
   a. John needs to apologize for me to forgive him.
   b. I don't care if John apologizes. It doesn't matter.

6. I have to go to work tomorrow whether I feel better or not.
   a. Whether I go to work or not depends on how I feel.
   b. I'm going to work tomorrow no matter how I feel.

❑ **Exercise 28. Looking at grammar.** (Chart 17-8)
Use the given information to complete sentences a. and b.

SITUATION 1: *Usually people need to graduate from school to get a good job. But it's different for Ed. Maybe Ed will graduate from school, and maybe he won't. It doesn't matter because he has a good job waiting for him in his father's business.*

   a. Ed will get a good job whether or not . . . .
      → *Ed will get a good job whether or not he graduates.*
   b. Ed will get a good job even if . . . .
      → *Ed will get a good job even if he doesn't graduate.*

SITUATION 2: *Cindy's uncle tells a lot of jokes. Sometimes they're funny, and sometimes they're not. It doesn't matter.*

   a. Cindy laughs at the jokes whether . . . or not.
   b. Cindy laughs at the jokes even if . . . .

SITUATION 3: *Maybe you are finished with the exam, and maybe you're not. It doesn't matter. The time is up.*

   a. You have to hand in your examination paper whether . . . or not.
   b. You have to hand in your examination paper even if . . . .

SITUATION 4: *It might snow, or it might not. We don't want to go camping in the snow, but it doesn't matter.*

   a. We're going to go camping in the mountains whether . . . or not.
   b. We're going to go camping in the mountains even if . . . .

SITUATION 5: *Max's family doesn't have enough money to send him to college. He would like to get a scholarship, but it doesn't matter because he's saved some money to go to school and has a part-time job.*

    a. Max can go to school whether or not . . . .
    b. Max can go to school even if . . . .

SITUATION 6: *Sometimes the weather is hot, and sometimes the weather is cold. It doesn't matter. My grandfather always wears his gray sweater.*

    a. My grandfather wears his gray sweater whether or not . . . .
    b. My grandfather always wears his gray sweater even if . . . .

SITUATION 7: *Your approval doesn't matter to me.*

    a. I'm going to marry Harry whether . . . or not.
    b. I'm going to marry Harry even if . . . .

❑ **Exercise 29. Warm-up.** (Chart 17-9)
Choose the sentence (1. or 2.) that has the same meaning as the given sentence.

If by chance you have trouble, you can reach me at this number.

1. In case you have trouble, you can reach me at this number.
2. When you have trouble, you can reach me at this number.

17-9 Adverb Clauses of Condition: Using *In Case*

(a) I'll be at my uncle's house *in case* you (should) need to reach me.	*In case* expresses the idea that something probably won't happen, but it might. *In case* means "if by chance this should happen."
	NOTE: Using *should* in an adverb clause emphasizes the speaker's uncertainty that something will happen.

❑ **Exercise 30. Looking at grammar.** (Chart 17-9)
Combine each pair of sentences. Begin your new sentence with *In case*.

1. You probably won't need to get in touch with me, but maybe you will. If so, I'll give you my phone number.
    → *In case you (should) need to get in touch with me, I'll give you my phone number.*

2. You probably won't need to see me, but maybe you will. If so, I'll be in my office tomorrow morning around ten.

3. I don't think you need any more information, but maybe you do. If so, you can call me.

4. You probably don't have any more questions, but maybe you do. If so, ask Dr. Smith.

5. Russ probably won't call, but maybe he will. If so, please tell him that I'm at the library.

6. You will probably be satisfied with your purchase, but maybe not. If not, you can return it to the store.

❏ **Exercise 31. Looking at grammar.** (Charts 17-8 and 17-9)
Complete the sentences with your own words. Work in pairs, in small groups, or as a class.

1. I have my umbrella with me just in case . . . .

2. It's a good idea for you to keep a written record of your credit card numbers in case . . . .

3. Our boss doesn't accept illness as an excuse for missing work. We have to go to work even if . . . .

4. I think I'd better clean up the apartment in case . . . .

5. Are you planning to apply for a scholarship? If so, ...

6. Do you have to work this Saturday? If not, ...

❏ **Exercise 32. Warm-up.** (Chart 17-10)
Choose the logical completions.

1. I'll be at work on time tomorrow if there (*is, isn't*) a lot of heavy traffic.

2. I'll be at work on time tomorrow unless there (*is, isn't*) a lot of heavy traffic.

3. We'll have the party outside unless it is (*rainy, sunny*).

4. We'll have the party inside unless it is (*rainy, sunny*).

17-10 Adverb Clauses of Condition: Using *Unless*	
(a) I'll go swimming tomorrow *unless* it's cold.	*unless* = *if . . . not*
(b) I'll go swimming tomorrow *if* it isn't cold.	In (a): *unless it's cold* means "if it isn't cold."
	Examples (a) and (b) have the same meaning.

❏ **Exercise 33. Looking at grammar.** (Chart 17-10)
Make sentences with the same meaning as the given sentences. Use **unless**.

1. I will go to the zoo if it isn't cold.
   → *I will go to the zoo unless it's cold.*

2. You can't travel abroad if you don't have a passport.

3. You can't get a driver's license if you're not at least sixteen years old.

4. If I don't get some new batteries for my camera, I won't be able to take pictures when Laura and Rob get here.

5. You'll get hungry during class if you don't eat breakfast.

❏ **Exercise 34. Looking at grammar.** (Chart 17-10)
Complete the sentences with your own words. Work in pairs, in small groups, or as a class.

1. Your letter won't be delivered unless . . . .
   → *Your letter won't be delivered unless it has the correct postage.*

2. I'm sorry, but you can't see the doctor unless . . . .

3. I can't graduate from school unless . . . .

4. . . . unless you put it in the refrigerator.

5. Unless it rains, ...

6. Certain species of animals will soon become extinct unless . . . .

7. . . . unless I get a raise in salary.

8. Tomorrow I'm going to . . . unless . . . .

9. The political situation in . . . will continue to worsen unless . . . .

10. Unless you . . . .

□ **Exercise 35. Warm-up.** (Chart 17-11)
Answer the questions about Scott.

SITUATION: Scott closes his bedroom window at night only if it's raining hard.

1. Does Scott close his bedroom window if the temperature is below freezing?

2. Does Scott close his bedroom window if it's windy outside?

3. Does Scott close his bedroom window if there's a light rain?

4. Does Scott close his bedroom window if there is a heavy rain?

17-11 Adverb Clauses of Condition: Using *Only If*

(a) The picnic will be canceled *only if it rains*. If it's windy, we'll go on the picnic. If it's cold, we'll go on the picnic. If it's damp and foggy, we'll go on the picnic. If it's unbearably hot, we'll go on the picnic.	*Only if* expresses the idea that there is only one condition that will cause a particular result.
(b) *Only if* it rains *will the picnic be canceled*.	When *only if* begins a sentence, the subject and verb of the main clause are inverted, as in (b).* No commas are used.

*Other subordinating conjunctions and prepositional phrases preceded by *only* at the beginning of a sentence require subject-verb inversion in the main clause:
   Only when the teacher dismisses us *can we stand* and *leave* the room.
   Only after the phone rang *did I realize* that I had fallen asleep in my chair.
   Only in my hometown *do I feel* at ease.

□ **Exercise 36. Looking at grammar.** (Chart 17-11)
Check (✓) the sentences that are true for this situation.

SITUATION: You can take Saturday off only if you work Thursday.

1. ____ You must work Thursday if you want Saturday off.

2. ____ You can take Saturday off if you work another day of your choice.

3. ____ If you work Thursday, you don't have to work Saturday.

4. ____ You can work Thursday, but it's not a requirement if you want Saturday off.

❏ **Exercise 37. Looking at grammar.** (Chart 17-11)

Part I. Read the situations and complete the sentences. Work in pairs, in small groups, or as a class.

SITUATION 1: *John must take an additional science class in order to graduate. That is the only condition under which he can graduate. If he doesn't take an additional science class, he can't graduate.*

    He can graduate only if . . . .
    → *He can graduate only if he takes an additional science class.*

SITUATION 2: *You have to have an invitation in order to go to the party. That is the only condition under which you will be admitted. If you don't have an invitation, you can't go.*

    You can go to the party only if . . . .

SITUATION 3: *You have to have a student visa in order to study here. Unless you have a student visa, you can't go to school here.*

    You can attend this school only if . . . .

SITUATION 4: *Jimmy's mother doesn't want him to chew gum, but sometimes he chews it anyway.*

    Jimmy . . . only if he's sure his mother won't find out.

SITUATION 5: *If you want to go to the movie, we'll go. If you don't want to go, we won't go.*

    We . . . only if you want to.

SITUATION 6: *The temperature has to reach 32°F / 0°C before water will freeze.*

    Water will freeze only if . . . .

SITUATION 7: *You must study hard. Then you will pass the exam.*

    Only if you study hard . . . .

SITUATION 8: *You have to have a ticket. Then you can get into the soccer stadium.*

    Only if you have a ticket . . . .

SITUATION 9: *His parents make Steve finish his homework before he can watch TV in the evening.*

    Only if Steve's homework is finished . . . .

SITUATION 10: *I have to get a job. Then I will have enough money to go to school.*

    Only if I get a job . . . .

Part II. Complete the sentences with your own words.

1. Yes, Paul, I will marry you — but only if . . . .
2. I . . . only if . . . .
3. Only if . . . .

❑ **Exercise 38. Looking at grammar.** (Charts 17-10 and 17-11)
Make sentences with the same meaning as the given sentences. Use **only if** and **unless**.

1. If you don't study hard, you won't pass the test.
   → *You will pass the test only if you study hard.*
   → *You won't pass the test unless you study hard.*
2. If I don't get a job, I can't pay my bills.
3. Your clothes won't get clean if you don't use soap.
4. I can't take any pictures if the flash doesn't work.
5. I don't wake up if the alarm clock doesn't ring.
6. If eggs aren't kept at the proper temperature, they won't hatch.
7. Don't borrow money from friends if you don't absolutely have to.
8. Anita doesn't talk in class if the teacher doesn't ask her specific questions.

❑ **Exercise 39. Looking at grammar.** (Charts 17-6 → 17-11)
Combine these two sentences using the words below the example.

It may or may not rain. The party will be held inside/outside.

Example: if
   → *If it rains, the party will be held inside.*
   → *If it doesn't rain, the party will be held outside.*

1. even if   3. in case   5. only if
2. whether or not   4. unless

❑ **Exercise 40. Reading and grammar.** (Chapter 17)
Part I. Read the passage about the ways people learn.

How Do People Learn Best?

How do people learn best? There is not one answer because much depends on individual learning styles and needs. Over 300 years ago, however, the noted inventor Benjamin Franklin made some observations regarding learning that still hold true for a great many learners today: "Tell me and I forget. Teach me and I remember. Involve me and I learn."

Imagine that you are learning how to fold a paper airplane. The person teaching you presents the information verbally. She begins by saying:

Benjamin Franklin

> Take a piece of paper.
> Fold it in half.
> Open the paper.
> Look at the crease in the middle.
> Now take one corner and fold it down along the crease.

The instructions continue this way. How well are you going to learn how to fold a paper airplane?

Now imagine that your instructor is standing before you with paper and gives the directions while folding the paper herself. Will this help you more?

Finally, imagine that both you and your instructor have paper. Each time she gives you instructions, both you and she fold your own papers.

Of the three methods, which one will be the most effective in helping you learn how to fold a paper airplane?

It's interesting to think about Benjamin Franklin's quote in relation to learning English. How do you learn English best? Is "being told" effective for you? What about "being taught"? How about "being involved"?

Part II. Think about your experiences learning English vocabulary and complete the sentences with your own words. Punctuate carefully.

1. I remember new words best when _____

2. I often forget the meanings of new words unless _____

3. Even if I _____

4. I _____ only if _____

5. If you want to increase your vocabulary, _____

   _____

6. If teachers want to help their class learn new vocabulary, they _____

   _____

7. Although _____

   _____

8. When I am involved in my learning, I feel _____

   _____

Chapter 18
Reduction of Adverb Clauses to Modifying Adverbial Phrases

❑ **Exercise 1. Warm-up.** (Charts 18-1 and 18-2)
Check (✓) the sentences that are grammatically correct.

1. ___✓___ While sitting at my desk, I fell asleep.
2. ___✓___ While I was sitting at my desk, I fell asleep.
3. _____ While was sitting at my desk, I fell asleep.
4. ___✓___ Before I went into the theater, I turned off my cell phone.
5. _____ Before go into the theater, I turned off my cell phone.
6. ___✓___ Before going into the theater, I turned off my cell phone.

18-1 Introduction

(a) Adverb clause:	*While I was walking* to class, I ran into an old friend.	In Chapter 13, we discussed changing adjective clauses to modifying phrases. (See Chart 13-11, p. 294.) Some adverb clauses may also be changed to modifying phrases, and the ways in which the changes are made are the same:
(b) Modifying phrase:	*While **walking** to class,* I ran into an old friend.	
(c) Adverb clause:	*Before I left for work,* I ate breakfast.	• If there is a **be** form of the verb, omit the subject of the dependent clause and **be** verb, as in (b). OR
(d) Modifying phrase:	*Before **leaving** for work,* I ate breakfast.	• If there is no **be** form of a verb, omit the subject and change the verb to **-ing**, as in (d).
(e) Change possible:	*While **I** was sitting in class,* **I** fell asleep. *While sitting in class,* **I** fell asleep.	An adverb clause can be changed to a modifying phrase **only when the subject of the adverb clause and the subject of the main clause are the same**.
(f) Change possible:	*While **Ann** was sitting in class,* **she** fell asleep. (clause) *While sitting in class,* **Ann** fell asleep.	A *modifying adverbial phrase* that is the reduction of an adverb clause *modifies the subject* of the main clause.
(g) No change possible:	*While **the teacher** was lecturing to the class,* I fell asleep.*	No reduction (i.e., change) is possible if the subjects of the adverb clause and the main clause are different, as in (g).
(h) *INCORRECT:*	~~While watching TV last night,~~ the phone rang.	In (h): *While watching* is called a "dangling modifier" or a "dangling participle," i.e., a modifier that is incorrectly "hanging alone" without an appropriate noun or pronoun subject to modify.

While lecturing to the class, **I fell asleep means "While **I** was lecturing to the class, **I** fell asleep."*

❏ **Exercise 2. Looking at grammar.** (Chart 18-1)
Check (✓) the sentences that are grammatically correct.

1. _____ While sitting at my computer, the fire alarm went off.
2. __✓__ While sitting at my computer, I heard the fire alarm go off.
3. _____ While standing on the top floor of the building, the crowd below looked like ants.
4. __✓__ While standing on the top floor of the building and looking down, Patrick suddenly felt dizzy.
5. __✓__ Before getting up, Mary likes to lie in her warm bed and plan her day.
6. _____ Before getting up, Mary's alarm clock went off three times by accident.
7. __✓__ While working on his new novel, William found himself telling the story of his childhood.
8. _____ After standing in line for hours to buy concert tickets, the theater manager told us the concert was sold out.

18-2 Changing Time Clauses to Modifying Adverbial Phrases

(a) Clause:	**Since Maria came** to this country, she has made many friends.	Adverb clauses beginning with **after**, **before**, **while**, and **since** can be changed to modifying adverbial phrases.
(b) Phrase:	**Since coming** to this country, Maria has made many friends.	
(c) Clause:	**After he (had) finished** his homework, Peter went to bed.	In (c): There is no difference in meaning between *After he finished* and *After he had finished*. (See Chart 3-5, p. 50.)
(d) Phrase:	**After finishing** his homework, Peter went to bed.	
(e) Phrase:	**After having finished** his homework, Peter went to bed.	In (d) and (e): There is no difference in meaning between *After finishing* and *After having finished*.
(f) Phrase:	Peter went to bed **after finishing** his homework.	The modifying adverbial phrase may follow the main clause, as in (f).

❏ **Exercise 3. Looking at grammar.** (Charts 18-1 and 18-2)
Underline the subject of the adverb clause and the subject of the main clause in each sentence. Change the adverb clauses to modifying adverbial phrases if possible.

1. While Joe was driving to school yesterday, he had an accident.
   → *While driving to school yesterday, Joe had an accident.*
2. While Joe was watching TV last night, the telephone rang. (*no change*)
3. Before I came to class, I had a cup of coffee.
4. Before the student came to class, the teacher had already given a quiz. (✕)
5. Since I came here, I have learned a lot of English.
6. Since Alberto opened his new business, he has been working 16 hours a day.
7. Omar left the house and went to his office after he (had) finished breakfast.

    X 8. Before the waiter came to our table, I had already made up my mind to order shrimp.

       9. You should always read a contract before you sign your name.

    ✓ 10. While Jack was trying to sleep last night, a mosquito kept buzzing in his ear.

      11. While Susan was climbing the mountain, she lost her footing and fell onto a ledge several
           feet below.

      12. After I heard Marika describe how cold it gets in Minnesota in the winter, I decided not to
           go there for my vacation in January.

❏ **Exercise 4. Let's talk: interview.** (Chart 18-2)
   Ask two classmates each question. Ask them to answer in complete sentences. Share some of
   their answers with the class.

   What do you do . . .
   1. before going to bed?   4. while sitting in class?
   2. after waking up?   5. before leaving school for the day?
   3. after arriving at school?   6. while preparing for a difficult exam?

❏ **Exercise 5. Warm-up.** (Charts 18-3 and 18-4)
   Read the sentences and answer the questions.

   1. Hiking through the woods yesterday, Alan saw a bear.
       QUESTION: Who was hiking through the woods?

   2. Walking through the woods, the bear spotted Alan.
       QUESTION: Who was walking through the woods?

18-3 Expressing the Idea of "During the Same Time" in Modifying Adverbial Phrases

(a) *While I was walking* down the street, *I* ran into an old friend.	Sometimes *while* is omitted, but the *-ing* phrase at the beginning of the sentence gives the same meaning (i.e., "during the same time").
(b) *While walking* down the street, *I* ran into an old friend.	
(c) *Walking* down the street, *I* ran into an old friend.	Examples (a), (b), and (c) have the same meaning.

18-4 Expressing Cause and Effect in Modifying Adverbial Phrases

(a) **Because she needed** some money to buy a book, *Sue* cashed a check. (b) **Needing** some money to buy a book, *Sue* cashed a check. (c) **Because he lacked** the necessary qualifications, *he* was not considered for the job. (d) **Lacking** the necessary qualifications, *he* was not considered for the job.	Often an **-ing** phrase at the beginning of a sentence gives the meaning of "because." Examples (a) and (b) have the same meaning. **Because** is not included in a modifying phrase. It is omitted, but the resulting phrase expresses a cause-and-effect relationship, as in (b) and (d).
(e) **Having seen** that movie before, *I don't want* to go again. (f) **Having seen** that movie before, *I didn't want* to go again.	**Having** + *past participle* gives the meaning not only of "because" but also of "before."
(g) **Because she was unable** to afford a car, *she* bought a bicycle. (h) **Being unable** to afford a car, *she* bought a bicycle. (i) **Unable** to afford a car, *she* bought a bicycle.	A form of **be** in the adverb clause may be changed to **being**. The use of **being** makes the cause-and-effect relationship clear. Examples (g), (h), and (i) have the same meaning.

❑ **Exercise 6. Looking at grammar.** (Charts 18-3 and 18-4)
Underline the modifying adverbial phrases and discuss their meanings. Which ones give the meaning of "because"? Which ones give the meaning of "while"? Do some of the sentences give the idea of both?

1. Driving to my grandparents' house last night, I saw a young woman who was selling flowers. I stopped so that I could buy some for my grandmother. (*Meaning* = "while")

2. Being a widow with three children, Mrs. Romero has no choice but to work. (B) W

3. Sitting on the airplane and watching the clouds pass beneath me, I let my thoughts wander to the new experiences that were in store for me during the next two years of living abroad.

4. Having guessed at the answers for most of the test, I did not expect to get a high score.

5. Realizing that I had made a dreadful mistake when I introduced him as George Johnson, I walked over to him and apologized. I know his name is John George.

6. Tapping his fingers loudly on the airline counter, Todd made his impatience known.

7. Having broken her arm in a fall, Elena had to learn to write with her left hand.

8. Lying on her bed in peace and quiet, Lisa soon forgot her troubles.

❑ **Exercise 7. Looking at grammar.** (Chart 18-4)
Change the adverb clauses to modifying adverbial phrases.

1. Because Sam didn't want to hurt her feelings, he didn't tell her the bad news.
    → *Not wanting to hurt her feelings, Sam didn't tell her the bad news.*

2. Because the little boy believed no one loved him, he ran away from home.

3. Because I had forgotten to bring a pencil to the examination, I had to borrow one.

4. Because Chelsea is a vegetarian, she does not eat meat.

❏ **Exercise 8. Looking at grammar.** (Charts 18-2 → 18-4)
Choose <u>all</u> the possible answers for each sentence.

1. Before _____ to you, I had never understood that formula.
   a. talked   b. talking   c. I talked

2. After _____ the chapter four times, I finally understood the author's theory.
   a. I read   b. read   c. reading

3. Since _____ his bachelor's degree, he has had three jobs, each one better than the last.
   a. he completed   b. completing   c. completed

4. _____ across Canada, I could not help being impressed by the great differences in terrain.
   a. Traveling   b. While I was traveling   c. While traveling

5. _____ national fame, the union leader had been an electrician in a small town.
   a. Before gaining   b. Gaining   c. Before he gained

6. _____ in an airplane before, the little girl was surprised and a little frightened when her ears popped.
   a. Had never flown   b. Having never flown   c. Because she had never flown

7. Before _____ vice-president of marketing and sales, Peter McKay worked as a sales representative.
   a. became   b. becoming   c. he became

8. _____ the cool evening breeze and listening to the sounds of nature, we lost track of time.
   a. Because enjoying   b. Enjoying   c. We were enjoying

9. _____ to spend any more money this month, Jim decided against going to a restaurant for lunch. He made himself a sandwich instead.
   a. Not wanting   b. Because he didn't want   c. Because not wanting

❏ **Exercise 9. Looking at grammar.** (Charts 18-3 and 18-4)
If possible, combine each pair of sentences by making a modifying phrase out of the first sentence.

1. The children had nothing to do. They were bored.
   → *Having nothing to do, the children were bored.*
2. The children were bored. I offered to play a game with them. (*no change*)
3. Anna kept one hand on the steering wheel. She paid the bridge toll with her free hand.
4. Anna kept one hand on the steering wheel. Bob put the money for the bridge toll in her free hand.
5. I heard that Nadia was in the hospital. I called her family to find out what was wrong.
6. We slowly approached the door to the hospital. The nurse stepped out to help us.
7. I live a long distance from my work. I have to commute daily by train.
8. Abdul lives a long distance from his work. His car is essential.
9. I am a married man. I have many responsibilities.
10. Martha was picking strawberries in the garden. A bumblebee stung her.
11. I recognized his face, but I had forgotten his name. I just smiled and said, "Hi."
12. Ann was convinced that she could never learn to play the piano. She stopped taking lessons.

Exercise 10. Game. (Charts 18-3 and 18-4)
Work in teams. Make sentences by combining the ideas in Column A and Column B. Use the idea in Column A as a modifying adverbial phrase. Show logical relationships. The first group to combine all the ideas correctly is the winner.

Example: Having sticky pads on their feet, flies can easily walk on the ceiling.

Column A

1. They have sticky pads on their feet.
2. She has done very well in her studies.
3. She was born two months prematurely.
4. He had done everything he could for the patient.
5. She had never eaten Thai food before.
6. He had no one to turn to for help.
7. They are extremely hard and nearly indestructible.
8. They are able to crawl into very small places.

Column B

a. Marta didn't know what to expect when she went to the Thai restaurant for dinner.
b. Mice can hide in almost any part of a house.
c. Sayid was forced to work out the problem by himself.
d. The doctor left to attend other people.
e. Nancy expects to be hired by a top company after graduation.
f. Diamonds are used extensively in industry to cut other hard minerals.
✓g. Flies can easily walk on the ceiling.
h. Monique needed special care for the first few days of her life.

Exercise 11. Looking at grammar. (Charts 18-1 → 18-4)
Check (✓) the sentences that are grammatically correct. Rewrite the incorrect sentences.

1. __✓__ After leaving the theater, we stopped at a coffee shop for a late-night snack.

2. _____ After leaving the theater, Tom's car wouldn't start, so we had to take a taxi home.
   → *After we left the theater, Tom's car wouldn't start, so we had to take a taxi home.*
   → *After leaving the theater, we discovered that Tom's car wouldn't start, so we took a taxi home.*

3. _____ Not wanting to interrupt the conversation, I stood quietly and listened until I could have a chance to talk.

4. _____ Being too young to understand death, my mother gave me a simple explanation of where my grandfather had gone.

5. _____ When asked to explain his mistake, the new employee cleared his throat nervously.

6. _____ While working in my office late last night, someone suddenly knocked loudly at my door and nearly scared me to death!

7. _____ After hurrying to get ready for the picnic, it began to rain just as we were leaving.

8. _____ While walking across the street at a busy intersection, a truck nearly hit me.

❑ **Exercise 12. Warm-up.** (Chart 18-5)
Which sentences have the same meaning?

1. When Sharon heard the news of her friend's death, she began to cry.
2. Upon hearing the news of her friend's death, Sharon began to cry.
3. On hearing the news of her friend's death, Sharon began to cry.

18-5	Using *Upon* + *-ing* in Modifying Adverbial Phrases	
(a)	***Upon reaching*** the age of 21, I received my inheritance.	Modifying adverbial phrases beginning with ***upon*** + ***-ing*** usually have the same meaning as adverb clauses introduced by ***when***.
(b)	***When I reached*** the age of 21, I received my inheritance.	Examples (a) and (b) have the same meaning.
(c)	***On reaching*** the age of 21, I received my inheritance.	***Upon*** can be shortened to ***on***. Examples (a), (b), and (c) all have the same meaning.

❑ **Exercise 13. Looking at grammar.** (Chart 18-5)
Make sentences using ***upon*** + ***-ing***.

1. When Carl saw his wife and child get off the airplane, he broke into a big smile.
   → *Upon seeing his wife and child get off the airplane, Carl broke into a big smile.*
2. When Tina crossed the marathon finish line, she fell in exhaustion.
3. When I looked in my wallet, I saw I didn't have enough money to pay my restaurant bill.

4. Sam found that he had made a math error when he re-read the data.
5. When you finish the examination, bring your paper to the front of the room.
6. There must have been 300 students in the room on the first day of class. The professor slowly read through the list of names. When I heard my name, I raised my hand to identify myself.
7. Captain Cook had been sailing for many weeks with no land in sight. Finally, one of the sailors shouted, "Land ho!" When he heard this, Cook grabbed his telescope and searched the horizon.

❑ **Exercise 14. Looking at grammar.** (Charts 18-1 → 18-5)
Change the adverb clause in each sentence to a modifying adverbial phrase if possible. Change punctuation, capitalization, and word order as necessary.

1. After it spends some time in a cocoon, a caterpillar will emerge as a butterfly.
   → *After spending some time in a cocoon, a caterpillar will emerge as a butterfly.*

2. When the movie started, it suddenly got very quiet inside the theater. (*no change*)

3. When we entered the theater, we handed the usher our tickets.
   → *Upon entering the theater, we handed the usher our tickets.*

4. Because I was unprepared for the test, I didn't do well.
   → *Being unprepared for the test, I didn't do well.* OR *Unprepared for the test, I didn't do well.*

5. Before I left on my trip, I checked to see what shots I would need.

6. Jane's family hasn't received any news from her since she arrived in Kenya two weeks ago.

7. Because I hadn't understood the directions, I got lost.

8. My father reluctantly agreed to let me attend the game after he had talked it over with my mother.

9. When I discovered I had lost my key to the apartment, I called the building superintendent.

10. Because the forest area is so dry this summer, it is prohibited to light campfires.

11. After we had to wait for more than half an hour, we were finally seated at the restaurant.

❑ **Exercise 15. Let's talk.** (Chapter 18)
Work in small groups. Imagine your friend is traveling to a foreign country and has never been abroad before. Give advice by making several suggestions for each item.

1. Before leaving on your trip, . . .
   → *you'll need to get a visa.*
   → *you should find out if you need immunizations.*
   → *give a friend or family member your itinerary.*
   → *don't forget to have someone pick up your mail.*
2. Upon arriving at the airport, . . .
3. After getting to your destination, . . .
4. When talking with the local people, . . .
5. While visiting tourist sites, . . .
6. Before leaving for home, . . .
7. In general, when traveling to a foreign country, . . .

❑ **Exercise 16. Listening.** (Chapter 18)

Listen to each conversation. Choose the sentence (a. or b.) that has the same meaning.

Example: You will hear: A: William, don't forget to pick up some groceries after work.
B: Oh yeah, thanks. That's the first thing I'll do when I leave the office.

You will choose: (a.) After leaving work, William will stop at the grocery store.
b. Before leaving work, William will pick up some groceries.

1. a. Fearing people will laugh at her if she plays the piano, Rose doesn't want to play at the family gathering.
   b. Knowing she plays beautifully, Rose is happy to play the piano at the family gathering.

2. a. Not wanting to upset him, Jan isn't going to talk to Thomas this afternoon.
   b. Hoping to change Thomas' work behavior, Jan is going to talk to him this afternoon.

3. a. Upon finding her wedding ring, Susan hid it in a box.
   b. On finding her wedding ring, Susan felt relieved.

4. a. Never having voted in an election, Sam is taking it very seriously.
   b. Having done a lot of research before choosing a candidate, Sam voted in the presidential election.

❑ **Exercise 17. Reading and grammar.** (Chapter 18)

Part I. Read the passage and underline the modifying adverbial phrases.

The First Telephone

Alexander Graham Bell, a teacher of the deaf in Boston, invented the first telephone. One day in 1875, while running a test on his latest attempt to create a machine that could carry voices, he accidentally spilled acid on his coat. Naturally, he called for his assistant, Thomas A. Watson, who was in another room. Bell said, "Mr. Watson, come here. I want you." Upon hearing words coming from the machine, Watson immediately realized that their experiments had at last been successful. He rushed excitedly into the other room to tell Bell that he had heard his words over the machine.

After successfully testing the new machine again and again, Bell confidently announced his invention to the world. For the most part, scientists appreciated his accomplishment, but the general public did not understand the revolutionary nature of Bell's invention. Believing the telephone was a toy with little practical application, most people paid little attention to Bell's announcement.

Part II. Read the statements. Circle "T" for true and "F" for false.

1. Bell was testing a machine when Watson made a discovery. T F
2. Watson heard words coming from the machine. T F
3. Watson tested the new device again and again. T F
4. Bell announced his phone was a toy. T F

❏ Exercise 18. Listening. (Chapter 18)

Part I. Look at the picture of the keyboard while listening to the lecture.

CD 2
Track 27

QWERTY keyboard

Part II. Read the statements. Circle "T" for true and "F" for false.

1. While working on a typewriter design, Sholes came up up with
    more than one pattern for the keyboard. T F
2. Upon discovering that the keys hit one another if the letters were
    in alphabetical order, Sholes developed a keyboard called
    "QWERTY." T F
3. Needing a keyboard that allowed typists to type letters as rapidly
    as possible, Sholes decided his design would be the best choice. T F
4. Having a long history of successful use, QWERTY is not likely to
    be replaced any time soon. T F

Chapter 19
Connectives That Express Cause and Effect, Contrast, and Condition

☐ **Exercise 1. Warm-up.** (Chart 19-1)
Which sentences express the same meaning as the given situation?

SITUATION: Monday was a holiday.
RESULT: All schools were closed.

1. All schools were closed on Monday because it was a holiday.
2. Because of the holiday, all schools were closed on Monday.
3. Due to the holiday, all schools were closed on Monday.
4. Due to the fact that it was a holiday, all schools were closed on Monday.
5. Because all schools were closed on Monday, it was a holiday.

19-1	Using *Because Of* and *Due To*	
(a)	*Because* the weather was cold, we stayed home.	*Because* introduces an adverb clause; it is followed by a subject and a verb, as in (a).
(b)	*Because of* the cold weather, we stayed home.	*Because of* and *due to* are phrasal prepositions; they are followed by a noun object, as in (b) and (c).
(c)	*Due to* the cold weather, we stayed home.	
(d)	*Due to the fact that* the weather was cold, we stayed home.	Sometimes (usually in more formal writing) *due to* is followed by a noun clause introduced by *the fact that*.
(e)	We stayed home *because of the cold weather.* We stayed home *due to the cold weather.* We stayed home *due to the fact that the weather was cold.*	Like adverb clauses, these phrases can also follow the main clause, as in (e).

☐ **Exercise 2. Looking at grammar.** (Charts 17-3 and 19-1)
Identify the cause and effect in each pair of sentences. Then combine the sentences with *because*.

1. Jon is a heavy smoker. Jon has breathing problems.
2. Martina feels homesick. Martina moved to a new town.
3. Mr. Jordan's house has no heat. Mr. Jordan lost his job.
4. Victor has gained weight. Victor is going to eat less.

❑ **Exercise 3. Looking at grammar.** (Charts 17-3 and 19-1)
Complete the sentences with *because* or *because of*.

1. We postponed our trip _____ the bad driving conditions.

2. Sue's eyes were red _____ she had been swimming in a chlorinated pool.

3. We can't visit the museum tomorrow _____ it isn't open.

4. Jim had to give up jogging _____ his sprained ankle.

5. _____ heavy fog at the airport, our plane was delayed for several hours.

6. _____ the elevator was broken, we had to walk up six flights of stairs.

7. Thousands of Irish people emigrated to the United States _____ the potato famine in Ireland in the mid-19th century.

❑ **Exercise 4. Looking at grammar.** (Chart 19-1)
Complete the sentences with the ideas in parentheses.

1. (*The traffic was heavy.*) We were late to the meeting due to _____*the heavy traffic*_____.

2. (*Bill's wife is ill.*) Bill has to do all of the cooking and cleaning because of _____
   _____.

3. (*It was noisy in the next apartment.*) I couldn't get to sleep last night because of
   _____.

4. (*Our parents are generous.*) Because of _____,
   all of the children in our family have received the best of everything.

5. (*Circumstances are beyond our control.*) Due to _____
   _____, our office is closed today.

❑ **Exercise 5. Warm-up.** (Chart 19-2)
Check (✓) the sentences that logically complete the idea of the given sentence.

Nadia likes fresh vegetables.

1. ____ Therefore, she has a vegetable garden in her yard.
2. ____ As a result, she doesn't grow her own vegetables.
3. ____ Therefore, she buys canned vegetables at the store.
4. ____ As a result, she buys produce from local farmers.
5. ____ She eats a lot of frozen vegetables, therefore.
6. ____ Consequently, she eats produce from her garden.

19-2 Cause and Effect: Using *Therefore, Consequently,* and *So*

(a) Al failed the test because he didn't study. (b) Al didn't study. *Therefore,* he failed the test. (c) Al didn't study. *Consequently,* he failed the test.	Examples (a), (b), and (c) have the same meaning. ***Therefore*** and ***consequently*** mean "as a result." In grammar, they are called *transitions* (or *conjunctive adverbs*). Transitions connect the ideas between two sentences. They are used most commonly in formal written English and rarely in spoken English.

(d) Al didn't study. *Therefore,* he failed the test.
(e) Al didn't study. He, *therefore,* failed the test.
(f) Al didn't study. He failed the test, *therefore.*
 	
POSITIONS OF A TRANSITION:
transition + S + V (+ rest of sentence)
    S + *transition* + V (+ rest of sentence)
    S + V (+ rest of sentence) + *transition*
	A transition occurs in the second of two related sentences.
	
	Notice the patterns and punctuation in the examples. A period (NOT a comma) is used at the end of the first sentence.* The transition has several positions in the second sentence. The transition is separated from the rest of the sentence by commas.

(g) Al didn't study, *so* he failed the test.	In (g): ***So*** is used as a *conjunction* between two independent clauses. It has the same meaning as ***therefore***. ***So*** is common in both formal written and spoken English. A comma usually precedes ***so*** when it connects two sentences, as in (g).

*A semicolon is also possible in this situation. See the footnote to Chart 19-3.

☐ **Exercise 6. Looking at grammar.** (Chart 19-2)
Rewrite the sentence with the given words. Punctuate carefully.

The children stayed home because a storm was approaching.

1. therefore   _____

2. consequently _____

3. so   _____

☐ **Exercise 7. Looking at grammar.** (Charts 17-3, 19-1, and 19-2)
Punctuate the sentences. Add capital letters as necessary. NOTE: Two sentences need no changes.

1. *adverb clause:*   Because it was cold she wore a coat.

2. *adverb clause:*   She wore a coat because it was cold.

3. *prepositional phrase:* Because of the cold weather she wore a coat.

4. *prepositional phrase:* She wore a coat because of the cold weather.

5. *transition:*   The weather was cold therefore she wore a coat.

6. *transition:*   The weather was cold she wore a coat therefore.

7. *conjunction:*   The weather was cold so she wore a coat.

Exercise 8. Looking at grammar. (Charts 17-3, 19-1, and 19-2)
Punctuate the sentences. Add capital letters as necessary.

1. Pat always enjoyed studying sciences in high school therefore she decided to major in biology in college.

2. Due to recent improvements in the economy fewer people are unemployed.

3. Last night's storm damaged the power lines consequently the town was without electricity.

4. Due to the snowstorm only five students came to class the teacher therefore canceled the class.

❏ **Exercise 9. Warm-up.** (Chart 19-3)
Check (✓) the sentences that have the correct punctuation.

1. _____ Doctors sometimes recommend yoga for their patients. Because it can lower stress.

2. _____ Because yoga can lower stress doctors sometimes recommend it for their patients.

3. _____ Yoga can lower stress. Doctors, therefore, sometimes recommend it for their patients.

4. _____ Yoga can lower stress, so doctors sometimes recommend it for their patients.

19-3 Summary of Patterns and Punctuation

Adverb Clauses	(a) **Because** it was hot**,** we went swimming. (b) We went swimming **because** it was hot.	An *adverb clause* may precede or follow an independent clause. PUNCTUATION: A comma is used if the adverb clause comes first.
Prepositions	(c) **Because of** the hot weather**,** we went swimming. (d) We went swimming **because of** the hot weather.	A *preposition* is followed by a noun object, not by a subject and verb. PUNCTUATION: A comma is usually used if the prepositional phrase precedes the subject and verb of the independent clause.
Transitions	(e) It was hot. **Therefore,** we went swimming. (f) It was hot. We**, therefore,** went swimming. (g) It was hot. We went swimming**, therefore**.	A *transition* is used with the second sentence of a pair. It shows the relationship of the second idea to the first idea. A transition is movable within the second sentence. PUNCTUATION: A period is used between the two independent clauses.* A comma may NOT be used to separate the clauses. Commas are usually used to set the transition off from the rest of the sentence.
Conjunctions	(h) It was hot**, so** we went swimming.	A conjunction comes between two independent clauses. PUNCTUATION: Usually a comma is used immediately in front of a conjunction.

*A semicolon (;) may be used instead of a period between the two independent clauses.

　　It was hot; therefore, we went swimming.
　　It was hot; we, therefore, went swimming.
　　It was hot; we went swimming, therefore.

In general, a semicolon can be used instead of a period between any two sentences that are closely related in meaning: *Peanuts are not nuts; they are beans.* Notice that a small letter, NOT a capital letter, immediately follows a semicolon.

❏ **Exercise 10. Looking at grammar.** (Charts 17-3 and 19-3)
Combine the sentences using the given words. Discuss correct punctuation.

We postponed our trip. The weather was bad.

Example: because → *We postponed our trip **because** the weather was bad.*
→ ***Because** the weather was bad, we postponed our trip.*

1. therefore
2. since
3. so
4. because of
5. consequently
6. due to the fact that

❏ **Exercise 11. Looking at grammar.** (Charts 17-3, 19-2, and 19-3)
Combine each pair of ideas with the words in parentheses.

1. My cell phone doesn't work. The battery is dead. (*because*)
   → *My cell phone doesn't work because the battery is dead.* OR
   → *Because the battery is dead, my cell phone doesn't work.*
2. Pat doesn't want to return to the Yukon to live. The winters are too severe. (*because*)
3. It is important to wear a hat on cold days. We lose sixty percent of our body heat through our head. (*since*)
4. Bill couldn't pick us up after the concert. His car wouldn't start. (*therefore*)
5. When I was in my teens and twenties, it was easy for me to get into an argument with my father. Both of us can be stubborn and opinionated. (*because*)
6. A camel can go completely without water for eight to ten days. It is an ideal animal for desert areas. (*due to the fact that*)
7. Robert emailed the software company for technical support. He got some new business software that didn't work. (*so*)
8. A tomato is classified as a fruit, but most people consider it a vegetable. It is often eaten in salads along with lettuce, onions, cucumbers, and other vegetables. (*since*)
9. There is consumer demand for ivory. Many African elephants are being slaughtered ruthlessly. Many people who care about saving these animals from extinction refuse to buy any item made from ivory. (*due to, consequently*)
10. Most 15th-century Europeans believed the world was flat and that a ship could conceivably sail off the end of the earth. Many sailors of the time refused to venture forth with explorers into unknown waters. (*because*)

❏ **Exercise 12. Warm-up.** (Chart 19-4)
Read about Alan and Lisa. Imagine their reactions as parents and complete the sentences with phrases in the list or your own ideas. What do you notice about *so/such* and the words in blue?

SITUATION: Alan and Lisa are the proud parents of triplets. Before their triplets were born, however, they were told they were going to have twins. Imagine their surprise when they found out they were the parents of three babies. Alan was incredibly happy. Lisa was utterly exhausted.

began to cry	couldn't laugh or cry	fell asleep
called friends	danced around the room	went into shock

1. Ed was *so* happy that he . . . .
2. Lisa was *so* tired that she . . . .
3. Ed was *such* a happy dad that he . . . .
4. Lisa was *such* a tired mom that she . . . .

19-4 Other Ways of Expressing Cause and Effect: Such ... That and So ... That

(a) Because the weather was nice, we went to the zoo. (b) It was *such nice weather that* we went to the zoo. (c) The weather was *so nice that* we went to the zoo.	Examples (a), (b), and (c) have the same meaning.
(d) It was *such good coffee that* I had another cup. (e) It was *such a foggy day that* we couldn't see the road.	*Such ... that* encloses a modified noun: *such + adjective + noun + that*
(f) The coffee is *so hot that* I can't drink it. (g) I'm *so hungry that* I could eat a horse. (h) She speaks *so fast that* I can't understand her. (i) He walked *so quickly that* I couldn't keep up with him.	*So ... that* encloses an adjective or adverb: $so + \left\{ \begin{array}{c} adjective \\ or \\ adverb \end{array} \right\} + that$
(j) She made *so many mistakes that* she failed the exam. (k) He has *so few friends that* he is always lonely. (l) She has *so much money that* she can buy whatever she wants. (m) He had *so little trouble* with the test *that* he left twenty minutes early.	*So ... that* is used with *many, few, much,* and *little.*
(n) It was *such a good book* (that) I couldn't put it down. (o) I was *so hungry* (that) I didn't wait for dinner to eat something.	Sometimes, primarily in speaking, *that* is omitted.

❏ **Exercise 13. Looking at grammar.** (Chart 19-4)
Complete the sentences with *so* or *such*.

1. It was ___such___ an enjoyable party that no one wanted to leave.

2. The party was ___so___ enjoyable that no one wanted to leave.

3. We had ___so___ much fun that no one wanted to leave.

4. Maya is _____ afraid of flying that she travels by train or bus.

5. You've been _____ kind that I don't know how to thank you.

6. The article had _____ little current information that it wasn't useful.

7. The teacher has repeated herself _____ many times that it's becoming a joke.

8. It was _____ a long trip abroad that I got very homesick.

9. My elderly aunt has _____ few friends that I am beginning to worry about her.

❏ **Exercise 14. Let's talk.** (Chart 19-4)
Work in small groups. Take turns making sentences using *so/such ... that* with the given ideas. Try to exaggerate your answers. Share your favorite sentences with the class.

Example: I'm hungry. In fact, I'm ....
→ *I'm* **so** *hungry. In fact, I'm* **so** *hungry* (**that**) *I could eat a horse.*

1. I'm really tired. In fact, I'm ....
2. I didn't expect it! I was really surprised. In fact, I was ....

3. I took a very slow bus to town. In fact, it was . . . .
4. I saw a shark while I was swimming in the ocean. I was frightened. In fact, I was . . . .
5. We rented a video. It was a very exciting movie. In fact, it was . . . .
6. The weather was really, really hot. In fact, it was . . . .
7. My wallet fell out of my pocket and I lost a lot of money. In fact, I lost . . . .
8. I ordered an expensive meal at a restaurant. The server brought a small plate with a tiny amount of food to your table. In fact, it was . . . .

❑ **Exercise 15. Looking at grammar.** (Chart 19-4)
Make sentences using *so* or *such* by combining the ideas in Column A and Column B.

Example: The wind was strong. → *The wind was **so** strong that it blew my hat off my head.*

Column A

1. The wind was strong.
2. The radio was too loud.
3. Olga did poor work.
4. The food was too hot.
5. There are many leaves on a single tree.
6. The tornado struck with great force.
7. Few students showed up for class.
8. Charles used too much paper when he was writing his report.

Column B

a. It burned my tongue.
b. She was fired from her job.
✓c. It blew my hat off my head.
d. The teacher postponed the test.
e. It is impossible to count them.
f. It lifted cars off the ground.
g. I couldn't hear what Michael was saying.
h. The wastepaper basket overflowed.

❑ **Exercise 16. Warm-up.** (Chart 19-5)
Check (✓) the sentences that correctly complete the given sentence.

Kay got a new job so that . . .

1. _____ she could be closer to home.
2. _____ she is very excited.
3. _____ her husband is taking her out to dinner to celebrate.
4. _____ she could earn more money.

19-5 Expressing Purpose: Using *So That*

(a) I turned off the TV **in order to** enable my roommate to study in peace and quiet.	**In order to** expresses *purpose*. (See Chart 15-1, p. 331.)
(b) I turned off the TV **so** (**that**) my roommate could study in peace and quiet.	In (a): I turned off the TV for a purpose. The purpose was to make it possible for my roommate to study in peace and quiet.

So That + *Can* or *Could*

(c) I'm going to cash a check **so that I can** buy my textbooks.	**So that** also expresses *purpose*.* It expresses the same meaning as **in order to**. The word "that" is often omitted, especially in speaking.
(d) I cashed a check **so that I could** buy my textbooks.	**So that** is often used instead of **in order to** when the idea of ability is being expressed. **Can** is used in the adverb clause for a present/future meaning.
	In (c): **so that I can buy** = in order to be able to buy
	Could is used after **so that** in past sentences, as in (d).**

So That + *Will / Would* or Simple Present

(e) I'll take my umbrella **so that I won't** get wet.	In (e): **so that I won't get wet** = in order to make sure that I won't get wet
(f) Yesterday I took my umbrella **so that I wouldn't** get wet.	**Would** is used in past sentences, as in (f).
(g) I'll take my umbrella **so that I don't** get wet.	In (g): It is sometimes possible to use the simple present after **so that** in place of **will**; the simple present expresses a future meaning.

*NOTE: *In order that* has the same meaning as *so that* but is less commonly used.

      Example: *I turned off the TV **in order that** my roommate could study in peace and quiet.*

Both *so that* and *in order that* introduce adverb clauses. It is unusual but possible to put these adverb clauses at the beginning of a sentence: ***So that** my roommate could study in peace and quiet, I turned off the TV.*

Also possible but less common: the use of **may or **might** in place of **can** or **could** (e.g., *I cashed a check **so that I might** buy my textbooks.*).

❑ **Exercise 17. Looking at grammar.** (Chart 19-5)
Combine each set of ideas by using *so* (*that*).

1. Please turn down the radio. I want to be able to get to sleep.

   → *Please turn down the radio so (that) I can get to sleep.*

2. My wife turned down the radio. I wanted to be able to get to sleep.

   → *My wife turned down the radio so (that) I could get to sleep.*

3. Put the milk in the refrigerator. We want to make sure it won't (OR doesn't) spoil.

   → *Put the milk in the refrigerator so (that) it won't (OR doesn't) spoil.*

4. I put the milk in the refrigerator. I wanted to make sure it didn't spoil.

   → *I put the milk in the refrigerator so (that) it wouldn't spoil.*

5. Please be quiet. I want to be able to hear what Sharon is saying.

6. I asked the children to be quiet. I wanted to be able to hear what Sharon was saying.

7. I'm going to cash a check. I want to make sure that I have enough money to go to the store.

8. I cashed a check yesterday. I wanted to make sure that I had enough money to go to the store.

9. Ann and Larry have a six-year-old child. Tonight they're going to hire a babysitter. They want to be able to go out with some friends.

10. Last week Ann and Larry hired a babysitter. They wanted to be able to go to a dinner party at the home of Larry's boss.

11. Be sure to put the meat in the oven at 5:00. You want to be sure that it will be (OR is) ready to eat by 6:30.

12. Yesterday I put the meat in the oven at 5:00. I wanted it to be ready to eat by 6:30.

13. I'm going to leave the party early. I want to be able to get a good night's sleep tonight.

14. When it started to rain, Harry opened his umbrella. He wanted to be sure he didn't get wet.

15. The little boy pretended to be sick. He wanted to stay home from school.

❏ **Exercise 18. Looking at grammar.** (Charts 19-2 and 19-5)
Add **that** to the sentence if **so** means **in order that**. If **so** means **therefore,** add a comma.

1. I borrowed some money so ∧ I could pay my rent.
   that

2. I didn't have enough money for a movie**,** so I went home and watched TV.

3. I need a visa so I can travel overseas.

4. I needed a visa so I went to the embassy to apply for one.

5. Marta is trying to improve her English so she can become a tour guide.

6. Olga wants to improve her English so she has hired a tutor.

7. Tarek borrowed money from his parents so he could start his own business.

8. I turned off the TV so I could concentrate on my paperwork.

❏ **Exercise 19. Warm-up.** (Chart 19-6)
Usually when someone breaks an arm, he/she goes to a doctor. That is expected behavior. Answer the same question about expected behavior for each statement. Circle *yes* or *no*.

	EXPECTED BEHAVIOR?	
1. Ron broke his arm, but he didn't go to the doctor.	yes	no
2. Joe went to the doctor because he broke his arm.	yes	no
3. Sue broke her arm, so she went to the doctor.	yes	no
4. Amy broke her arm; nevertheless, she didn't go to the doctor.	yes	no
5. Despite having a broken arm, Rick didn't go to the doctor.	yes	no
6. Eva was in so much pain from her broken arm that she went to the doctor.	yes	no
7. Jeff broke his arm; therefore, he went to the doctor.	yes	no

19-6 Showing Contrast (Unexpected Result)

All of these sentences have the same meaning. The idea of cold weather is contrasted with the idea of going swimming. Usually if the weather is cold, one does not go swimming, so going swimming in cold weather is an "unexpected result." It is surprising that the speaker went swimming in cold weather.

Adverb Clauses	*even though*	(a) ***Even though*** *it was cold,* I went swimming.
	although	(b) ***Although*** *it was cold,* I went swimming.
	though	(c) ***Though*** *it was cold,* I went swimming.
Conjunctions	*but . . . anyway*	(d) It was cold, ***but*** I went swimming ***anyway***.
	but . . . still	(e) It was cold, ***but*** I ***still*** went swimming.
	yet . . . still	(f) It was cold, ***yet*** I ***still*** went swimming.
Transitions	*nevertheless*	(g) It was cold. ***Nevertheless***, I went swimming.
	nonetheless	(h) It was cold; ***nonetheless***, I went swimming.
	however . . . still	(i) It was cold. ***However***, I ***still*** went swimming.
Prepositions	*despite*	(j) I went swimming ***despite*** the cold weather.
	in spite of	(k) I went swimming ***in spite of*** the cold weather.
	despite the fact that	(l) I went swimming ***despite the fact that*** the weather was cold.
	in spite of the fact that	(m) I went swimming ***in spite of the fact that*** the weather was cold.

❑ **Exercise 20. Looking at grammar.** (Charts 19-2 and 19-6)
Complete the sentences with ***inside*** or ***outside*** to make logical statements.

1. It rained, but we still had our wedding _____.

2. It rained, so we had our wedding _____.

3. It rained; nevertheless, we had our wedding _____.

4. Though it rained, we had our wedding _____.

5. Even though it rained, we had our wedding _____.

6. Although it rained, we had our wedding _____.

7. Despite the fact that it rained, we had our wedding _____.

8. It rained; therefore, we had our wedding _____.

❑ **Exercise 21. Looking at grammar.** (Chart 19-6)
Complete the sentences with ***am*** or ***am not*** to make logical statements.

1. The roads are icy; nevertheless, I _____ going shopping.

2. Though the roads are icy, I _____ staying home.

3. Even though the roads are icy, I _____ going shopping.

4. I _____ going shopping although the roads are icy.

5. The roads are icy, yet I _____ going shopping anyway.

6. Despite the fact that the roads are icy, I _____ staying home.

7. In spite of the icy roads, I _____ going shopping.

Exercise 22. Looking at grammar. (Chart 19-6)
Complete the sentences with the given words. Notice the use of punctuation and capitalization.

Part I. Complete the sentences with *but, even though*, or *nevertheless*.

1. Bob ate a large dinner. _____, he is still hungry.

2. Bob ate a large dinner, _____ he is still hungry.

3. Bob is still hungry _____ he ate a large dinner.

4. I had a lot of studying to do, _____ I went to a movie anyway.

5. I had a lot of studying to do. _____, I went to a movie.

6. _____ I had a lot of studying to do, I went to a movie.

7. I finished all of my work _____ I was very sleepy.

8. I was very sleepy, _____ I finished all of my work anyway.

9. I was very sleepy. _____, I finished all of my work.

Part II. Complete the sentences with *yet, although*, or *however*.

10. I washed my hands. _____, they still looked dirty.

11. I washed my hands, _____ they still looked dirty.

12. _____ I washed my hands, they still looked dirty.

13. Diana didn't know how to swim, _____ she jumped into the pool.

14. _____ Diana didn't know how to swim, she jumped into the pool.

15. Diana didn't know how to swim. _____, she jumped into the pool.

❑ **Exercise 23. Looking at grammar.** (Chart 19-6)
Add commas, periods, and capital letters as necessary. Do not add, omit, or change any words.

1. Anna's father gave her some good advice nevertheless she did not follow it.
   → *Anna's father gave her some good advice.* N*evertheless,* *she did not follow it.*

2. Anna's father gave her some good advice but she didn't follow it.

3. Even though Anna's father gave her some good advice she didn't follow it.

4. Anna's father gave her some good advice she did not follow it however.

5. Thomas was thirsty I offered him some water he refused it.

6. Thomas refused the water although he was thirsty.

7. Thomas was thirsty nevertheless he refused the glass of water I brought him.

8. Thomas was thirsty yet he refused to drink the water that I offered him.

❑ **Exercise 24. Looking at grammar.** (Chart 19-6)
Combine the sentences using the given words. Discuss correct punctuation. Use the negative if necessary to make a logical statement.

His grades were low. He was admitted to the university.

1. even though
2. but . . . anyway
3. yet . . . still

4. nonetheless
5. despite
6. because of

❑ **Exercise 25. Warm-up.** (Chart 19-7)
Read the question and the answers that follow. Which answers express "direct contrast," i.e., the idea that "this" is the opposite of "that"?

hurricane

tornado

What is the difference between hurricanes and tornadoes?

1. Hurricanes develop over warm oceans while tornadoes form over land.
2. Hurricanes develop while they are traveling over warm ocean water.
3. Hurricanes develop over warm oceans, but tornadoes form over land.
4. Hurricanes develop over warm oceans; however, tornadoes form over land.
5. Hurricanes develop over warm oceans; on the other hand, tornadoes form over land.

19-7 Showing Direct Contrast

All of the sentences have the same meaning: "This" is the opposite of "that."

Adverb Clauses	*while*	(a) Mary is rich, **while** *John is poor.** (b) John is poor, **while** *Mary is rich.*
Conjunctions	*but*	(c) Mary is rich, **but** *John is poor.* (d) John is poor, **but** *Mary is rich.*
Transitions	*however* *on the other hand*	(e) Mary is rich; **however**, *John is poor.* (f) John is poor; *Mary is rich,* **however**. (g) Mary is rich. *John,* **on the other hand**, *is poor.* (h) John is poor. *Mary,* **on the other hand**, *is rich.*

*Sometimes a comma precedes a *while*-clause that shows direct contrast. A comma helps clarify that *while* is being used to express contrast rather than time. The use of a comma in this instance is a stylistic choice by the writer.

❑ **Exercise 26. Looking at grammar.** (Chart 19-7)
Make two sentences with the same meaning as the given sentence. Use *however* or *on the other hand*. Punctuate carefully.

1. Florida has a warm climate, while Alaska has a cold climate.
2. While Fred is a good student, his brother is lazy.
3. Elderly people in my country usually live with their children, but the elderly in the United States often live by themselves.

❑ **Exercise 27. Looking at grammar.** (Chart 19-7)
Complete the sentences with your own words.

1. Some people really enjoy swimming, while others . . . *are afraid of water.*
2. In the United States, people drive on the right-hand side of the road. However, people in . . . .
3. While my desk always seems to be a mess, my . . . .
4. My oldest son is shy, while my youngest son . . . .

❑ **Exercise 28. Let's talk or write.** (Chart 19-7)
Part I. Read the information below about extroverts and introverts. Make several sentences with the words in the list, either orally or in writing using the words *but, however, on the other hand,* or *while*.

General Characteristics of Extroverts and Introverts

Extroverts . . .
  like to be the center of attention.
  like to talk more than listen.
  enjoy meeting people.
  prefer being active.
  like to work in groups.
  don't always think before speaking.
  don't mind noise.
  like crowds.
  are energized by being with others.

Introverts . . .
  are uncomfortable being the center of attention.
  like to listen more than talk.
  are reserved when meeting people.
  like to spend time alone.
  don't like to work in groups.
  think carefully before speaking.
  prefer the quiet.
  avoid crowds.
  can find it tiring to spend time with others.

Examples:
  → *Extroverts like to talk more than listen,* **while** *introverts like to listen more than talk.*
  → *Introverts like to listen more than talk. Extroverts,* **however,** *like to talk more than listen.*

Part II. Are you an extrovert or introvert? Compare yourself to someone you know who is different from you. Make several sentences.

❑ **Exercise 29. Let's talk.** (Chart 19-7)
Think of two different countries you are familiar with. How are they different? Use *while, however, on the other hand,* and *but*. Work in pairs, in small groups, or as a class.

1. size
2. population
3. food
4. time of meals
5. economic system
6. educational system
7. role of women
8. language
9. educational costs
10. medical care
11. public transportation
12. dating customs

Exercise 30. Warm-up. (Chart 19-8)
Choose the logical verb for each sentence: ***can*** or ***can't***.

SITUATION: Sarah drinks coffee every morning. It wakes her up.

1. If Sarah drinks coffee in the morning, she   *can / can't*   wake up quickly.

2. Unless Sarah drinks coffee in the morning, she   *can / can't*   wake up quickly.

3. Sarah drinks coffee every morning; otherwise, she   *can / can't*   wake up quickly.

4. Sarah drinks coffee in the morning, or else she   *can / can't*   wake up quickly.

19-8	Expressing Conditions: Using *Otherwise* and *Or (Else)*	
Adverb Clauses	(a) *If* I don't eat breakfast, I get hungry. (b) You'll be late *if* you don't hurry. (c) You'll get wet *unless* you take your umbrella.	*If* and *unless* state conditions that produce certain results. (See Charts 17-6 and 17-10, pp. 377 and 382.)
Transitions	(d) I always eat breakfast. *Otherwise*, I get hungry during class. (e) You'd better hurry. *Otherwise*, you'll be late. (f) Take your umbrella. *Otherwise*, you'll get wet.	*Otherwise* expresses the idea "if the opposite is true, then there will be a certain result." In (d): *otherwise* = if I don't eat breakfast
Conjunctions	(g) I always eat breakfast, *or (else)* I get hungry during class. (h) You'd better hurry, *or (else)* you'll be late. (i) Take your umbrella, *or (else)* you'll get wet.	*Or else* and *otherwise* have the same meaning.

❑ **Exercise 31. Looking at grammar.** (Chart 19-8)
Make sentences with the same meaning as the given sentence. Use ***otherwise***.

1. If I don't call my mother, she'll start worrying about me.
   → *I am going to / should / had better / have to / must call my mother. Otherwise, she'll start worrying about me.*

2. If you don't leave now, you'll be late for class.

3. Unless you have a ticket, you can't get into the theater.

4. You can't enter that country unless you have a passport.

5. If Tom doesn't get a job soon, his family won't have enough money for food.

6. Only if you speak both Japanese and Chinese fluently will you be considered for that job.★

7. Mary can go to school only if she gets a scholarship.

8. If I don't wash my clothes tonight, I won't have any clean clothes to wear tomorrow.

★Notice that the subject and verb in the main clause are inverted because the sentence begins with *only if*. See Chart 17-11, p. 383.

19-9 Summary of Connectives: Cause and Effect, Contrast, and Condition

	Adverb Clause Words	Transitions	Conjunctions	Prepositions
Cause and Effect	because so (that) since now that	therefore consequently	so	because of due to
Contrast	even though while although though	however nevertheless nonetheless on the other hand	but (. . . anyway) yet (. . . still)	despite in spite of
Condition	if in case unless only if even if whether or not	otherwise	or (else)	

❑ **Exercise 32. Looking at grammar.** (Chart 19-9)
Using the two ideas of "to study" and "to pass or fail the exam," complete the sentences. Punctuate and capitalize as necessary.

1. Because I did not study _, I failed the exam._ _____

2. I failed the exam because _____

3. Although I studied _____

4. I did not study therefore _____

5. I did not study however _____

6. I studied nevertheless _____

7. Even though I did not study _____

8. I did not study so _____

9. Since I did not study _____

10. If I study for the exam _____

11. Unless I study for the exam _____

12. I must study otherwise _____

13. Even if I study _____

14. I did not study consequently _____

15. I did not study nonetheless _____

16. I will probably fail the exam whether _____

17. Only if I study _____

18. I studied hard yet _____

19. You'd better study or else _____

❏ **Exercise 33. Listening.** (Chart 19-9)
Listen to each sentence and choose the logical completion (a. or b.).

Example: You will hear: I was exhausted when I got home, but . . .
You will choose: (a.) I didn't take a nap.   b. I took a nap.

1. a. my back gets sore.   b. my back doesn't get sore.

2. a. my old one works fine.   b. my old one doesn't work.

3. a. I hurry.   b. I don't hurry.

4. a. I hurried.   b. I didn't hurry.

5. a. our offices are hot.   b. our offices aren't hot.

6. a. the noise bothers me.   b. the noise doesn't bother me.

7. a. I fell asleep during dinner.   b. I didn't fall asleep during dinner.

❏ **Exercise 34. Game.** (Charts 17-2, 19-4, and 19-9)
Work in teams. Combine these two ideas using the words below the example. The time is now, so use present and future tenses. The team that correctly combines the most sentences wins.

to go (or not to go) to the beach \ hot, cold, nice weather

Example: because
→ ***Because*** *the weather is cold, we aren't going to go to the beach.*
→ *We're going to go to the beach **because** the weather is hot.*

1. so . . . that	8. because of	15. therefore
2. so	9. consequently	16. only if
3. nevertheless	10. as soon as	17. nonetheless
4. despite	11. such . . . that	18. in spite of
5. now that	12. since	19. even if
6. once	13. but . . . anyway	20. yet . . . still
7. although	14. unless	21. whether . . . or not

❑ **Exercise 35. Reading.** (Chart 19-9)

Part I. Read the passage comparing optimists and pessimists.

Optimists vs. Pessimists

Have you ever heard the expression that a glass is half full or half empty? If not, imagine that you are looking at a glass that is filled exactly halfway with liquid. Now, is the glass half full or half empty to you? People who say it is half full are called optimists, while people who say it is half empty are called pessimists. In simple terms, optimists see the best in the world, while pessimists see the worst.

One of the clearest ways to see the differences between the two is to look at the way optimists and pessimists explain events. When something bad happens, optimists tend to see the event as a single event which does not affect other areas of their lives. For example, Sarah is an optimistic person. When she gets a low grade on a test, she will say something like this to herself: "Oh well, that was one test I didn't do well on. I wasn't feeling well that day. I have another test in a few weeks. I'll do better on that one."

Pessimists, on the other hand, will feel that an event is just one of a string of bad events affecting their lives, and that they're somehow the cause of it. Let's take a look at Susan. She is a pessimist. When she gets a low grade on a test, she might say: "I failed again. I never do well on tests. I'm stupid. I should just quit trying." And when something does go well for Susan, she often attributes her success to luck. She may say, "I was just lucky that time," and she doesn't expect to do well again. While optimists don't see themselves as failures, pessimists do.

Research has shown that optimism can be a learned trait and that, despite their upbringing, people can train themselves to respond to events in more positive terms. For example, Paul has a tendency to react negatively to events. The first thing he has to do is become conscious of that behavior. Once he identifies how he is reacting, he can reframe his thoughts in more positive terms, as Sarah did when she failed the test. As Paul begins to do more of this, he forms new patterns of response, and over time these responses become more automatic. Gradually he can develop a more positive outlook on life.

What about you? How do you see life? Is the glass half full or half empty?

Part II. Complete the sentences with information from the reading.

1. Optimists think positively about life, while . . . .
2. An optimist may do poorly on a test; nevertheless, ...
3. Things sometimes go well for a pessimist; however, ...
4. Pessimists see themselves as failures; on the other hand, ...
5. Optimists don't see a single event affecting other areas of their lives; consequently, ...
6. Optimists see the best in the world; therefore, ...
7. Optimists see the best in the world; however, ...
8. Although people may have been raised as pessimists, ...
9. If a pessimist wants to change how he reacts, ...

Exercise 36. Listening. (Chapters 17 → 19)

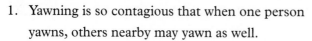

CD 2
Track 29

Part I. Answer these questions. Then listen to the lecture with your book closed.

1. What makes you yawn?
2. Do you yawn when others around you yawn?

Part II. Open your book and read the statements. Circle "T" for true and "F" for false.

1. Yawning is so contagious that when one person
   yawns, others nearby may yawn as well.   T   F

2. According to the speaker, people are not necessarily
   tired even though they may yawn.   T   F

3. According to the speaker, people yawn
   only if others around them yawn.   T   F

4. It's been proven that unless people yawn,
   they can't stay awake.   T   F

5. It's possible that at some point in history, people
   yawned so that they could stay awake and keep others
   awake in times of danger.   T   F

6. According to the speaker, if you are talking to people
   and they begin yawning, you can be certain that they
   have become bored by you.   T   F

❑ **Exercise 37. Check your knowledge.** (Chapters 1 → 19)
These sentences are taken from student writing. You are the editor for these students. Rewrite the sentences, correcting errors, combining ideas, and making whatever revisions in phrasing or vocabulary you feel will help the writers say what they intended to say.

Example: My idea of the most important thing in life. It is to be healthy. Because a person
        can't enjoy life without health.
   → *In my opinion, the most important thing in life is good health because a person cannot
      enjoy life fully without it.*

1. We went shopping after ate dinner. But the stores were closed. We had to go back home

   even we hadn't found what were we looking for.

2. I want explain that I know a lot of grammars but is my problem I haven't enough

   vocabularies.

3. When I got lost in the bus station a kind man helped me, he explained how to read the

   huge bus schedule on the wall. Took me to the window to buy a ticket and showed me

   where was my bus, I will always appreciate his kindness.

4. I had never understand the important of know English language. Until I worked at a large international company.

5. Since I was young my father found an American woman to teach me and my brothers English, but when we move to other town my father wasn't able to find other teacher for other five years.

6. I was surprised to see the room that I was given at the dormitory. Because there aren't any furniture, and dirty.

7. When I meet Mr. Lee for the first time, we played video games at the student center even though we can't communicate very well, but we had a good time.

8. Because the United States is a large and also big country. It means that they're various kinds of people live there and it has a diverse population.

9. My grammar class was start at 10:35. When the teacher was coming to class, she returned the last quiz to my classmates and I. After we have had another quiz.

10. If a wife has a work, her husband should share the houseworks with her. If both of them help, the houseworks can be finish much faster.

11. The first time I went skiing. I was afraid to go down the hill. But then I think to myself, "Why not? Give it a try. You'll make it!" After stand around for ten minutes without moving. Finally, I decided go down that hill.

❑ **Exercise 38. Listening and writing.** (Chapter 19)

Listen to each passage twice. Then work together in pairs or small groups to write out the passage. Summarize what you heard. Then listen again and revise your writing as necessary.

CD 2
Track 30

PASSAGE 1: Turtles
PASSAGE 2: Boy or Girl?

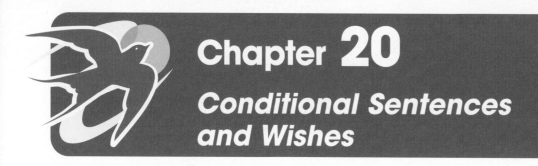

Chapter 20

Conditional Sentences and Wishes

❏ **Exercise 1. Warm-up.** (Chart 20-1)
Each sentence talks about a "condition" and the "result" of this condition. <u>Underline</u> the result clause in each sentence. Notice the verbs in blue. In which sentence does a past verb refer to present or future time?

1. If I have extra money, <u>I usually buy computer equipment with it.</u>
2. I will buy a new laptop computer next month if I have some extra money.
3. If I had some extra money, I would buy a new laptop today or tomorrow.
4. I would have bought a new laptop last month if I had had some extra money.

20-1	Overview of Basic Verb Forms Used in Conditional Sentences			
Situation	***If*-clause**	**Result clause**	**Examples**	
True in the Present/Future	simple present	*will* + *simple form*	If I *have* enough time, I *watch* TV every evening. If I *have* enough time, I *will watch* TV later on tonight.	
Untrue in the Present/Future	simple past	*would* + *simple form*	If I *had* enough time, I *would watch* TV now or later on.	
Untrue in the Past	past perfect	*would have* + *past participle*	If I *had had* enough time, I *would have watched* TV yesterday.	

❏ **Exercise 2. Looking at grammar.** (Chart 20-1)
Complete the sentences with the verbs in parentheses.

1. I usually send my parents an email every week. That is a true fact. In other words:

   If I (*have*) _____*have*_____ enough time, I (*send*) _____*send*_____ my parents an email **every week**.

2. I may have enough time to send my parents an email later tonight. I want to send them an email tonight. Both of those things are true. In other words:

   If I (*have*) _____*have*_____ enough time, I (*send*) _____*will send*_____ my parents an email **later tonight**.

3. I don't have enough time right now, so I won't send my parents an email. I'll try to do it later. I want to email them, but the truth is that I just don't have enough time right now. In other words:

    If I (*have*) ___had___ enough time **right now**, I (*send*) ___would send___ my parents an email.

4. I won't have enough time tonight, so I won't send my parents an email. I'll try to do it tomorrow. I want to email them, but the truth is that I just won't have enough time. In other words:

    If I (*have*) ___had___ enough time **later tonight**, I (*send*) ___would send___ my parents an email.

5. I wanted to send my parents an email last night, but I didn't have enough time. In other words:

    If I (*have*) ___had had___ enough time, I (*send*) ___would have sent.___ my parents an email **last night**.

❏ **Exercise 3. Warm-up.** (Chart 20-2)
Discuss the differences in meaning, if any, in each pair of sentences.

1. a. If it rains, the streets get wet.
    b. If it rains tomorrow, the streets will get wet.

2. a. If you heat water, it boils.
    b. If you heat water, it will boil.

3. a. If it should rain tomorrow, we'll cancel the picnic.
    b. If it rains tomorrow, we'll cancel the picnic.

20-2 True in the Present or Future

(a) If I *don't eat* breakfast, I always *get* hungry during class.	In conditional sentences that express true, factual ideas in the present/future, the *simple present* (not the simple future) is used in the *if*-clause.
(b) Water *freezes* OR *will freeze* if the temperature *reaches* 32°F/0°C.	The result clause has various possible verb forms. A result clause verb can be:
(c) If I *don't eat* breakfast tomorrow morning, I *will get* hungry during class.	• the *simple present,* to express a habitual activity or situation, as in (a).
(d) If it *rains,* we *should stay* home. If it *rains,* I *might decide* to stay home. If it *rains,* we *can't go.* If it *rains,* we*'re going to stay* home.	• either the *simple present* or the *simple future,* to express an established, predictable fact or general truth, as in (b). • the *simple future,* to express a particular activity or situation in the future, as in (c).
(e) If anyone *calls,* please *take* a message.	• *modals* and *phrasal modals* such as **should, might, can, be going to,** as in (d).* • an *imperative* verb, as in (e).
(f) If anyone *should call,* please take a message.	Sometimes **should** is used in an *if*-clause. It indicates a little more uncertainty than the use of the simple present, but basically the meaning of examples (e) and (f) is the same.

*See Chart 9-1, p. 157, for a list of modals and phrasal modals.

❏ **Exercise 4. Let's talk.** (Chart 20-2)
Answer the questions. Work in pairs, in small groups, or as a class.

1. If it's cold tomorrow, what are you going to wear to class?
2. If it's cold, what do you usually wear?
3. Fish can't live out of water. If you take a fish out of water, what will happen/what happens?
4. If I want to learn English faster, what should I do?
5. Tell me what to do, where to go, and what to expect if I visit your hometown as a tourist.

❏ **Exercise 5. Looking at grammar.** (Chart 20-2)
Choose the correct verb for the result clauses. In some cases, both answers are correct.

1. If I find out the answer, I   *will let / let*   you know.
2. If I have extra time, I   *tutor / am going to tutor*   students in math.
3. If it snows, the roads   *are / will be*   closed.
4. If you run up a hill, your heart   *beats / will beat*   fast.
5. If it should rain tomorrow, we   *might change / will change*   our plans.
6. If my cell phone battery goes dead, I   *will recharge / would recharge*   it.

❏ **Exercise 6. Listening.** (Chart 20-2)
If + *pronoun* can be difficult to hear at the beginning of sentences because these words are generally unstressed. Additionally, *if* at the beginning of a sentence is often reduced to /f/.

CD 2
Track 31   Listen to the sentences spoken in casual, relaxed English. Complete the sentences with the non-reduced forms of the words you hear.

Example: You will hear: If I hear anything, I'll tell you.
              You will write: _____*If I hear*_____ anything, I'll tell you.

1. _____ too fast, please tell me.
2. _____ married, everyone will be shocked.
3. _____ okay, I'll ask for some advice.
4. _____ to quit, I hope he lets us know soon.
5. _____, we'll need to try something else.
6. _____ harder, I'm sure she'll succeed.
7. _____ the job, I'll call you right away.

❏ **Exercise 7. Warm-up.** (Chart 20-3)
Choose the correct completions.

1. If Tom were a teacher, he would teach law.
   a. Tom   *is / isn't*   a teacher.
   b. Tom   *teaches / doesn't teach*   law.

2. If it were 5:00, we could leave.
   a. It   *is / isn't*   5:00.
   b. We   *can / can't*   leave now.

20-3 Untrue (Contrary to Fact) in the Present or Future

(a) If I *taught* this class, I *wouldn't give* tests.	In (a): In truth, I don't teach this class.
(b) If he *were* here right now, he *would help* us.	In (b): In truth, he is not here right now.
(c) If I *were* you, I *would accept* their invitation.	In (c): In truth, I am not you.
	NOTE: **Were** is used for both singular and plural subjects. **Was** (with *I, he, she, it*) is sometimes used in informal speech: *If I was you, I'd accept their invitation.*
COMPARE: (d) If I had enough money, I *would* buy a car. (e) If I had enough money, I *could* buy a car.	In (d): The speaker wants a car but doesn't have enough money. **Would** expresses desired or predictable results. In (e): The speaker is expressing one possible result. **could** = *would be able to;* **could** expresses possible options.

❑ **Exercise 8. Looking at grammar.** (Charts 20-2 and 20-3)
Complete the sentences with the verbs in parentheses.

1. If I have enough apples, I (*bake*) _____will bake_____ an apple pie this afternoon.

2. If I had enough apples, I (*bake*) _____would bake / could bake_____ an apple pie.

3. I will fix your bicycle if I (*have*) _____have_____ a screwdriver of the proper size.

4. I would fix your bicycle if I (*have*) _____had_____ a screwdriver of the proper size.

5. I (*go*) _____will go_____ to a movie tonight if I don't have any homework to do.

6. I (*go*) _____would go_____ to a movie tonight if I didn't have any homework to do.

7. Sally always answers the phone if she (*be*) _____is_____ in her office.

8. Sally would answer the phone if she (*be*) _____were_____ in her office right now.

❑ **Exercise 9. Let's talk.** (Chart 20-3)
Discuss the questions. Work in small groups or as a class.

Under what conditions, if any, would you . . .
1. exceed the speed limit while driving?
2. lie to your best friend?
3. disobey an order from your boss?
4. steal food?
5. carry a friend on your back?
6. not pay your rent?

❑ **Exercise 10. Looking at grammar.** (Charts 20-2 and 20-3)
Complete the sentences with the verbs in parentheses. Work in pairs or small groups.

1. I (*be, not*) _____ a student in this class if English (*be*) _____ my native language.

2. Most people know that oil floats on water. If you pour oil on water, it (*float*)

_____ .

3. If there (*be*) _____ no oxygen on earth, life as we know it (*exist, not*)

   _____ .

4. My evening newspaper has been late every day this week. If the paper (*arrive, not*)

   _____ on time today, I'm going to cancel my subscription.

5. If I (*be*) _____ a bird, I (*want, not*)

   _____ to live my whole life in a cage.

6. How long (*human beings, live*) _____

   _____ if all diseases in the world were

   completely eradicated?

7. If you boil water, it (*disappear*) _____

   into the atmosphere as vapor.

8. If people (*have*) _____ paws instead of hands with fingers and opposable

   thumbs, the machines we use in everyday life (*have to*) _____

   be constructed very differently. We (*be, not*) _____

   able to turn knobs, push small buttons, or hold tools and utensils securely.

❏ **Exercise 11. Let's talk: interview.** (Chart 20-3)
Find a partner to interview. Give him/her a fact. Ask your partner to make an unreal "if" statement. Change roles after item 3. Share some of the statements with the class.

Example: Ocean water is salty.
   → *If ocean water weren't salty, people could drink it and there would be enough water for everyone in the world.*

Facts:
1. There is gravity on the earth.
2. People don't have wings.
3. Cars can't fly.
4. Children don't get everything they want.
5. Guns exist.
6. There isn't enough food on the earth for everyone.

❏ **Exercise 12. Warm-up.** (Chart 20-4)
Check (✓) the sentences that have a past meaning.

1. _____ If Ann were available, she would help us.

2. _____ If Ann had been available, she would have helped us.

3. _____ If Ann is available, she will help us.

4. _____ If Ann had been available, she could have helped us.

20-4 Untrue (Contrary to Fact) in the Past

(a) If you **had told** me about the problem, I **would have helped** you.	In (a): In truth, you did not tell me about it.
(b) If they **had studied**, they **would have passed** the exam.	In (b): In truth, they did not study. Therefore, they failed the exam.
(c) If I **hadn't slipped** on the stairs, I **wouldn't have broken** my arm.	In (c): In truth, I slipped on the stairs. I broke my arm.
	NOTE: The auxiliary verbs are often reduced in speech. "If you'd told me, I would've helped you (OR I-duv helped you)."*
COMPARE:	In (d): **would** expresses a desired or predictable result.
(d) If I had had enough money, I **would** have bought a car.	In (e): **could** expresses a possible option.
(e) If I had had enough money, I **could** have bought a car.	**could have bought** = would have been able to buy

*In casual, informal speech, some native speakers sometimes use **would have** in an *if*-clause: *If you **would've told** me about the problem, I would've helped you.* This verb form usage is generally considered to be grammatically incorrect in standard English, but it occurs fairly commonly.

❏ **Exercise 13. Looking at grammar.** (Chart 20-4)
Complete the sentences with a factual or truthful statement.

1. If I had worn a jacket, I wouldn't have been so cold at the park, but the truth is . . . .
   → *I didn't wear a jacket.*
2. If Martin hadn't become a soccer player, he would have been a soccer coach, but the truth is . . . .
3. If I hadn't answered my cell phone while I was driving, I wouldn't have caused the accident, but the truth is . . . .
4. If Professor Stevens had given a fair test, more students would have passed, but the truth is . . . .

❏ **Exercise 14. Looking at grammar.** (Charts 20-1 → 20-4)
Underline the clause that expresses a condition. Write "T" if the condition is a true condition (i.e., a condition that exists in fact). Write "U" if the condition is untrue (i.e., a condition that does not exist in fact). Then decide if the sentence refers to present/future or past time.

1. __T__ If the weather is warm, we'll eat outdoors.   (present/future)   past

2. __U__ If the weather were warm, we would eat outdoors.   (present/future)   past

3. __U__ If the weather had been warm, we would have eaten outdoors.   present/future   past

4. __U__ If I had more money, I would work less.   present/future   past

5. __U__ If I had had more money, I would have worked less.   present/future   past

6. __T__ If I take time off from work, I feel more relaxed.   present/future   past

7. __U__ If I hadn't had to work, I could have seen you.   present/future   past

8. __U__ If I didn't have to work, I could see you.   present/future   past

❑ **Exercise 15. Looking at grammar.** (Charts 20-1 → 20-4)
Complete each sentence with *would do, will do,* or *would have done*.

1. Rita believes in hard work and wants her children to work hard. She always tells them,

    "If you work hard every day, you _____ well."

2. Scott is smart, but he doesn't work very hard. As a result, he is not very successful at

    his job. His co-workers often tell him, "If you worked hard every day, you

    _____ well."

3. Mark planned to study hard for a test yesterday, but some friends called, and he decided to

    go out with them. He didn't do well on his test the next day. His teacher told him, "If you

    had worked hard yesterday, you _____ well on the test."

❑ **Exercise 16. Looking at grammar.** (Charts 20-1 → 20-4)
Complete the sentences with the verbs in parentheses.

1. If I (*have*) ___have___ enough money, I will go with you.

2. If I (*have*) ___had___ enough money, I would go with you.

3. If I (*have*) ___had had___ enough money, I would have gone with you.

4. If the weather is nice tomorrow, we (*go*) ___will go___ to the zoo.

5. If the weather were nice today, we (*go*) ___would go___ to the zoo.

6. If the weather had been nice yesterday, we (*go*) ___would have gone___ to the zoo.

7. If Sally (*be*) ___is___ at home tomorrow, I am going to visit her.

8. Jim isn't home right now. If he (*be*) ___were___ at home
   right now, I (*visit*) ___would visite___ him.

9. Linda wasn't at home yesterday. If she (*be*)
   ___had been___ at home yesterday, I (*visit*)
   ___would have visited.___ her.

10. Last night Alex ruined his sweater when he washed it.
    If he (*read*) ___had read.___ the label, he (*wash, not*)
    ___might not have washed.___ it in hot water.

Exercise 17. Looking at grammar. (Charts 20-1 → 20-4)
Answer the questions with *yes* or *no*.

1. If the weather had been good yesterday, we would not have canceled the picnic.

    a. Was the picnic canceled? ___yes___

    b. Was the weather good? ___no___

2. If I had an envelope and a stamp, I would mail this letter today.

    a. Do I have an envelope and a stamp right now? _____

    b. Do I want to mail this letter today? _____

    c. Am I going to mail this letter today? _____

3. Ann would have made it to class on time this morning if the bus hadn't been late.

    a. Did Ann try to make it to class on time? _____

    b. Did Ann make it to class on time? _____

    c. Was the bus late? _____

4. If I didn't have any friends, I would be lonely.

    a. Am I lonely? _____

    b. Do I have friends? _____

❑ **Exercise 18. Let's talk.** (Chart 20-4)
Work with a partner. Speaker A gives the cue. Speaker B begins the response with *But if I had known*.

Example:
SPEAKER A (*book open*):   There was a test yesterday. You didn't know that, so you didn't study.
SPEAKER B (*book closed*):   But if I had known (that there was a test yesterday), I would have
                    studied.

1. Your friend was in the hospital. You didn't know that, so you didn't visit her.
2. I've never met your friend. You didn't know that, so you didn't introduce me.
3. There was a meeting last night. You didn't know that, so you didn't go.
4. Your friend's parents are in town. You didn't know that, so you didn't invite them to dinner.

Change roles.
5. I wanted to go to the soccer game. You didn't know that, so you didn't buy a ticket for me.
6. I was at home last night. You didn't know that, so you didn't visit me.
7. Your sister wanted a gold necklace for her birthday. You didn't know that, so you didn't buy her one.
8. I had a problem. You didn't know that, so you didn't offer to help.

Exercise 19. Let's listen and talk. (Chart 20-4)

Part I. Answer this question: Why do you think dinosaurs became extinct? Then close your book and listen to the short talk on dinosaurs.

CD 2
Track 32

Part II. Open your book and read the statements. Circle "T" for true and "F" for false.

1. According to one theory, if an asteroid had collided with the earth,
   several disastrous changes in the earth's climate would have taken place. T F

2. This theory suggests that if an asteroid had not collided with the earth,
   dinosaurs would still exist. T F

Part III. Discuss these questions.

1. If dinosaurs still existed, what do you think the world would be like?
2. Would it be possible for dinosaurs and human beings to coexist on the same planet?

Exercise 20. Listening. (Charts 20-1 → 20-4)

In conditional sentences, /h/ is often dropped in the auxiliary verbs **have** and **had**. Listen to the sentences spoken in casual, relaxed English. Complete the sentences with the non-reduced forms of the words you hear.

CD 2
Track 33

SITUATION: Jon told several good friends a lie, and they recently found out. Here are their reactions:

Example: You will hear: If he had been truthful, he wouldn't have lost my trust.
You will write: _____*If he had been*_____ truthful, _____*he wouldn't have lost*_____ my trust.

1. _____ the truth sooner, _____ differently.

2. _____ him, _____ so foolish.

3. _____ me what a great guy Jon was, _____
   _____ him so easily.

4. _____ another person, _____ so shocked.

5. _____ , _____ more respect for him.

424 CHAPTER 20

○ **Exercise 21. Looking at grammar.** (Charts 20-1 → 20-4)
Complete the sentences with the verbs in parentheses.

1. You should tell your father exactly what happened. If I (*be*) _____ *were* _____ you, I (*tell*) _____ *would ~~told~~ tell* _____ him the truth as soon as possible.

2. If I (*have*) _____ *had ~~had~~* _____ my camera with me yesterday, I (*take*) _____ *would have taken* _____ a picture of Alex standing on his head.

3. I'm almost ready to plant my garden. I have a lot of seeds. Maybe I have more than I need. If I (*have*) _____ *have* _____ more seeds than I need, I (*give*) _____ *will give* _____ some to my neighbor.

4. George has only two pairs of socks. If he (*have*) _____ *~~have~~ had* _____ more than two pairs of socks, he (*have to, not*) _____ *would not have to* _____ wash his socks so often.

5. The cowboy pulled his gun to shoot at the rattlesnake, but he was too late. If he (*be*) _____ *~~were~~ had been* _____ quicker to pull the trigger, the snake (*bite, not*) _____ *might not have bitten* _____ him on the foot. It's a good thing he was wearing heavy leather boots.

6. What (*we, use*) _____ *~~could we used~~ (do we use* _____ to look at ourselves when we comb our hair if we (*have, not*) _____ *~~have to don't have~~ didn't* _____ mirrors?

7. It's been a long drought. It hasn't rained for over a month. If it (*rain, not*) _____ *~~doesn't rains~~* _____ soon, a lot of crops (*die*) _____ *will die* _____. If the crops (*die*) _____ *die* _____, many people (*go*) _____ *will go* _____ hungry this coming winter.

8. A: Shhh! Your father is taking a nap. Uh-oh. You woke him up.
   B: Gee, I'm sorry, Mom. If I (*realize*) _____ *had realised* _____ he was sleeping, I (*make, not*) _____ *would ~~not have~~ made* _____ so much noise when I came in.

9. A: Since I broke my foot, I haven't been able to get to the basement to wash my clothes.
   B: Why didn't you say something? I (*come*) _____ *~~will will came~~* _____ over and *could have* (*wash*) _____ *~~wash~~ wash* _____ them for you if you (*tell*) _____ *~~tell~~ had told* _____ me.
   A: I know you (*come*) _____ *~~will~~ come* _____ right away if I (*call*) _____ *call* _____ you. I guess I didn't want to bother you.
   B: Nonsense! What are good neighbors for?

❏ **Exercise 22. Listening.** (Charts 20-1 → 20-4)

CD 2
Track 34

Listen to the statements and answer the questions.

Example: You will hear: If Bob had asked me to keep the news about his marriage a secret, I
wouldn't have told anybody. I know how to keep a secret.

You will answer: a. Did I tell anybody the news? ____yes____

b. Did Bob ask me to keep it a secret? ____no____

1. a. Am I going to go to the art museum? _____

b. Do I have enough time? _____

2. a. Did Mrs. Jones receive immediate medical attention? _____

b. Did she die? _____

3. a. Am I a carpenter? _____

b. Do I want to build my own house? _____

c. Am I going to build my own house? _____

4. a. Was the hotel built to withstand an earthquake? _____

b. Did the hotel collapse? _____

❏ **Exercise 23. Looking at grammar.** (Charts 20-1 → 20-4)

Complete each sentence with an appropriate auxiliary verb.

1. I don't have a pen, but if I _____*did*_____, I would lend it to you.

2. He is busy right now, but if he _____*weren't*_____, he would help us.

3. I didn't vote in the election, but if I _____*had*_____, I would have voted for Senator Todd.

4. I don't have enough money, but if I _____*had*_____, I would buy that book.

5. The weather is cold today, but if it _____*weren't*_____, I'd go swimming.

6. She didn't come, but if she _____*had/did*_____, she would have met my brother.

7. I'm not a good cook, but if I _____*were*_____, I would make all of my own meals.

8. He didn't go to a doctor, but if he _____*had gone*_____, the cut on his hand wouldn't have
gotten infected.

9. I always pay my bills. If I _____*didn't*_____, I'd get in a lot of trouble.

10. Helium is lighter than air. If it _____*weren't*_____, a helium-filled balloon wouldn't float
upward.

11. I called my husband to tell him I would be late. If I _____*hadn't*_____, he would have gotten
worried about me.

❑ **Exercise 24. Let's talk: pairwork.** (Charts 20-1 → 20-4)
Work with a partner. Speaker A asks the questions. Speaker B begins the answers with
No, but.

Example:
SPEAKER A (*book open*): Do you have a dollar?
SPEAKER B (*book closed*): No, but if I did (No, but if I had a dollar), I would lend it to you.

Change roles.

1. Are you rich?
2. Do you have a car?
3. Are you a bird?
4. Did you forget to bring a pen to class today?
5. Do you have your own airplane?
6. Are you the teacher of this class?

7. Are you at home right now?
8. Do you speak (*another language*)?
9. Did you forget to bring your grammar book to class today?
10. Is the weather hot/cold today?
11. Do you live in (*a different city*)?
12. Are you hungry?

❑ **Exercise 25. Warm-up.** (Chart 20-5)
Match the true or factual sentences in Column A to the conditional sentences in Column B.

Column A

1. I was painting my apartment when you asked me to go to a movie.
2. I am painting my apartment right now.

Column B

a. If I weren't painting my apartment, I would go to a movie with you.
b. If I hadn't been painting my apartment, I would have gone to a movie with you.

20-5 Using Progressive Verb Forms in Conditional Sentences

Notice the use of progressive verb forms in these examples. Even in conditional sentences, progressive verb forms are used in progressive situations. (See Chart 1-2, p. 3, for a discussion of progressive verbs.)

(a)	True:	It *is raining* right now, so I *will not go* for a walk.
(b)	Conditional:	If it *were not raining* right now, I *would go* for a walk.
(c)	True:	It *was raining* yesterday afternoon, so I *did not go* for a walk.
(d)	Conditional:	If it *had not been raining*, I *would have gone* for a walk.

❑ **Exercise 26. Looking at grammar.** (Chart 20-5)
Change the statements to conditional sentences.

1. You weren't listening, so you didn't understand the directions. But . . . .
   → *if you had been listening, you would have understood the directions.*
2. You aren't wearing a coat, so you're cold. But . . . .
3. Joe got a ticket because he was driving too fast. But . . . .
4. I'm enjoying myself, so I won't leave. But . . . .
5. You were sleeping, so I didn't tell you the news as soon as I heard it. But . . . .

Exercise 27. Looking at grammar. (Chart 20-5)
Complete each sentence with the correct form of the verb in parentheses. Make untrue or contrary-to-fact statements.

1. It's snowing. We can't go to the park.

   If it (*snow*) _____weren't snowing_____, we could go to the park.

2. It wasn't snowing. We went to the park.

   If it (*snow*) _____had been snowing_____,
   we wouldn't have gone to the park.

3. Elena just got out of the shower. She's
   drying her hair with a hair dryer, so she can't
   hear the phone ring.

   If Elena (*dry*) _____didn't dry / weren't dry_____
   her hair, she could hear the phone ring.

4. Elena was waiting for a phone call from Tom, but as it happened, she was drying her hair when he called and couldn't hear the phone ring.

   If Elena (*dry*) _____had not dried_____ her hair when Tom called, she could have heard the phone ring.

5. Max is at a party at his friend's apartment, but he's not having any fun. He wants to leave.

   Max wouldn't want to leave early if he (*have*) _____had_____ fun.

6. Mrs. Chang was talking on her cell phone while she was driving and wasn't paying enough attention to traffic. When the car in front of her stopped, she crashed into it.

   If Mrs. Chang (*talk*) _____had not talked_____ on her cell phone, she probably wouldn't have gotten into an accident.

◻ **Exercise 28. Warm-up.** (Chart 20-6)
Choose the correct time words.

1. If I had done my homework (*now / earlier*), I would know the answers (*now / earlier*).

2. Anita wouldn't be sick (*now / earlier*) if she had followed the doctor's orders (*now / earlier*).

20-6 Using "Mixed Time" in Conditional Sentences

Frequently the time in the *if*-clause and the time in the result clause are different: one clause may be in the present and the other in the past. Notice that past and present times are mixed in these sentences.

(a) True:	I *did not eat* breakfast several hours ago, so I *am* hungry now.	
(b) Conditional:	If I *had eaten* breakfast several hours ago, I *would not be* hungry now.	
	(past)	(present)

(c) True:	He *is not* a good student. He *did not study* for the test yesterday.	
(d) Conditional:	If he *were* a good student, he *would have studied* for the test yesterday.	
	(present)	(past)

❑ **Exercise 29. Looking at grammar.** (Chart 20-6)
Change the statements to conditional sentences. Begin each one with **But**.

1. I'm hungry now because I didn't eat dinner.
   → *But if I'd eaten dinner, I wouldn't be hungry now.*
2. The room is full of flies because you left the door open.
3. You are tired this morning because you didn't go to bed at a reasonable hour last night.
4. I didn't finish my report yesterday, so I can't begin a new project today.
5. I'm not you, so I didn't tell him the truth.
6. I don't know anything about plumbing, so I didn't fix the leak in the sink myself.
7. Anita got sick because she didn't follow the doctor's orders.

❑ **Exercise 30. Warm-up.** (Chart 20-7)
The following sentences are correct. Make sentences with the same meaning using *if*. Notice the order of the words in blue.

1. Were I the teacher, I would give fewer tests.
2. Had I known about your problem, I would have helped you.
3. Should anyone come, please tell them I'm asleep.

20-7 Omitting *If*	
(a) *Were I* you, I wouldn't do that.	With **were**, **had** (past perfect), and **should**, sometimes *if* is omitted and the subject and verb are inverted.
(b) *Had I known,* I would have told you.	In (a): **Were I you** = *if I were you*
(c) *Should anyone call,* please take a message.	In (b): **Had I known** = *if I had known*
	In (c): **Should anyone call** = *if anyone should call*

❑ **Exercise 31. Looking at grammar.** (Chart 20-7)
Make sentences with the same meaning by omitting *if*.

1. If you should need more money, go to the bank before six o'clock.
   → *Should you need more money, go to the bank before six o'clock.*
2. If I were you, I wouldn't do that.
3. If they had realized the danger, they would have done it differently.
4. If I were your teacher, I would insist you do better work.
5. If you should change your mind, please let me know immediately.
6. She would have gotten the job if she had been better prepared.
7. Your boss sounds like a real tyrant. If I were you, I would look for another job.
8. I'll be out of the office until June 12th. If you should need to reach me, I'll be at our company headquarters in Seoul.
9. The artists and creative thinkers throughout the history of the world have changed all of our lives. If they had not dared to be different, the history of civilization would have to be rewritten.
10. If there should be a global nuclear war, life on earth as we know it would end forever.

□ **Exercise 32. Listening.** (Chart 20-7)

CD 2
Track 35

Choose the sentence that best expresses the meaning of the sentence you hear.

Example: You will hear: Should you need help, I'll be in the room next door.
You will choose: a. I'll be helping others in the room.
　　　　　　　　 (b.) I'm available to help you.
　　　　　　　　　c. You shouldn't ask me for help.
　　　　　　　　　d. Do you need help from me?

1. a. I get a lot of speeding tickets.
    b. I was driving too fast.
    c. I like to drive fast.
    d. I didn't get a ticket.

2. a. You shouldn't call me on my cell.
    b. Did you have questions?
    c. Call me soon.
    d. Call me if you have questions.

3. a. We're glad you told us.
    b. We were happy to help you.
    c. We needed to know earlier.
    d. Why did you tell us so soon?

4. a. I took the fastest way to the theater.
    b. I didn't take the fastest way.
    c. The theater was too far away.
    d. I took several different routes.

5. a. We stayed home.
    b. We didn't stay home.
    c. Someone warned us.
    d. Several people warned us.

6. a. Are we rich?
    b. Rich people live in houses overlooking the ocean.
    c. We aren't rich.
    d. We live in a house overlooking the ocean.

□ **Exercise 33. Warm-up.** (Chart 20-8)
Read the paragraph. Check (✓) the sentences that are true.

　　One night a fire started in Janet's apartment. A blanket on the sofa got too close to an electric heater. Janet was in a deep sleep and wasn't aware of the fire. Fortunately, her neighbors saw smoke coming out of the window and threw rocks at her bedroom window to wake her up. Janet was very grateful that she wasn't killed or injured in the fire.

1. _____ Janet would have kept sleeping, but the neighbors woke her up.

2. _____ Janet would have awakened without her neighbors' help.

3. _____ Janet was awakened by her neighbors; otherwise, she wouldn't have woken up.

20-8	Implied Conditions	
(a) I **would have gone** with you, *but I had to study.* (b) I never **would have succeeded** *without your help.*	Often the *if*-clause is implied, not stated. Conditional verbs are still used in the result clause. In (a): the implied condition = *if I hadn't had to study* In (b): the implied condition = *if you hadn't helped me*	
(c) She ran; *otherwise,* she **would have missed** her bus.	Conditional verbs are frequently used following **otherwise**. In (c), the implied *if*-clause = *if she had not run*	

430 CHAPTER 20

❏ **Exercise 34. Looking at grammar.** (Chart 20-8)
Identify the implied conditions by making sentences using *if*-clauses.

1. I would have visited you, but I didn't know that you were at home.
   → *I would have visited you if I had known you were at home.*
2. It wouldn't have been a good meeting without Rosa.
   → *It wouldn't have been a good meeting if Rosa hadn't been there.*
3. I would have answered the phone, but I didn't hear it ring.
4. I couldn't have finished the work without your help.
5. I like to travel. I would have gone to Nepal last summer, but I didn't have enough money.
6. I stepped on the brakes. Otherwise, I would have hit the child on the bicycle.
7. Olga turned down the volume on the CD player. Otherwise, the neighbors probably would have called to complain about the noise.
8. Tarek would have finished his education, but he had to quit school and find a job in order to support his family.

❏ **Exercise 35. Listening.** (Chart 20-8)

CD 2
Track 36

Choose the statement (a. or b.) that is true for each sentence you hear. In some cases both answers are correct.

Example: You will hear: I canceled your dentist appointment for Tuesday. Otherwise, you would have had two appointments in one day.
You will choose: a. I thought you needed two appointments.
　　　　　　　　　(b.) I didn't think you wanted two appointments.

1. a. If I had had your number, I would have called.
   b. I didn't have your number; otherwise, I would have called.

2. a. If my parents hadn't helped me, I wouldn't have gone to college.
   b. If I hadn't gone to college, my parents wouldn't have helped me.

3. a. I picked up your clothes.
   b. I wasn't able to pick up your clothes.

4. a. If someone had told us about the party, we would have come.
   b. We came to the party even though you didn't tell us about it.

5. a. If I'd had your advice, I would have known what to do.
   b. Because of your advice, I knew what to do.

❏ **Exercise 36. Looking at grammar.** (Charts 20-1 → 20-8)
Complete each sentence with the verb in parentheses. Some of the verbs are passive.

1. If I could speak Japanese, I (*spend*) _____ next year studying in Japan.

2. Had I known Mr. Jung was in the hospital, I (*send*) _____ him a note and some flowers.

3. We will move into our new house next month if it (*complete*) _____ _____ by then.

4. It's too bad that it's snowing. If it (*snow, not*) _____, we could go for a drive.

5. I was very tired. Otherwise, I (*go*) _____ to the party with you last night.

6. I'm glad I have so many friends and such a wonderful family. Life without friends or family (*be*) _____ lonely for me.

7. If you (*sleep, not*) _____ last night when we arrived, I would have asked you to go with us, but I didn't want to wake you up.

8. Bill has such a bad memory that he (*forget*) _____ his head if it (*be, not*) _____ attached to his body.

9. A: What would you be doing right now if you (*be, not*) _____ in class?

   B: I (*sleep*) _____.

10. A: Boy, is it ever hot today!

    B: You said it! If there (*be*) _____ only a breeze, it (*be, not*) _____ _____ quite so unbearable.

11. A: Hi. Sorry I'm late.

    B: That's okay.

    A: I (*be*) _____ here sooner, but I had car trouble.

12. A: Want to ride on the roller coaster?

    B: No way! I (*ride, not*) _____ on the roller coaster even if you paid me a million dollars!

13. A: Are you coming to the party?

    B: I don't think so, but if I change my mind, I (*tell*) _____ you.

☐ **Exercise 37. In your own words.** (Charts 20-1 → 20-8)
Complete the sentences with your own words, either orally or in writing. If written, add commas as necessary.

1. If it hadn't rained . . . .
2. If it weren't raining . . . .
3. You would have passed the test had . . . .
4. It's a good thing we took a map with us. Otherwise . . . .

5. Without electricity modern life . . . .
6. If you hadn't reminded me about the meeting tonight . . . .
7. Should you need any help . . . .
8. If I could choose any profession I wanted . . . .
9. If I were at home right now . . . .
10. Without your help yesterday . . . .
11. Were I you . . . .
12. What would you do if . . . .
13. If I had the chance to live my childhood over again . . . .
14. Had I known . . . .
15. Can you imagine what life would be like if . . . .

❏ **Exercise 38. Let's talk.** (Charts 20-1 → 20-8)
Explain what you would do in these circumstances. Work in pairs or small groups.

Example:
SPEAKER A (*book open*): Suppose the student sitting next to you drops her pen.
                          What would you do?
SPEAKER B (*book closed*): I would pick it up for her.

1. Suppose/pretend there is a fire in this building right now. What would you do?
2. Suppose there is a fire in your room or apartment or house. You have time to save only one thing. What would you save?
3. Suppose you go to the bank to cash a check for (twenty dollars). The bank teller cashes your check and you leave, but when you count the money, you find she gave you (thirty dollars) instead of (twenty). What would you do?
4. Same situation, but she gave you only (fifteen dollars) instead of (twenty).
5. John was cheating during an examination. Suppose you were the teacher and you saw him. What would you have done?
6. You are at a party. A man starts talking to you, but he is speaking so fast that you can't catch what he is saying. What would you do?
7. Late at night you're driving your car down a deserted street. You're all alone. In an attempt to avoid a dog in the road, you swerve and hit a parked car. You know that no one saw you. What would you do?
8. Ricardo goes to a friend's house for dinner. His friend serves a dish that he can't stand/doesn't like at all. What if you were Ricardo?
9. Suppose you go to another city to visit a friend. You have never been there before. Your friend said he would meet you at the airport, but he's not there. You wait a long time, but he never shows up. You try to call him, but nobody answers the phone. Now what?

❏ **Exercise 39. Warm-up.** (Chart 20-9)
Which sentences are true for you? Circle *yes* or *no*. What do you notice about the words in blue?

1. I wish I were someplace else right now.	yes	no
2. I wish I could travel all around the world next year.	yes	no
3. I wish I had learned English when I was a child.	yes	no

20-9 Verb Forms Following *Wish*

Wish is used when the speaker wants reality to be different, to be exactly the opposite.

	"True" Statement	Verb Form Following *Wish*	*Wish* is followed by a noun clause. (See Chart 12-5, p. 253.) Past verb forms, similar to those in conditional sentences, are used in the noun clause.
A Wish about the Future	(a) She *will not tell* me. (b) He *isn't going to be* here. (c) She *can't come* tomorrow.	I *wish* (that) she *would tell* me. I *wish* he *were going to be* here. I *wish* she *could come* tomorrow.	For example, in (a): *would*, the past form of *will*, is used to make a wish about the future.
A Wish about the Present	(d) I *don't know* French. (e) It *is raining* right now. (f) I *can't speak* Japanese.	I *wish* I *knew* French. I *wish* it *weren't raining* right now. I *wish* I *could speak* Japanese.	In (d): the simple past (*knew*) is used to make a wish about the present.
A Wish about the Past	(g) John *didn't come*. (h) Mary *couldn't come*.	I *wish* John *had come*.* I *wish* Mary *could have come*.	In (g): the past perfect (*had come*) is used to make a wish about the past.

*Sometimes in very informal speaking: *I wish John **would have** come.*

❑ **Exercise 40. Looking at grammar.** (Chart 20-9)
Complete the sentences with an appropriate verb form.

1. Our classroom doesn't have any windows. I wish our classroom _____*had*_____ windows.

2. The sun isn't shining. I wish the sun _____ right now.

3. I didn't go shopping. I wish I _____ shopping.

4. I don't know how to dance. I wish I _____ how to dance.

5. It's cold today. I'm not wearing a coat. I wish I _____ a coat.

6. I don't have enough money to buy that book. I wish I _____ enough money.

7. I can't go with you tomorrow, but I wish I _____.

8. My friend won't ever lend me his car. I wish he _____ me his car for my date tomorrow night.

9. Mrs. Takasawa isn't coming to dinner with us tonight. I wish she _____ _____ to dinner with us.

10. The teacher is going to give an exam tomorrow. I wish he _____ _____ us an exam tomorrow.

11. You can't meet my parents. I wish you _____ them, but they're out of town.

12. Khalid didn't come to the meeting. I wish he _____ to the meeting.

13. I'm not lying on a sunny beach. I wish I _____ on a sunny beach.

Exercise 41. Let's talk: interview. (Chart 20-9)
Ask two classmates each question. Share some of their answers with the class.

1. What is something you can't do but you wish you could do?
2. What do you wish you were doing right now?
3. What is something you don't have but wish you had?
4. What is something that didn't happen yesterday but that you wish had happened?
5. What is something you don't know but wish you knew?
6. What is something that has never happened in your life but that you wish would happen?
7. What is something that happened in your life but that you wish had not happened?
8. What is something you have to do but wish you didn't have to do?
9. What is something that will not happen tomorrow but that you wish would happen?
10. What is something you were unable to do yesterday but you wish you could have done?

❏ **Exercise 42. Looking at grammar.** (Chart 20-9)
Complete the sentences with an appropriate auxiliary verb.

1. I'm not at home, but I wish I _____*were*_____.

2. I don't know her, but I wish I _____*did*_____.

3. I can't sing well, but I wish I _____*could*_____.

4. I didn't go, but I wish I _____*had*_____.

5. He won't talk about it, but I wish he _____*would*_____.

6. I didn't read that book, but I wish I _____.

7. I want to go, but I can't. I wish I _____.

8. I don't have a bicycle, but I wish I _____.

9. He didn't buy a ticket to the game, but he wishes he _____.

10. It probably won't happen, but I wish it _____.

11. He isn't old enough to drive a car, but he wishes he _____.

12. They didn't go to the movie, but they wish they _____.

13. I don't have a driver's license, but I wish I _____.

14. I'm not living in an apartment, but I wish I _____.

❏ **Exercise 43. Warm-up.** (Chart 20-10)
Choose the correct time word for each sentence. What do you notice about the verbs in blue and the tenses?

1. Jim's neighbors play loud music. He wishes they were quieter (*now / soon*).
2. Jim's neighbors are going to move. He wishes they would move (*soon / last week*).

20-10 Using *Would* to Make Wishes about the Future

(a) It is raining. I *wish* it *would stop*. (*I want it to stop raining.*) (b) I'm expecting a call. I *wish* the phone *would ring*. (*I want the phone to ring.*)	*Would* is usually used to indicate that the speaker wants something to happen or someone other than the speaker to do something in the future. The wish may or may not come true (be realized).
(c) It's going to be a good party. I *wish* you *would come*. (d) We're going to be late. I *wish* you *would hurry*.	In (c) and (d): *I wish you would* . . . is often used to make a request.

❑ **Exercise 44. Looking at grammar.** (Charts 20-9 and 20-10)
Use the given information to answer each pair of questions. Use *wish* + *would*.

Example:
TOM: Why are you watching the telephone?
SUE: I'm waiting to hear from Sam. I want him to call me. I need to talk to him right now. We had an argument. I need to make sure everything's okay.

    (a) What does Sue want to happen in the near future?
      → *She* **wishes** *the phone* **would** *ring.*
    (b) What else does Sue wish?
      → *She* **wishes** *Sam* **would** *call her. She wishes she could talk to Sam right now. She probably wishes she and Sam hadn't had an argument.*

1. ANNA: Can't you come to the concert? Please change your mind. I'd really like you to come.
    YOKO: No, I can't. I have to work.

    (a) What does Anna want Yoko to do?
    (b) What else does Anna wish?

2. Helen is a neat and orderly person. Judy, her roommate, is messy. Judy never picks up after herself. She leaves dirty dishes in the sink. She drops her clothes all over the apartment. She never makes her bed. Helen nags Judy to pick up after herself.

    (a) What does Helen want Judy to do?
    (b) What does Judy probably wish?

❑ **Exercise 45. Listening.** (Charts 20-9 and 20-10)
CD 2
Track 37
Listen to the sentences spoken in casual, relaxed English. Complete the sentences with the non-reduced forms of the words you hear.

Example: You will hear: I wish I didn't need so much sleep. I could get so much more done in a day!
           You will write: I wish I ____*didn't need*____ so much sleep.

1. Alice doesn't like her job as a nurse. She wishes _____

    to nursing school.

2. A: I wish _____ go to work today.

    B: So do I. I wish _____ a holiday.

3. We had a good time in the mountains over vacation. I wish _____
   with us. If _____ with us, _____
   a good time.

4. I know that something's bothering you. I wish _____
   me what it is. Maybe I can help.

5. A: My feet are killing me! I wish _____ more comfortable shoes.

   B: Yeah, me too. I wish _____ that we were going to have
      to walk this much.

❑ **Exercise 46. Let's talk.** (Charts 20-9 and 20-10)
Answer the questions. Use *wish*. Work in pairs, in small groups, or as a class.

1. Where do you wish you were right now? What do you wish you were doing?
2. Are you pleased with the weather today, or do you wish it were different?
3. Look around this room. What do you wish were different?
4. Is there anything you wish were different about the place you are living?
5. What do you wish were different about this city/town?
6. What do you wish were different about this country?
7. What do you wish were different about a student's life? about a worker's life?
8. Your friend gave you his phone number, but you didn't write it down because you thought you would remember it. Now you have forgotten the number. What do you wish?
9. You didn't eat breakfast/lunch/dinner before you came to class. Now you are hungry. What do you wish?
10. (____) stayed up very late last night. Today she is tired and sleepy. What does she probably wish?

❑ **Exercise 47. Let's talk or write.** (Chapter 20)
Answer the questions, either orally or in writing. If orally, work in pairs, in small groups, or as a class.

1. If you could have free service for the rest of your life from a chauffeur, cook, housekeeper, or gardener, which would you choose? Why?
2. If you had to leave your country and build a new life, where would you go? Why?
3. If you had control of all medical research in the world and, by concentrating funds and efforts, could find the cure for only one disease in the next 25 years, which disease would you select? Why?
4. You have promised to spend an evening with your best friend. Then you discover you have the chance to spend the evening with (*name of a famous person*). Your friend is not invited. What would you do? Why?
5. Assume that you have a good job. If your boss told you to do something that you think is wrong, would you do it? Why or why not? (You understand that if you don't do it, you will lose your job.)
6. If you had to choose among perfect health, a loving family, and wealth (and you could have only one of the three during the rest of your life), which would you choose? Why?

Appendix
Supplementary Grammar Charts

UNIT A: Basic Grammar Terminology

A-1 Subjects, Verbs, and Objects

(a) $\overset{S}{\text{Birds}}$ $\overset{V}{\text{fly.}}$
(noun) (verb)

Almost all English sentences contain a subject (**S**) and a verb (**V**). The verb may or may not be followed by an object (**O**).

(b) The $\overset{S}{\text{baby}}$ $\overset{V}{\text{cried.}}$
(noun) (verb)

VERBS: Verbs that are not followed by an object, as in (a) and (b), are called "intransitive verbs."

Common intransitive verbs: *agree, arrive, come, cry, exist, go, happen, live, occur, rain, rise, sleep, stay, walk.*

(c) The $\overset{S}{\text{student}}$ $\overset{V}{\text{needs}}$ a $\overset{O}{\text{pen.}}$
(noun) (verb) (noun)

Verbs that are followed by an object, as in (c) and (d), are called "transitive verbs."

Common transitive verbs: *build, cut, find, like, make, need, send, use, want.*

(d) My $\overset{S}{\text{friend}}$ $\overset{V}{\text{enjoyed}}$ the $\overset{O}{\text{party.}}$
(noun) (verb) (noun)

Some verbs can be either intransitive or transitive.
    Intransitive: *A student studies.*
    Transitive: *A student studies books.*

SUBJECTS AND OBJECTS: The subjects and objects of verbs are nouns (or pronouns).

Examples of nouns: *person, place, thing, John, Asia, pen, information, appearance, amusement.*

A-2 Adjectives

(a) Ann is an *intelligent* student.
    (adjective) (noun)

(b) The *hungry* child ate fruit.
    (adjective) (noun)

Adjectives describe nouns. In grammar, we say that adjectives modify nouns. The word *modify* means "change a little." Adjectives give a little different meaning to a noun: *intelligent student, lazy student, good student.*

Examples of adjectives: *young, old, rich, beautiful, brown, French, modern.*

(c) I saw some *beautiful* pictures.
    INCORRECT: beautiful-s- pictures

An adjective is neither singular nor plural. A final **-s** is never added to an adjective.

A-3 Adverbs

(a) He walks *quickly*. 　　　　　(adverb) (b) She opened the door *quietly*. 　　　　　　　　　　　　(adverb)	Adverbs modify verbs. Often they answer the question "How?" In (a): *How does he walk?* Answer: *Quickly.* Adverbs are often formed by adding *-ly* to an adjective. 　　Adjective:　*quick* 　　Adverb:　　*quickly*
(c) I am *extremely happy*. 　　　　(adverb)　(adjective)	Adverbs are also used to modify adjectives, i.e., to give information about adjectives, as in (c).
(d) Ann will come *tomorrow*. 　　　　　　　　　　(adverb)	Adverbs are also used to express time or frequency. Examples: *tomorrow, today, yesterday, soon, never, usually, always, yet.*
MIDSENTENCE ADVERBS: (e) Ann *always comes* on time. (f) Ann *is always* on time. (g) Ann *has always come* on time. (h) *Does she always come* on time?	Some adverbs may occur in the middle of a sentence. Midsentence adverbs have usual positions; they 　• come in front of simple present and simple past verbs (except *be*), as in (e); 　• follow *be* (simple present and simple past), as in (f); 　• come between a helping verb and a main verb, as in (g). In a question, a midsentence adverb comes directly after the subject, as in (h).

Common midsentence adverbs

ever	usually	generally	seldom	never	already
always	often	sometimes	rarely	not ever	finally
	frequently	occasionally	hardly ever		just
					probably

A-4　Prepositions and Prepositional Phrases

Common prepositions

about	at	beyond	into	since	up
above	before	by	like	through	upon
across	behind	despite	near	throughout	with
after	below	down	of	till	within
against	beneath	during	off	to	without
along	beside	for	on	toward(s)	
among	besides	from	out	under	
around	between	in	over	until	

S　　　V　　PREP　　O of PREP (a) The student studies *in* the library. 　　　　　　　　　　　　　　　　　(noun) 　　　　S　　V　　　O　PREP　O of PREP (b) We enjoyed the party *at* your house. 　　　　　　　　　　　　　　　　(noun)	An important element of English sentences is the prepositional phrase. It consists of a preposition (PREP) and its object (O). The object of a preposition is a noun or pronoun. In (a): *in the library* is a prepositional phrase.
(c) We went　*to the zoo*　*in the afternoon*. 　　　　　　　(Place)　　　　(Time) (d) *In the afternoon,* we went to the zoo.	In (c): In most English sentences, "place" comes before "time." In (d): Sometimes a prepositional phrase comes at the beginning of a sentence.

A-5 The Verb *Be*

(a) John *is* **a student**.
        (be)   (noun)
 	
(b) John *is* **intelligent**.
        (be) (adjective)
 	
(c) John *was* **at the library**.
        (be) (prep. phrase)
	A sentence with **be** as the main verb has three basic patterns:
	
	In (a): **be** + *a noun*
	In (b): **be** + *an adjective*
	In (c): **be** + *a prepositional phrase*

(d) Mary **is** *writing* a letter. (e) They **were** *listening* to some music. (f) That letter **was** *written* by Alice.	**Be** is also used as an auxiliary verb in progressive verb tenses and in the passive. In (d): **is** = *auxiliary;* **writing** = *main verb*

Tense Forms of *Be*

	SIMPLE PRESENT	SIMPLE PAST	PRESENT PERFECT
Singular	*I* **am** *you* **are** *he, she, it* **is**	*I* **was** *you* **were** *he, she, it* **was**	*I* **have been** *you* **have been** *he, she, it* **has been**
Plural	*we, you, they* **are**	*we, you, they* **were**	*we, you, they* **have been**

A-6 Linking Verbs

(a) The soup *smells* *good*. (linking verb) (adjective) (b) This food ***tastes delicious***. (c) The children ***feel happy***. (d) The weather ***became cold***.	Other verbs like **be** that may be followed immediately by an adjective are called "linking verbs." An adjective following a linking verb describes the subject of a sentence.* Common verbs that may be followed by an adjective: • *feel, look, smell, sound, taste* • *appear, seem* • *become* (and *get, turn, grow* when they mean "become")

*COMPARE:
  (1) *The man looks angry.* → An adjective (**angry**) follows **look**. The adjective describes the subject (**the man**). **Look** has the meaning of "appear."
  (2) *The man looked at me angrily.* → An adverb (**angrily**) follows **look at**. The adverb describes the action of the verb. **Look at** has the meaning of "regard, watch."

Ann *is* ***at the laudromat***.
She ***looks*** very ***busy***.

UNIT B: Questions

B-1 Forms of Yes/No and Information Questions

A yes/no question = a question that may be answered by *yes* or *no*
> A: Does he live in Chicago?
> B: Yes, he does. OR No, he doesn't.

An information question = a question that asks for information by using a question word
> A: Where does he live?
> B: In Chicago.

Question word order = (*Question word*) + *helping verb* + *subject* + *main verb*

Notice that the same subject-verb order is used in both yes/no and information questions.

(Question Word)	Helping Verb	Subject	Main Verb	(Rest of Sentence)	
(a) (b) Where	Does does	she she	live live?	there? 	If the verb is in the simple present, use **does** (with *he, she, it*) or **do** (with *I, you, we, they*) in the question. If the verb is simple past, use **did**. Notice: The main verb in the question is in its simple form; there is no final *-s* or *-ed*.
(c) (d) Where	Do do	they they	live live?	there? 	
(e) (f) Where	Did did	he he	live live?	there? 	
(g) (h) Where	Is is	he he	living living?	there? 	If the verb has an auxiliary (a helping verb), the same auxiliary is used in the question. There is no change in the form of the main verb. If the verb has more than one auxiliary, only the first auxiliary precedes the subject, as in (m) and (n).
(i) (j) Where	Have have	they they	lived lived?	there? 	
(k) (l) Where	Can can	Mary Mary	live live?	there? 	
(m) (n) Where	Will will	he he	be living be living?	there? 	

(o) Who
 (p) Who
	Ø
	 can
		Ø
		 Ø
			lives
			 come?
				there?
				
					If the question word is the subject, usual question-word order is not used; **does, do,** and **did** are not used. The verb is in the same form in a question as it is in a statement.
					
					     Statement: *Tom came.*
					     Question: *Who came?*

(q) (r) Where	Are are	they they?	Ø Ø	there? 	Main verb **be** in the simple present (*am, is, are*) and simple past (*was, were*) precedes the subject. It has the same position as a helping verb.
(s) (t) Where	Was was	Jim Jim?	Ø Ø	there? 	

	Question	Answer	
When	(a) **When** did they arrive? **When** will you come?	Yesterday. Next Monday.	**When** is used to ask questions about *time*.
Where	(b) **Where** is she? **Where** can I find a pen?	At home. In that drawer.	**Where** is used to ask questions about *place*.
Why	(c) **Why** did he leave early? **Why** aren't you coming with us?	Because he's ill. I'm tired.	**Why** is used to ask questions about *reason*.
How	(d) **How** did you come to school? **How** does he drive?	By bus. Carefully.	**How** generally asks about *manner*.
	(e) **How much** money does it cost? **How many** people came?	Ten dollars. Fifteen.	**How** is used with **much** and **many**.
	(f) **How old** are you? **How cold** is it? **How soon** can you get here? **How fast** were you driving?	Twelve. Ten below zero. In ten minutes. 50 miles an hour.	**How** is also used with adjectives and adverbs.
	(g) **How long** has he been here? **How often** do you write home? **How far** is it to Miami from here?	Two years. Every week. 500 miles.	**How long** asks about *length of time*. **How often** asks about *frequency*. **How far** asks about *distance*.
Who	(h) **Who** can answer that question? **Who** came to visit you?	I can. Jane and Eric.	**Who** is used as the subject of a question. It refers to people.
	(i) **Who** is coming to dinner tonight? **Who** wants to come with me?	Ann, Bob, and Al. We do.	**Who** is usually followed by a singular verb even if the speaker is asking about more than one person.
Whom	(j) **Who(m)** did you see? **Who(m)** are you visiting?	I saw George. My relatives.	**Whom** is used as the object of a verb or preposition. In everyday spoken English, **whom** is rarely used; **who** is used instead. **Whom** is used only in formal questions.
	(k) **Who(m)** should I talk *to?* *To* **whom** should I talk? (formal)	The secretary.	NOTE: **Whom**, not **who**, is used if preceded by a preposition.
Whose	(l) **Whose** book did you borrow? **Whose** key is this? (**Whose** is this?)	David's. It's mine.	**Whose** asks questions about *possession*.

(continued)

	Question	Answer	
What	(m) *What* made you angry? *What* went wrong?	His rudeness. Everything.	**What** is used as the subject of a question. It refers to things.
	(n) *What* do you need? *What* did Alice buy?	I need a pencil. A book.	**What** is also used as an object.
	(o) *What* did he talk *about*? *About what* did he talk? (formal)	His vacation.	
	(p) *What kind of* soup is that? *What kind of* shoes did he buy?	It's bean soup. Sandals.	**What kind of** asks about the particular variety or type of something.
	(q) *What did* you *do* last night? *What is* Mary *doing*?	I studied. Reading a book.	**What** + *a form of* **do** is used to ask questions about activities.
	(r) *What countries* did you visit? *What time* did she come? *What color* is his hair?	Italy and Spain. Seven o'clock. Dark brown.	**What** may accompany a noun.
	(s) *What is* Ed *like*?	He's kind and friendly.	**What** + **be like** asks for a general description of qualities.
	(t) *What is* the weather *like*?	Hot and humid.	
	(u) *What does* Ed *look like*?	He's tall and has dark hair.	**What** + **look like** asks for a physical description.
	(v) *What does* her house *look like*?	It's a two-story,* red brick house.	
Which	(w) I have two pens. *Which pen* do you want? *Which one* do you want? *Which do* you want?	The blue one.	**Which** is used instead of **what** when a question concerns choosing from a definite, known quantity or group.
	(x) *Which book* should I buy?	That one.	
	(y) *Which countries* did he visit? *What countries* did he visit?	Peru and Chile.	In some cases, there is little difference in meaning between **which** and **what** when they accompany a noun, as in (y) and (z).
	(z) *Which class* are you in? *What class* are you in?	This class.	

*American English: *a two-**story** house*.
British English: *a two-**storey** house*.

B-3 Shortened Yes/No Questions

(a) *Going to bed now?* = *Are you going to bed now?* (b) *Finish your work?* = *Did you finish your work?* (c) *Want to go to the movie with us?* = *Do you want to go to the movie with us?*	Sometimes in spoken English, the auxiliary and the subject *you* are dropped from a yes/no question, as in (a), (b), and (c).

B-4 Negative Questions

(a) *Doesn't she live* in the dormitory? (b) *Does she not live* in the dormitory? (very formal)	In a yes/no question in which the verb is negative, usually a contraction (e.g., *does* + *not* = *doesn't*) is used, as in (a). Example (b) is very formal and is usually not used in everyday speech. Negative questions are used to indicate the speaker's idea (i.e., what she/he believes is or is not true) or attitude (e.g., surprise, shock, annoyance, anger).
(c) Bob returns to his dorm room after his nine o'clock class. Matt, his roommate, is there. Bob is surprised. Bob says, "*What are you doing here? Aren't you supposed to be in class now?*"	In (c): Bob believes that Matt is supposed to be in class now. *Expected answer:* **Yes.**
(d) Alice and Mary are at home. Mary is about to leave on a trip, and Alice is going to take her to the airport. Alice says, "*It's already two o'clock. We'd better leave for the airport. Doesn't your plane leave at three?*"	In (d): Alice believes that Mary's plane leaves at three. She is asking the negative question to make sure that her information is correct. *Expected answer:* **Yes.**
(e) The teacher is talking to Jim about a test he failed. The teacher is surprised that Jim failed the test because he usually does very well. The teacher says: "*What happened? Didn't you study?*"	In (e): The teacher believes that Jim did not study. *Expected answer:* **No.**
(f) Barb and Ron are riding in a car. Ron is driving. He comes to a corner where there is a stop sign, but he does not stop the car. Barb is shocked. Barb says, "*What's the matter with you? Didn't you see that stop sign?*"	In (f): Barb believes that Ron did not see the stop sign. *Expected answer:* **No.**

B-5 Tag Questions

(a) Jack *can* come, *can't* he? (b) Fred *can't* come, *can* he?	A tag question is a question added at the end of a sentence. Speakers use tag questions mainly to make sure their information is correct or to seek agreement.*

AFFIRMATIVE SENTENCE + NEGATIVE TAG → AFFIRMATIVE ANSWER EXPECTED

Mary *is* here,	*isn't* she?	Yes, she is.
You *like* tea,	*don't* you?	Yes, I do.
They *have left,*	*haven't* they?	Yes, they have.

NEGATIVE SENTENCE + AFFIRMATIVE TAG → NEGATIVE ANSWER EXPECTED

Mary *isn't* here,	*is* she?	No, she isn't.
You *don't like* tea,	*do* you?	No, I don't.
They *haven't left,*	*have* they?	No, they haven't.

(c) *This/That* is your book, isn't *it?* *These/Those* are yours, aren't *they?*	The tag pronoun for **this/that** = **it**. The tag pronoun for **these/those** = **they**.
(d) *There is* a meeting tonight, *isn't there?*	In sentences with **there** + **be**, **there** is used in the tag.
(e) *Everything* is okay, isn't *it?* (f) *Everyone* took the test, didn't *they?*	Personal pronouns are used to refer to indefinite pronouns. **They** is usually used in a tag to refer to **everyone**, **everybody**, **someone**, **somebody**, **no one**, **nobody**.
(g) *Nothing is* wrong, *is* it? (h) *Nobody called* on the phone, *did* they? (i) You*'ve never been* there, *have* you?	Sentences with negative words take affirmative tags.
(j) *I am* supposed to be here, *am I not?* (k) *I am* supposed to be here, *aren't I?*	In (j): **am I not?** is formal English. In (k): **aren't I?** is common in spoken English.

*A tag question may be spoken:
   (1) with a rising intonation if the speaker is truly seeking to ascertain that his/her information, idea, belief is correct (e.g., *Ann lives in an apartment, doesn't she?*); OR
   (2) with a falling intonation if the speaker is expressing an idea with which she/he is almost certain the listener will agree (e.g., *It's a nice day today, isn't it?*).

Jim *could* use some help, *couldn't* he?

UNIT C: Contractions

C   Contractions

IN SPEAKING: In everyday spoken English, certain forms of **be** and auxiliary verbs are usually contracted with pronouns, nouns, and question words.

IN WRITING: (1) In written English, contractions with pronouns are common in informal writing, but they're not generally acceptable in formal writing.

(2) Contractions with nouns and question words are, for the most part, rarely used in writing. A few of these contractions may be found in quoted dialogue in stories or in very informal writing, such as a chatty letter to a good friend, but most of them are rarely if ever written.

In the following, quotation marks indicate that the contraction is frequently spoken but rarely, if ever, written.

	With Pronouns	**With Nouns**	**With Question Words**
am	*I'm* reading a book.	Ø	*"What'm"* I supposed to do?
is	*She's* studying. *It's* going to rain.	My *"book's"* on the table. *Mary's* at home.	*Where's* Sally? *Who's* that man?
are	*You're* working hard. *They're* waiting for us.	My *"books're"* on the table. The *"teachers're"* at a meeting.	*"What're"* you doing? *"Where're"* they going?
has	*She's* been here for a year. *It's* been cold lately.	My *"book's"* been stolen! *Sally's* never met him.	*Where's* Sally been living? *What's* been going on?
have	*I've* finished my work. *They've* never met you.	The *"books've"* been sold. The *"students've"* finished the test.	*"Where've"* they been? *"How've"* you been?
had	*He'd* been waiting for us. *We'd* forgotten about it.	The *"books'd"* been sold. *"Mary'd"* never met him before.	*"Where'd"* you been before that? *"Who'd"* been there before you?
did	Ø	Ø	*"What'd"* you do last night? *"How'd"* you do on the test?
will	*I'll* come later. *She'll* help us.	The *"weather'll"* be nice tomorrow. *"John'll"* be coming soon.	*"Who'll"* be at the meeting? *"Where'll"* you be at ten?
would	*He'd* like to go there. *They'd* come if they could.	My *"friends'd"* come if they could. *"Mary'd"* like to go there too.	*"Where'd"* you like to go?

UNIT D: Negatives

D-1 Using *Not* and Other Negative Words

(a) AFFIRMATIVE: The earth is round. (b) NEGATIVE: The earth is *not* flat.	*Not* expresses a *negative* idea.

		AUX + *NOT* + MAIN VERB			
(c)	I	will	not	go	there.
	I	have	not	gone	there.
	I	am	not	going	there.
	I	was	not		there.
	I	do	not	go	there.
	He	does	not	go	there.
	I	did	not	go	there.

Not immediately follows an auxiliary verb or *be*.

NOTE: If there is more than one auxiliary, *not* comes immediately after the first auxiliary: *I will not be going there.*

Do or *does* is used with *not* to make a simple present verb (except *be*) negative.

Did is used with *not* to make a simple past verb (except *be*) negative.

Contractions of auxiliary verbs with *not*

are not = aren't*	has not = hasn't	was not = wasn't
cannot = can't	have not = haven't	were not = weren't
could not = couldn't	had not = hadn't	will not = won't
did not = didn't	is not = isn't	would not = wouldn't
does not = doesn't	must not = mustn't	
do not = don't	should not = shouldn't	

(d) I almost *never* go there.
I have *hardly ever* gone there.
	In addition to *not*, the following are negative adverbs:
	   never, rarely, seldom
	   hardly (ever), scarcely (ever), barely (ever)

(e) There's *no* chalk in the drawer.	*No* also expresses a negative idea.

COMPARE: *NOT* VS. *NO* (f) I *do not have* any money. (g) I have *no money*.	*Not* is used to make a verb negative, as in (f). *No* is used as an adjective in front of a noun (e.g., *money*), as in (g). NOTE: Examples (f) and (g) have the same meaning.

*Sometimes in spoken English you will hear "ain't." It means "am not," "isn't," or "aren't." *Ain't* is not considered proper English, but many people use *ain't* regularly, and it is also frequently used for humor.

D-2 Avoiding Double Negatives

(a) INCORRECT: I ~~don't~~ have ~~no~~ money. (b) CORRECT: I *don't* have *any money*. CORRECT: I have *no money*.	Sentence (a) is an example of a "double negative," i.e., a confusing and grammatically incorrect sentence that contains two negatives in the same clause. One clause should contain only one negative.*

*Negatives in two different clauses in the same sentence cause no problems; for example:
   *A person who **doesn't** have love **can't** be truly happy.*
   *I **don't** know why he **isn't** here.*

D-3 Beginning a Sentence with a Negative Word

(a) *Never will I do* that again! (b) *Rarely have I eaten* better food. (c) *Hardly ever does he come* to class on time.	When a negative word begins a sentence, the subject and verb are inverted (i.e., question word order is used).*

*Beginning a sentence with a negative word is relatively uncommon in everyday usage; it is used when the speaker/writer wishes to emphasize the negative element of the sentence and be expressive.

UNIT E: Preposition Combinations

E Preposition Combinations with Adjectives and Verbs

A
be absent from
be accused of
be accustomed to
be acquainted with
be addicted to
be afraid of
    agree with
be angry at, with
be annoyed with, by
    apologize for
    apply to, for
    approve of
    argue with, about
    arrive in, at
be associated with
be aware of

B
    believe in
    blame for
be blessed with
be bored with, by

C
be capable of
    care about, for
be cluttered with
be committed to
    compare to, with
    complain about, of
be composed of
be concerned about
be connected to
    consist of
be content with
    contribute to
be convinced of
be coordinated with
    count (up)on
be covered with
be crowded with

D
    decide (up)on
be dedicated to
    depend (up)on
be devoted to
be disappointed in, with
be discriminated against
    distinguish from
be divorced from
be done with

    dream of, about
be dressed in

E
be engaged in, to
be envious of
be equipped with
    escape from
    excel in, at
be excited about
    excuse for
be exhausted from
be exposed to

F
be faithful to
be familiar with
    feel like
    fight for
be filled with
be finished with
be fond of
    forget about
    forgive for
be friendly to, with
be frightened of, by
be furnished with

G
be gone from
be grateful to, for
be guilty of

H
    hide from
    hope for

I
be innocent of
    insist (up)on
be interested in
    introduce to
be involved in

J
be jealous of

K
    keep from
be known for

L
be limited to
be located in
    look forward to

M
be made of, from
be married to

O
    object to
be opposed to

P
    participate in
be patient with
be pleased with
be polite to
    pray for
be prepared for
    prevent from
    prohibit from
be protected from
be proud of
    provide with

Q
be qualified for

R
    recover from
be related to
be relevant to
    rely (up)on
be remembered for
    rescue from
    respond to
be responsible for

S
be satisfied with
be scared of, by
    stare at
    stop from
    subscribe to
    substitute for
    succeed in

T
    take advantage of
    take care of
    talk about, of
be terrified of, by
    thank for
    think about, of
be tired of, from

U
be upset with
be used to

V
    vote for

W
be worried about

UNIT F: The Subjunctive in Noun Clauses

F Using the Subjunctive in Noun Clauses

(a) The teacher *demands* that we *be* on time.	A subjunctive verb uses the simple form of a verb. It does not have present, past, or future forms; it is neither singular nor plural.
(b) I *insisted* that he *pay* me the money.	
(c) I *recommended* that she *not go* to the concert.	Sentences with subjunctive verbs generally *stress importance or urgency*. A subjunctive verb is used in *that*-clauses that follow the verbs and expressions listed below.
(d) *It is important* that they *be told* the truth.	
	In (a): *be* is a subjunctive verb; its subject is *we*.
	In (b): *pay* (not *pays*, not *paid*) is a subjunctive verb; it is in its simple form, even though its subject (*he*) is singular.
	Negative: *not* + *simple form,* as in (c).
	Passive: *simple form of be* + *past participle,* as in (d).
(e) I *suggested* that she *see* a doctor.	*Should* is also possible after *suggest* and *recommend*.*
(f) I *suggested* that she *should see* a doctor.	

Common verbs and expressions followed by the subjunctive in a noun clause

advise (that)	propose (that)	it is critical (that)	it is important (that)
ask (that)	recommend (that)	it is essential (that)	it is necessary (that)
demand (that)	request (that)	it is imperative (that)	it is vital (that)
insist (that)	suggest (that)		

*The subjunctive is more common in American English than British English. In British English, ***should*** + *simple form* is more usual than the subjunctive: *The teacher **insists** that we **should be** on time.*

UNIT G: Troublesome Verbs

G *Raise / Rise, Set / Sit, Lay / Lie*

Transitive	Intransitive	
(a) *raise, raised, raised* Tom *raised his hand.*	(b) *rise, rose, risen* The sun *rises* in the east.	***Raise***, ***set***, and ***lay*** are *transitive* verbs; they are followed by an object.
		Rise, ***sit***, and ***lie*** are intransitive; they are NOT followed by an object.*
(c) *set, set, set* I *will set the book* on the desk.	(d) *sit, sat, sat* I *sit* in the front row.	In (a): ***raised*** is followed by the object ***hand***.
		In (b): ***rises*** is not followed by an object.

(e) *lay, laid, laid*
I *am laying the book* on the desk.
	(f) *lie,*** *lay, lain*
	He *is lying* on his bed.
		NOTE: ***Lay*** and ***lie*** are troublesome for native speakers too and are frequently misused.
		    lay = *put*
		    lie = *recline*

*See Appendix Chart A-1 for information about transitive and intransitive verbs.

*****Lie*** is a regular verb (*lie, lied*) when it means "not tell the truth": *He **lied** to me about his age.*

Listening Script

Please note: You may want to pause the audio after each item or in longer passages so that there is enough time to complete each task.

Chapter 12: Noun Clauses

Exercise 11, p. 248.

1. A: It's a beautiful day. Let's walk over to Lakeside Park. It's not far from here, is it?
   B: Gosh, I don't know how far it is.

2. A: Do you want to walk to the farmers' market with me tomorrow morning? They have lots of fresh fruits and vegetables.
   B: Gee, I don't know. Maybe. How far is it?

3. A: That was a terrible movie!
   B: I agree. I don't know why we watched the whole thing.

4. A: I watched an awful movie on TV last night.
   B: Well, if it was awful, why did you watch it?

5. A: Is Jeannie going to be 49 or 50 this year?
   B: I don't know. I can never remember how old she is.

6. A: Excuse me. I'm still unsure about the pronunciation of that word.
   B: Which one?
   A: This one right here. How is this word pronounced?

7. A: You look upset.
   B: I am. I'm very upset.
   A: So, what is the problem?

Exercise 41, p. 264.

1. I'm not going to the personnel meeting because I have to finish a report.
2. I can't lend Marta any money because my wallet is in my coat pocket back at home.
3. Someone in this room is wearing very strong perfume. It's giving me a headache.
4. Hi, Emma. I'll meet you at the coffee shop at 9:00. I promise not to be late.
5. I'm considering looking for a new job. What do you think I should do?
6. We are going to be late for the concert. My wife has to attend a business function after work.

Chapter 13: Adjective Clauses

Exercise 5, p. 271.

Part I.
1. He has a friend who'll help him.
2. He has a friend who's helping him.
3. He has a friend who's helped him.
4. He has friends who're helping him.
5. He has friends who've helped him.
6. He has a friend who'd helped him.
7. He has a friend who'd like to help him.

Part II.
8. We know a person who'll be great for the job.
9. We know a person who'd like to apply for the job.
10. That's the man who's giving the speech at our graduation.
11. I know a nurse who's traveled around the world helping people.
12. Let's talk to the people who're planning the protest march.
13. There are people at the factory who've worked there all their adult lives.
14. The doctor who'd been taking care of my mother retired.

Exercise 19, p. 278.

1. I met the man who's going to become the new manager of our department.
2. I know someone who's never flown in an airplane.
3. I talked to the man whose wife was in the car accident on Fifth Street yesterday. She's in the hospital, but she's going to be okay.
4. I forget the name of the woman who's going to call you later — Mrs. Green or Mrs. White or something like that.
5. I need to hurry. The neighbor whose bike I borrowed is waiting for me to return it.
6. I got an email from a friend who's studying in Malaysia. It was really good to hear from her.
7. I recently heard from a friend who's been out of the country for over two months. He finally sent me an email.

8. I'm thinking about getting a pet. There's a woman at work whose dog just had puppies. I might adopt one.

Exercise 21, 279.
1. That's the person who's going to help us.
2. That's the person whose help we need.
3. I'd like to introduce you to a teacher who's spent time in Africa.
4. I'd like to introduce you to the teacher whose husband is from Africa.
5. The company is looking for a person who's bilingual.
6. The company is looking for a person whose native language is Arabic.
7. The company is looking for a person who's had a lot of experience in sales.
8. They want to hire a person who's familiar with their sales territory.

Exercise 29, p. 281.
1. The man who organized the community dinner is a friend of mine.
2. Two people died in the accident that blocked all lanes of the highway for two hours.
3. The small town where I was born is now a large city.
4. The music teacher who directs the school band plays in a rock band on weekends.
5. The camera that Jack gave me for my birthday takes excellent digital pictures.
6. My neighbor often drops in for a visit about the time when we would like to sit down to dinner.

Exercise 33, p. 284.
A: Do you see that guy who's wearing the baseball cap?
B: I see two guys that're wearing baseball caps. Do you mean the one whose T-shirt says "Be Happy"?
A: Yeah, him. Do you remember him from high school? He looks a little different now, doesn't he? Isn't he the one whose wife joined the circus?
B: Nah, I heard that story too. That was just a rumor. When the circus was in town last summer, his wife spent a lot of time there, so people started wondering why. Some people started saying she was working there as a performer. But the truth is that she was only visiting a cousin who's a manager for the circus. She just wanted to spend time with him while he was in town.
A: Well, you know, it was a story that sounded pretty fishy to me. But people sure enjoyed talking about it. The last thing that I heard was that she'd learned how to eat fire and swallow swords!
B: Rumors really take on a life of their own, don't they?!

Exercise 36, p. 286.
1. Did you hear about the man who rowed a boat across the Atlantic Ocean?
2. My uncle, who loves boating, rows his boat across the lake near his house nearly every day.

3. Tea, which is a common drink throughout the world, is made by pouring boiling water onto the dried leaves of certain plants.
4. Tea which is made from herbs is called herbal tea.
5. Toys which contain lead paint are unsafe for children.
6. Lead, which can be found in paint and plastics, is known to cause brain damage in children.

Exercise 39, p. 288.
1. My mother looked in the fruit basket and threw away the apples that were rotten.
2. My mother looked in the fruit basket and threw away the apples, which were rotten.
3. The students who had done well on the test were excused from class early.
4. The students, who had done well on the test, were excused from class early.

Exercise 52, p. 295.
1. The fence surrounding our house is made of wood.
2. The children attending that school receive a good education.
3. Dr. Stanton, the president of the university, will give a speech at the commencement ceremonies.
4. Our solar system is in a galaxy called the Milky Way.

Exercise 56, p. 297.
Animals and Earthquakes

Whether or not animals can predict earthquakes has been widely debated for hundreds of years. In fact, as far back as 373 B.C. villagers reported that hundreds of animals deserted the Greek town of Helice a few days before an earthquake destroyed it. There are other interesting phenomena that scientists have noted. For example, before an earthquake, dogs may begin barking or howling for no reason; chickens might stop laying eggs; and some pets will go into hiding.

In Asia in 2004, many animals that were accustomed to being on the beach in the early morning refused to go there the morning of the big tsunami. In Thailand, a herd of buffalo on a beach noticed or heard something which made them run to the top of a hill before the tsunami was anywhere in sight. The villagers who followed them were saved.

What causes this strange behavior in animals? One theory is that they can sense the earth move before people can. There are vibrations deep in the earth that begin before an earthquake can be detected. Another idea is that the energy in the air changes and that animals are disturbed by these changes.

Some scientists dismiss these ideas, while others believe that they are worth researching further. Those scientists who have witnessed this strange animal behavior are certain that animals are far more sensitive to subtle changes in the earth than people are and that studying their behavior can be useful in the prediction of earthquakes.

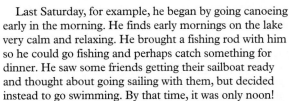

Chapter **14**: Gerunds and Infinitives, Part 1

Exercise 6, p. 305.
1. A: I'm sorry I'm late.
   B: No problem. We have lots of time.
2. A: I finished the project early.
   B: That's great you got it done so quickly.
3. A: I hate to do housework.
   B: I know. I do too. It's a lot of work.
4. A: You were a big help. Thanks.
   B: Sure. I was happy to help out.
5. A: Your report isn't finished. What's your excuse?
   B: Uh, well, sorry. I don't really have one.
6. A: How do you like the food here?
   B: It's too spicy. I can't eat much of it.
7. A: How was your weekend? Did you go away for the holiday?
   B: No. I got the flu and spent the whole weekend in bed.

Exercise 13, p. 308.
1. A: What should we do tomorrow night?
   B: Let's just stay home and watch a movie. There's nothing I like to do better on a weekend.
   A: Sounds good to me.
2. A: I was really looking forward to the hike up to Skyline Ridge to see the mountains, but I guess we're not going to get there this month.
   B: It doesn't look like it. I don't think there's any hope. It's supposed to rain the rest of this week and into next week.
3. A: Do you want to take a break?
   B: No, we have to finish this report by 5:00. We don't have time for a break.
4. A: Let's go into the city this weekend. There's a great concert at the park. And it's free!
   B: Great idea! Who's playing?
5. A: Gosh, I'd really like to go out this evening, but I have all this work to do. I have three papers due, and I haven't begun to write any of them.
   B: I know how you feel. I'm way behind in my homework too.
6. A: I just heard that there's an accident on the freeway and nothing's moving. I don't want our drive home to take hours.
   B: Me neither. Let's not leave the office for another couple of hours. We can get caught up on our work.
   A: Good idea. I have so much to do.

Exercise 17, p. 309.
Ron's Busy Saturday

Ron is an active individual. On his days off, he likes to do several activities in one day. His friends can't keep up with him.

Last Saturday, for example, he began by going canoeing early in the morning. He finds early mornings on the lake very calm and relaxing. He brought a fishing rod with him so he could go fishing and perhaps catch something for dinner. He saw some friends getting their sailboat ready and thought about going sailing with them, but decided instead to go swimming. By that time, it was only noon!

After lunch, he went biking in the hills behind his town. He cooked a fish that he had caught for dinner, and it was delicious. Later, some friends called to invite him out, so he finished the day by going dancing with them.

Exercise 22, p. 312.
1. I have a terrible memory. I can't even remember my children's birthdays.
2. My teenage son tried to hide his report card, but I caught him.
3. I'm in a hurry in the mornings. I always stand at the kitchen counter and eat my breakfast.
4. Foreign languages are hard for me to learn.
5. I sat in traffic for two hours. It was a waste of time.
6. We sang songs on the bus trip. It was fun.
7. I looked all over for Tom. He was studying in the library.
8. There was a line to buy movie tickets. I had to wait for an hour.

Exercise 31, p. 318.
1. Joan remembered to call her husband before she left work yesterday.
2. Rita remembered going to the farmers' market with her grandmother.
3. Roger stopped smoking when the doctor told him he had heart disease.
4. Mr. and Mrs. Olson stopped to eat before the movie.
5. I regret leaving school before I graduated.

Chapter **15**: Gerunds and Infinitives, Part 2

Exercise 14, p. 336.
1. That dinner was delicious, Nancy.
2. Do you leave your daughter home alone when you go out?
3. I think our English is getting a lot better, but learning a second language isn't easy.
4. I used a new laundry detergent on these shirts. How did it work?
5. Mr. Jones is 99 years old. He's too old to drive.
6. We need 20 big envelopes, but we only have 10.

Exercise 36, p. 348.
An Issue in Health Care: Illiteracy

According to some estimates, well over half of the people in the world are functionally illiterate. This means that they are unable to perform everyday tasks because they can't read, understand, and respond appropriately to information. One of the problems this creates in health care is that millions of people are not able to read directions on medicine bottles or packages. Imagine being a parent with a sick child and being unable to read the directions on a medicine bottle. We all know that it is important for medical directions to be understood clearly. One solution is pictures. Many medical professionals are working today to solve this problem by using pictures to convey health-care information.

Exercise 39, p. 350.

Protecting Yourself in a Lightning Storm

Lightning storms can occur suddenly and without warning. It's important to know how to stay safe if you're outside when a storm begins. Some people stand under trees or in open shelters like picnic areas in order to protect themselves. They are surprised to hear that this can be a fatal mistake. Tall objects are likely to attract lightning, so when you are out in the open, you should try to make yourself as small as possible. Crouching down or curling up into a ball lessens the chance that a lightning bolt will strike you. Finding a depression in the ground to hide in, like a hole or a ditch, is even better.

Being inside a building is safer than being outside, but it's not without dangers. Be careful to stay away from doors and windows. If you're talking on a phone with a cord, hang up. Lightning has been known to travel along a phone cord and strike the person holding the phone. Even TVs can conduct lightning through the cable or antenna, so it's a good idea to stay away from the television. It's also inadvisable to take a shower or bath since plumbing can conduct electricity from lightning. How safe are cars? Surprisingly, the inside of a car is safe as long as it has a metal roof, but avoid touching any part of the car that leads to the outside.

There's a 30/30 rule regarding lightning. As soon as you see lightning, begin counting the seconds until you hear thunder. If you hear thunder before you reach 30, this means you need to seek shelter immediately. Additionally, even if the storm has passed, you want to stay in a protected place for 30 minutes after you hear the last sounds of thunder or have seen the last flashes of lightning. Many lightning deaths, in fact more than half in the United States, occur after a storm has passed.

Chapter 16: Coordinating Conjunctions

Exercise 5, p. 354.
1. My bedroom has a bed, a desk, and a lamp.
2. The price of the meal includes a salad, a main dish, and dessert.
3. The price of the meal includes a salad and a main dish.
4. Elias waited for his son, wife, and daughter.
5. Elias waited for his son's wife and daughter.
6. Susan raised her hand, snapped her fingers, and asked a question.

7. Red, yellow, gold, and olive green are the main colors in the fabric.
8. I love films full of action, adventure, and suspense.
9. I love action and adventure films.
10. Travel is fatal to prejudice, bigotry, and narrow-mindedness.

Exercise 14, p. 359.
1. Ben will call either Mary or Bob.
2. Both my mother and father talked to my teacher.
3. Simon saw not only a whale but also a dolphin.
4. Our neighborhood had neither electricity nor water after the storm.
5. Either Mr. Anderson or Ms. Wiggins is going to teach our class today.

Exercise 16, p. 360.

Bats

(1) What do people in your country think of bats? Are they mean and scary creatures, or are they symbols of both happiness and luck?

(2) In Western countries, many people have an unreasoned fear of bats. According to scientist Dr. Sharon Horowitz, bats are not only harmless but also beneficial mammals. "When I was a child, I believed that a bat would attack me and tangle itself in my hair. Now I know better," said Dr. Horowitz.

(3) Contrary to popular Western myths, bats do not attack humans. Although a few bats may have diseases, they are not major carriers of rabies or other frightening diseases. Bats help natural plant life by pollinating plants, spreading seeds, and eating insects. If you get rid of bats that eat overripe fruit, then fruit flies can flourish and destroy the fruit industry.

(4) According to Dr. Horowitz, bats are both gentle and trainable pets. Not many people, however, own or train bats, and bats themselves prefer to avoid people.

Exercise 19, p. 362.
1. Both Jamal and I had many errands to do yesterday. Jamal had to go to the post office and the bookstore. I had to go to the post office, the travel agency, and the bank.
2. Roberto slapped his hand on his desk in frustration. He had failed another examination and had ruined his chances for a passing grade in the course.
3. When Alex got home, he took off his coat and tie, threw his briefcase on the kitchen table, and opened the refrigerator looking for something to eat. Ann found him sitting at the kitchen table when she got home.
4. When Tara went downtown yesterday, she bought birthday presents for her children, shopped for clothes, and saw a movie at the theater. It was a busy day, but she felt fine because it ended on a relaxing note.
5. It was a wonderful picnic. The children waded in the stream, collected rocks and insects, and flew kites. The teenagers played an enthusiastic game of

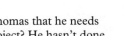

baseball. The adults busied themselves preparing the food, supervising the children, and playing some volleyball.

Exercise 21, p. 363.

Butterflies

A butterfly is a marvel. It begins as an ugly caterpillar and turns into a work of art. The sight of a butterfly floating from flower to flower on a warm, sunny day brightens anyone's heart. A butterfly is a charming and gentle creature. Caterpillars eat plants and cause damage to some crops, but adult butterflies feed principally on nectar from flowers and do not cause any harm. When cold weather comes, some butterflies travel great distances to reach tropical climates. They can be found on every continent except Antarctica. Because they are so colorful and beautiful, butterflies are admired throughout the world.

Chapter 17: Adverb Clauses

Exercise 11, p. 372.

Cultural Misunderstandings

Since Marco and Anya came to this country, they've had some memorable misunderstandings due to language and culture. The first time Marco met someone at a party, he was asked "How's it going?" Marco thought that the person was asking him about leaving, and that seemed very strange.

Once, Anya walked into class, and a native speaker said, "Hi. How are you?" When Anya started to give a long answer, the native speaker looked at her rather oddly. This happened several times until Anya learned she was just supposed to say something like "Okay" or "Fine, thanks. And you?"

Another time, Marco was at a restaurant and wanted to get the server's attention. He snapped his fingers. The server was not pleased.

Since coming here, Marco and Anya have learned that cultural misunderstandings are a normal part of learning another language. They can be valuable and even entertaining learning experiences. Marco and Anya just smile at these misunderstandings now.

Chapter 18: Reduction of Adverb Clauses to Modifying Adverbial Phrases

Exercise 16, p. 395.

1. A: I don't want to play the piano at the family gathering. I don't play well enough. People will laugh at me.
   B: Oh, Rose, don't be silly. You play beautifully. Everyone will love hearing you.

2. A: Jan, are you going to tell Thomas that he needs to do more work on the project? He hasn't done his share. He's being really lazy.
   B: Well, he'll probably get upset, but I'm going to talk with him about it this afternoon.

3. A: I'm so relieved that I found my wedding ring. It'd been missing for a month. The next time I take it off, I'm going to put it in a box on top of my dresser drawer.
   B: That sounds like a wise thing to do, Susan. It'd be terrible to lose your wedding ring again.

4. A: This is the first year I'm eligible to vote in the presidential election. I'm going to research all the candidates extensively.
   B: They have very different positions, Sam. It's good to get as much information as you can.

Exercise 18, p. 396

The QWERTY Keyboard

Do you know why the letters on an English language keyboard are placed where they are? Take a minute and look at the second row on the keyboard in the picture. Notice that Q-W-E-R-T-Y are the first six letters beginning on the left. In fact, the keyboard is called "QWERTY." As you look at all the letters on the keyboard, does it seem to make any sense to you? Many people have wondered about this rather strange placement of keys, but as it turns out, there is a logical reason for the design.

A man named Christopher Sholes, the inventor of the typewriter, came up with this keyboard in the 1860s. Wanting to create a logical design, Sholes first placed the letters in alphabetical order on his typewriter. He put two rows from A to Z on the keyboard.

But Sholes found there was a problem. The letters were on typebars — typebars, by the way, are also called keys — and some of these keys crashed into one another. This happened when letters that often occur together in words, like "s" and "l," were near each other on the keyboard. The keys tended to hit each other and get stuck, and the typist would have to stop and pull them apart.

Trying to figure out a way to keep the keys from hitting one another, Sholes made a list of letters commonly used together in English, like the pair I already mentioned, "s" and "l," or, for example, "q" and "u." He then rearranged these letters so they would be on opposite sides of the keyboard. If you look at a keyboard, "q" is on the left side and "u" is on the right side. He put the keys that were most likely to be hit one after the other on opposite sides of the keyboard. This keyboard became known as QWERTY.

Nowadays, with computers, we don't have to worry about keys crashing into one another, so QWERTY is not necessarily the fastest and most efficient keyboard. Other people have come up with alternative keyboard patterns, but so far, none has gained much popularity. Having survived since the 1860s, QWERTY has demonstrated its longevity. It does not appear that it is going to be replaced any time soon by a faster, more efficient keyboard.

Chapters 17 and 18

LISTENING SCRIPT **455**

Chapter 19: Connectives That Express Cause and Effect, Contrast, and Condition

Exercise 33, p. 412.
1. Because I lift heavy boxes at work, . . .
2. I bought a new TV even though . . .
3. Even if I'm late for work, . . .
4. I was late for work this morning; nevertheless, . . .
5. The air-conditioning has been broken; therefore, . . .
6. Although I live in a noisy city, . . .
7. I was so tired last night that . . .

Exercise 36, p. 414.
Why We Yawn

Have you ever noticed that when a person near you yawns, you may start yawning too? This is called contagious yawning. *Contagious* in this sense means that the behavior spreads: when one person does something like yawn, it can cause others to do the same thing.

There are various theories about why people yawn. One popular idea is that yawning brings more oxygen into the brain to wake people up. Is that what you have thought? But in 2007, researchers at a university in New York came up with a new idea: yawning helps cool the brain.

Scientists found that people yawned more frequently in situations where their brains were warmer. The idea is that yawning cools the brain by increasing blood flow and bringing cooler air into the body. Cooler brains work better than warmer ones.

This may also help explain why yawning is contagious. People are more awake when their brains are cooler. As people evolved over time, contagious yawning helped people stay awake. This was important in times of danger. It's very possible that the person yawning could have been signaling to others to stay awake.

The next time you are talking to someone and that person yawns, you can tell yourself that he or she actually wants to stay awake, not go to sleep.

Exercise 38, p. 415.
Passage 1: Turtles

Turtles have survived on earth for more than 200 million years, but now many species face extinction. People in many parts of the world use them for food and for traditional medicine, so the demand for them is high. In spite of international trade laws that protect them, illegal traffic in turtles is increasing.

Passage 2: Boy or Girl?

Research shows that many parents prefer to have a boy rather than a girl because boys are expected to become better economic providers for their parents in their old age. In developed countries, however, more women than men go to a university. It's possible that in some places more women than men will be prepared for the high-paying jobs of the 21st century.

Chapter 20: Conditional Sentences and Wishes

Exercise 6, p. 418.
1. If I'm talking too fast, please tell me.
2. If we get married, everyone will be shocked.
3. If it's okay, I'll ask for some advice.
4. If he's planning to quit, I hope he lets us know soon.
5. If it's not working, we'll need to try something else.
6. If she works harder, I'm sure she'll succeed.
7. If I should get the job, I'll call you right away.

Exercise 19, p. 424.
The Extinction of Dinosaurs

There are several scientific theories as to why dinosaurs became extinct. One theory has to do with asteroids. Asteroids, as you may know, are rocky objects that orbit the sun. According to this theory, an asteroid collided with the earth millions of years ago, causing disastrous changes in the earth's climate, such as tsunamis, high winds, and dust in the atmosphere that blocked the sun. As a result, dinosaurs could no longer survive. Some scientists believe that if this asteroid had not collided with the earth, dinosaurs would not have become extinct.

Exercise 20, p. 424.
1. If I had known the truth sooner, I would have acted differently.
2. If we hadn't believed him, we wouldn't have felt so foolish.
3. If you hadn't told me what a great guy Jon was, I wouldn't have believed him so easily.
4. If it had been another person, I wouldn't have been so shocked.
5. If he hadn't lied, I would have had more respect for him.

Exercise 22, p. 426.
1. If I had enough time, I'd go to the art museum this afternoon. I love going to art museums.
2. Mrs. Jones is really lucky. If she hadn't received immediate medical attention, she would have died.
3. If I were a carpenter, I'd build my own house. I'd really enjoy that.
4. So many people died unnecessarily in the earthquake. If the hotel had been built to withstand an earthquake, it wouldn't have collapsed.

Exercise 32, p. 430.
1. If I hadn't been driving so fast, I wouldn't have gotten a speeding ticket.
2. Should you have questions, give me a call on my cell.
3. Had you told us sooner, we could have helped you.
4. If there had been a faster way to get to the theater, I would have taken it.

5. Had anyone warned us about the situation, we would have stayed home.
6. Were we rich, we would live in a house overlooking the ocean.

Exercise 35, p. 431.

1. I would have called, but I left your number at home.
2. I couldn't have gone to college without my parents' financial help.
3. I ran out of time. Otherwise, I would have picked up your clothes from the cleaners.
4. We would have come to the party, but no one told us about it.
5. Without your advice, I wouldn't have known what to do.

Exercise 45, p. 436.

1. Alice doesn't like her job as a nurse. She wishes she hadn't gone to nursing school.
2. A: I wish we didn't have to go to work today.
   B: So do I. I wish it were a holiday.
3. We had a good time in the mountains over vacation. I wish you had come with us. If you had come with us, you would have had a good time.
4. I know that something's bothering you. I wish you would tell me what it is. Maybe I can help.
5. A: My feet are killing me! I wish I had worn more comfortable shoes.
   B: Yeah, me too. I wish I had known that we were going to have to walk this much.

Index

Accustomed to, 302 *(Look on page 302.)*	The numbers following the words listed in the index refer to page numbers in the text.
Correlative conjunctions, 358*fn.* *(Look at the footnote on page 358.)*	The letters *fn.* mean "footnote." Footnotes are at the bottom of a chart or the bottom of a page.

H

Have, has, helping vs. main verb, 277*fn.*
Have/has/had:
    causative, 344
    contracted, 447–448
Help, 343
How, 443
However:
    -ever word, 268
    transition, 406, 408

I

If, 249, 253 (SEE ALSO Adverb clauses,
        conditions; Conditional sentences;
        Noun clauses)
If-clauses, 377–378, 416, 430
If . . . not, 382
Imperative sentences, 261
In case, 381
Indefinite pronouns, modified by adjective
        clauses, 283
Independent clauses, defined, 242, 270
    combining with conjunctions, 361
Indirect speech, 258*fn.*
Infinitives, defined, 313
    following adjectives, 333
    with causative *get,* 344
    with *it,* 322
    following *need,* 339
    negative form, 313
    past, passive, 338
    purpose (*in order to*), 317, 331
    with question words, 252
    in reported speech, 261*fn.*
    as subjects, 322
    with *too/enough,* 335
    verbs followed by, 313, 317
        list, 325
Information questions, 442–444
-Ing forms:
    go + *-ing,* 309
    special expressions followed by (e.g., *have*
        fun doing), 309
    upon + *-ing,* 393
    uses of, 301*fn.*
    verbs of perception, + *-ing* (e.g., *see her*
        walking), 341
    (SEE ALSO Gerunds; Present participle)
In order that, 404*fn.*
In order to, 307*fn.,* 317, 331, 404
In spite of, 406

Intend, 313*fn.*
Intransitive verbs, defined, 439
Inverted commas, 258*fn.*
Inverted word order:
    after negatives, 448
    after *only if,* 383
It:
    with infinitives, 322
    with noun clauses, 253

J

Just, meaning *immediately,* 369*fn.*

L

Lay/lie, 450
Let + simple form, 343
Linking verbs, 441
-Ly, adverb form, 440

M

Main clauses (SEE Independent clauses)
Make, causative (e.g., *make them do it*), 344
Midsentence adverbs, 440
Might, in reported speech, 261
Modal auxiliaries in reported speech, 261
Modify, defined, 439
Modifying phrases:
    reduction of adjective clauses, 294
    reduction of adverb clauses,
        387–388, 393

N

Need, verb forms following, 339
Negative(s), 448
    word order in negative questions, 247*fn.*
Neither . . . nor, 358
Nevertheless/nonetheless, 404
No, 448
Nor, 352
Not, 448
Not only . . . but also, 358
Noun(s), defined, 439
Noun clauses, defined, 242
    with *it,* 253
    with question words, 244
    reduced to infinitive phrases, 261
    reported speech, sequence of tenses, 261
    subjunctive in, 450
    with *that,* 253
    with *the fact that,* 253, 397

with *whether/if*, 249
after *wish*, 434
word order in, 244
Now that, 373

O

Object(s), defined, 439
of a preposition, 274, 302
Object pronouns, 261*fn.*, 274
Once, 368
Only if, 383
On the other hand, 408
Or, 352
Or else, 410
Otherwise, 410, 430

P

Paired conjunctions (e.g., *both . . . and*), 358
Parallel structure, 352, 354
Participial phrases (SEE Modifying phrases)
Participles (SEE ALSO Modifying phrases;
        Present participle)
Passive:
    with causative verbs (e.g., *have it done*), 344
    gerunds, (e.g., *being done*), 338
    infinitives (e.g., *to be done*), 338
Periods, 361, 400
Phrasal verb, defined, 307*fn.*
Phrases, defined, 242*fn.*
    prepositional, 440
    reduction of adjective clauses, 294
    reduction of adverb clauses,
        387–390, 393
    reduction of noun clauses, 249
Possessive:
    in adjective clauses (*whose*), 277, 443
    pronouns/adjectives (*mine, my,* etc.), 277
    in questions (*whose*), 443
Prefer, 317*fn.*
Preposition(s):
    combinations followed by gerunds, 302
    combinations with adjectives and
        verbs, 449
    as connectives, 411
    list, 440
Prepositional phrases, 440
Present participle:
    vs. gerund, 301*fn.*
    in reduction of adjective clauses, 294
    in reduction of adverb clauses, 388

special expressions followed by (e.g., *have
        fun doing*), 310
with verbs of perception (e.g., *watch
        someone doing*), 341
Progressive verbs, 427
Pronouns:
    indefinite, 283
    object, 261*fn.*, 274
    possessive, 277
    relative (SEE Adjective clauses)
    subject, 270
Punctuation:
    adjective clauses, 285
    adjective phrases, 294
    adverb clauses, 365, 400
    conjunctions, 400
    independent clauses, 361
    parallel structure, 348
    quoted speech, 258
    transitions, 399–400
    (SEE ALSO Apostrophes; Commas; Periods;
        Quotation marks; Semicolons)

Q

Quantity (SEE Expressions of quantity)
Questions:
    information, 442–444
    negative, 445
        word order in, 247*fn.*
    tag, 446
    word order in, 442
    yes/no, 442, 445
Question words:
    with infinitives, 252
    in noun clauses, 244
    in questions, 443–444
Quotation marks, 258
Quoted speech, 258

R

Raise/rise, 450
Reduction:
    of adjective clauses, 294
    of adverb clauses, 387–390, 393
    of noun clauses, 261
Relative clauses, 270 (SEE ALSO Adjective clauses)
Relative pronouns, 270
Regret, 317
Remember/forget, 317
Reported speech, 261